The Mediocracy

The Mediocracy

French Philosophy since the mid-1970s

———————◆———————

DOMINIQUE LECOURT

Translated by Gregory Elliott

VERSO
London · New York

This book is supported by the French Ministry for Foreign Affairs as part of
the Burgess Programme, headed for the French Embassy in London by
the Institut Français du Royaume Uni

ǁ institut français

This edition first published by Verso 2001
© Verso 2001
Translation © Gregory Elliott 2001
First published as *Les piètres penseurs*
© Flammarion 1999
Appendix first published as *Dissidence ou révolution?*
by François Maspero, 1978
© Dominique Lecourt

Verso
UK: 6 Meard Street, London W1V 3HR
US: 180 Varick Street, New York, NY 10014–4606

Verso is the imprint of New Left Books

ISBN 1–85984–793–5

British Library Cataloguing in Publication Data
A catalogue record for this book is available from the British Library

Library of Congress Cataloging-in-Publication Data
A catalog record for this book is available from the Library of Congress

Typeset in Perpetua by M Rules
Printed and bound in Great Britain by
Biddles Ltd, Guildford and King's Lynn

To Thomas, Matthieu and Pascal

Contents

Preface to the English Edition

Twenty years separate the two texts you are about to read. Both take the form of polemics, written while I was engaged in research on the philosophical dimensions and political implications of scientific thought. But neither indulges in polemic for polemic's sake. Instead – or so it seems to me – they attest to the consistency of a certain practice of philosophy.

This is a practice that does not dissociate analysis of the statements produced and refined by philosophers from analysis of the conjuncture in which they are destined to signify and to act. It has determined my choice of topics over the years.

In 1976, I completed and published a book on the history of Lysenkoism on which I had been working for four years. The case of Lysenko interested me because it represented a historical enigma. How could a powerful state like the USSR, which had just demonstrated its enormous technological capabilities during the war, completely destroy its research in genetics in 1948, and wreck its agriculture through the application of a so-called 'proletarian science' of heredity? But it was the role assigned to the official philosophy of the Soviet state in this tragedy – the famous 'dialectical materialism' – that was of particular interest. It seemed to me urgent for those affiliated to Marxism to steer clear of this philosophy – not only in order to avoid any repetition of such horrors, but to lift the dead weight of moral and political conformism oppressing the peoples of the countries of 'really existing socialism'. I proposed to resume and extend the critique of the presuppositions of political economy, grasping them by their philosophical roots in order to challenge the economism that seemed to have triumphed, in East and West alike, courtesy of 'peaceful coexistence'.

I wrote *Dissidence ou révolution?* in the winter of 1977–78. It was published in spring 1978 against the advice of Althusser, who had written a brilliant preface to my previous book. François Maspero accepted it for his *Cahiers libres* series, though not without enduring, more or less stoically, violent reproaches from the director of the *Théorie* collection. Althusser did not want someone he considered one of his own to intervene publicly against the 'New Philosophers'. Although he had been very upset by the publication of André Glucksmann's book *Les maîtres penseurs* in 1977, he reckoned that there were no grounds for taking the group seriously as such. But it would not be long before he recognized that he had underestimated the ideological and political impact of the media and commercial operation mounted around the 'New Philosophy'. Preoccupied with what was then called the 'international Communist movement', he was about to publish the series of sensational articles in *Le Monde* (24–27 April 1978) entitled 'Ce qui ne peut plus durer dans le parti communiste'. Because of my rebellion, a certain coldness had set in between us. And I can still see myself coming across the first of those articles on the front page of *Le Monde*, displayed in a newspaper kiosque on the Champs-Élysées. Spotting the headline ('Ce qui ne peut plus durer … '), I could not help thinking: Althusser … . It would not take long for history to prove me right, in a tragic fashion I could never have imagined.

Rereading this little book today, I still experience the feeling that gripped me as I wrote it: a world was in the process of toppling, and we would need to forge new intellectual instruments to understand what was transpiring, as if fortuitously. At the risk of immodesty, I must confess that I am far from dissatisfied with the verdict I ventured in the heat of the moment: my closing chapter anticipated 'The America in Our Heads'. It is certainly installed there now – for worse as well as for better.

On the other hand, I would not seek to hide my embarrassment at the body of the text. In a note to *Les piètres penseurs*, I share my retrospective irritation with its 'stereotyped language'. This is not simply a matter of style. Through an overdose of 'class' terminology, it seems to me to be intent on counterposing the image of a living and even combative Marxism to those who were proclaiming the death of Marx. But at the prompting of my chosen adversaries, in reality I was content to frame my philosophical analysis in a rather conventional geopolitical perspective, which I set against theirs. Had I practised the method I preached – the rectification of Marxist concepts in and through their confrontation with the concrete – the conjunctural analyses in which I inscribed my intervention would have been enriched.

Twenty years separate my first pamphlet and *Les piètres penseurs*. The title, which assonates ironically with *Les maîtres penseurs*, indicates that I conceived it in the same vein as *Dissidence ou révolution?*. I would have no difficulty demonstrating the brutality with which these two decades put my consistency to the test. The murder of

Hélène Althusser by her husband in the early hours of a November morning in 1980 was a source of immense grief to me. Appointed by my friend as his legal representative, I soon became familiar with the machinery of the psychiatric and judicial institutions. Moreover, in the emotional intensity of what was an intellectually intolerable situation, I found myself compelled to reflect further on the practice of a psychoanalyst whom I had taken the step of alerting about the state of his illustrious patient a fortnight earlier, and who had dispatched me rather condescendingly.

On 21 May 1981, in his absence and in haste, I cleared out the flat at the École normale supérieure which Althusser had occupied with his companion, while he remained confined at the Sainte Anne hospital. That evening I watched on television the ceremony all of left-wing France was waiting for: François Mitterrand's ascent, rose in hand, to the Panthéon, and then his descent into the crypt dedicated to the great men of our history.

Anyone who has read *Dissidence ou révolution?* will readily appreciate why I entertained few illusions about the Left's arrival in power. To my mind, it came too late to embody a future for France that was substantially different from its immediate past. I remained all the more cautious because, as editor of a collection at Albin Michel sponsored by Jean-Edern Hallier, I was – without knowing it – subject in the early months to the ostracism directed at all those whose names featured in the writer's address book. It was Jean-Pierre Chevènement – the new Minister for Research, and one of the main architects of Mitterrand's victory – who drew me out. In 1978 he had read *Dissidence ou révolution?*, and I received a surprise invitation to lunch at the National Assembly from someone who was then merely the young and brilliant Deputy for Belfort. We had maintained bonds of friendship, reinforced by my family roots in Franche-Comté. Together with François Châtelet, Jacques Derrida and Jean-Pierre

Faye, he charged me with setting up the novel institution that was to be the Collège international de philosophie, which will soon mark its twentieth anniversary. Because of my interests and previous work, my role would be to establish links between philosophers and scientists. The framework of the Collège proved unconducive to this. And so, still enjoying the support of Jean-Pierre Chevènement, I created another structure – what is today the Association Diderot – the initial inspiration for which came from the neurologist Alain Prochiantz, my contemporary at the École normale supérieure.

The period between 1982 and 1989 was thus very rich in experience: both as a founder of two institutions whose activities involved long-term projects designed to counteract the shortcomings of the French university system; and as a member on several occasions of the Conseil national des universités and the national committee of the Centre national de la recherche scientifique – bastions of that very system.

For eight years I did not write or publish anything. But I had a privileged vantage point from which to observe the collapse of academic Marxism; the survival and then revival of the phenomenological current, which underwent a spectacular theological 'turn' during the 1980s; the blaze of postmodernism, which died down as rapidly as it had flared up; and then the institutional ascendancy of philosophers identifying with logical positivism, Popperianism, or analytical philosophy.

The rise of sociologists or anthropologists of science contributed to the recession of the French tradition of historical epistemology without completely marginalizing it, given the links with scientists and doctors it maintained under the vigilant eyes of Georges Canguilhem and François Dagognet.

As I anticipated at the end of my 1978 text, Anglo-Saxon political philosophy of a liberal inspiration has had a strong impact in

France in the wake of historiographical work challenging the ortho-dox, *marxisant* interpretation of the French Revolution. François Furet drove Albert Soboul from the front of the stage. Tocqueville opened the door of our republic of letters to John Rawls, who was belatedly translated into French.

Reading the recent attacks on French philosophy in the United States, one has the impression that this profound transformation is very poorly appreciated in the Anglo-Saxon countries. The picture of French philosophy implicitly painted by Alain Sokal and Jean Bricmont's choice of targets in *Intellectual Impostures* seems outdated. In *Les piètres penseurs*, by contrast, I have sought to register the set of forces that have contributed to the formation of a new intellectual landscape in France. Following the ill-fated Gilles Châtelet in his lampoon *Vivre et penser comme des porcs* (1998), I argue that the media celebrity of a few personalities derives from their philosophical ori-entation. Regardless of whether their references are Kantian, Stoic, or Epicurean, their discourse presents itself as a discourse of order, consensus, or consolation. The word 'wisdom' unites them. It carries with it the injunction for everyone to remain in their place and – above all – to rest content with the mediocrity of their position. Nothing would be worse in their eyes than to imagine changing the world through audacious and rigorous thinking. We would only engender new monsters!

The trap set by Sokal for Francophile American intellectuals, and the attack he launched with Jean Bricmont on a heteroclite crowd of French philosophers from the 1970s, have a compound effect attuned to the milieu of academic philosophy. In response to the instances of scientistic imprudence – certainly deplorable – with which these thinkers believed they had to pay for their theoretical audacity, *Intellectual Impostures* sounds like a summons to retreat. As you will see in *Les piètres penseurs*, I still prefer ambition and risk.

For that reason, I find the English title of this collection apt. Like that of my last book, it contains a play on words. Mediocrity as a shared ideal is its main target. The media are content with this ideal, and diffuse it. It is up to us to mount some kind of resistance.

D. L.

3 March 2000

The Mediocracy

Prologue

I love my country. So when I see it nursing old nationalist hatreds, or indulging in the morbid fantasies of a lethal racism, I also have occasion to detest it. But I will never adopt that tone of lofty contempt employed by influential technocrats at the slightest provocation to bemoan the fact that 'this country', as they put it, balks at submitting respectfully to their admirable authority.

Absorbed in their servile admiration for the triumphant Anglo-Saxon world, in particular they have no inkling of the world renown of French thinkers. Yet this remains so strong, even in the USA, that they are regularly the target of concerted attacks over there, as we saw again recently with the 'Sokal affair'.[1] It will, however, have been noted that those who found themselves in the firing line once more belong to what is conventionally called the ''60s generation': a daring group of thinkers whose starting point

1 See Yves Jeanneret, *L'affaire Sokal ou la querelle des impostures*, Presses Universitaires de France, Paris 1998.

was the simple idea that, in order to change the world, it is necessary to interpret it; and that, in order to interpret it in depth, it is necessary to want to change it. Heirs to a great tradition, the more 'political' among them inscribed this idea in the perspective of revolution.

These thinkers imposed their radicalism to such an extent that their opponents revived a virulently counter-revolutionary strain of thought in response. At the beginning of the 1960s, 'conservative' was reputedly a typically British, grey word in France, foreign to our political lexicon. Liberalism was reckoned American and, moreover, archaic; the possibility of a Reagan had not as yet been envisaged. Social democracy was good for the Federal Republic of Germany and the Scandinavian countries. In short, there was a time when lukewarm water was not popular in our country!

Today, we are swimming in it. And any intellectuals who claim to connect up their thought with a project geared to changing society are considered suspect, potentially dangerous or virtually raving. Only experts of all kinds are regarded as respectable – in the front rank, the economists and political pundits who hold forth. Specialists in predictions invariably contradicted by the facts, they brandish their statistics as thought. They never utter a word, even by way of apology, about their errors. The popularity of the terms 'pragmatism' and 'realism' – the only thing disabused politicians of all stripes ever invoke – is symptomatic of our society's intellectual abdication. It now seems as if the only people it recognizes as thinkers are a few moralists who are praised to the skies. Having adopted the stance of spectators on the world, the latter confine themselves at best to commenting on current events, when they are not content to parade their own moods on the public stage. Indignation, compassion and admonition represent their preferred register.

Hence the disquiet expressed by some young people who work alongside me during the celebration of the thirtieth anniversary of May 1968, so powerfully orchestrated in the media. What have you done with yourself in the last thirty years?, they have asked insistently. What have you done for us? What is the point of the incessant spectacle being staged by some people? Can it simply be attributed to the novel power of the media, to the operation of networks of influence, institutionalized cronyism and creeping corruption? Why, seemingly, does no original thinking emerge? Should we renounce any purchase on a world whose poverty, meanness and violence we deplore?

In the pages that follow I have tried, as best I can, to answer these questions, which involve the future. I have endeavoured to unravel the threads of the history that has led numerous French intellectuals to set themselves no higher ambition than acquiring the social status of 'opinion-maker', as they say in the marketplace. I have had to retrace the itinerary that has seen them graduate from repudiation of their intellectual guides [*maîtres-à-penser*], formerly branded by one of them 'master thinkers' [*maîtres penseurs*] – totalitarianism-mongers – to a renunciation of any inventive thinking.

A thinker who abandons the thought for which he has been assigned responsibility, and is no longer concerned to extend and develop it, I brand a mediocre thinker [*piètre penseur*]. In my view, the era of the 'master thinkers' has been followed by that of the 'mediocrities'.

Even so, we should have a bit of a laugh. They are so serious! The times may seem very sombre. Silently, however, the labour of thought has, as always, continued its work. I shall resist announcing a new dawn. But we may at least be able to shed some light on things.

1

Baby Boom

Young people, I understand your confusion, your irritation, your bitterness even. You have just had a breathtaking commemoration of May '68 inflicted on you by those who occupy pride of place in the media. You've got the message: We old hands, who've seen it all before, have discovered everything and understood everything! Even our errors should redound to our credit. They consecrate our judgements as self-confessed 'penitents'. In short, this world is *our* world. It's up to you to find a place in it. One condition: be good! And don't complain. You've got a choice between two models: pliable asceticism or moderate hedonism.

You protest? Aren't we going to let you fashion your own life? Are we going to declare everything you attempt, imagine or undertake null and void in advance?

You are right. But do not lament, for you would be quite wrong to take the triumphant discourses of the puffed-up people now offering you instruction at their word. The past thirty years have not simply witnessed the rise to social prominence of a self-assured generation. We should recall, as has Jean-Paul Dollé in his superb book on Pierre Goldmann,[2] the names of all those who did not swallow it, and of all those for whom things did not turn out well. First of all, the insubordinate and those who held themselves aloof, in the background or in reserve. We should also salute those damaged in the course of the experience, who lost the use of speech, or those who one day preferred to take their own lives – our friends Nicos Poulantzas or Michel Pêcheux,[3] and so many others. Yes, so many others – those murdered in cold blood and those who, in the early hours, were plunged irrevocably back into the night of a lethal madness: Althusser. . . .

But have no fear: I am not going to lapse into pathos. It is simply that the picture that has been painted of a generation of self-satisfied Rastignacs is, in my view, nothing but an imposture. To speak in a postmodernist idiom, let us say that it is the mini-'grand narrative' constructed retrospectively by some in order to enlist their contemporaries in the legitimation of their (good) fortune. No, as it happens, we have not understood everything. That is why it will be necessary one day to write another history, to get the measure not only of the successes – they do exist! – but also of the failures and, above all, of the incompetence of those who so readily say 'we' in the name of others. It is not true that there is no longer anything to be understood; there is evidently a lot still to be done.

---

2 *L'insoumis. Vies et légendes de Pierre Goldmann*, Grasset, Paris 1997.

3 Nicos Poulantzas: Greek sociologist and philosopher. Settled in Paris in 1960 and met Althusser in 1966. Committed suicide in 1979.

   Michel Pêcheux: student at the École normale supérieure (1959) and 'Althusserian' philosopher. Gravitated towards psychology (Lacan), complicating his relationship with Althusser. Committed suicide in 1983.

I do not think I am too badly placed to venture a judgement on this history, since I did, after all, participate in it – and occasionally found myself in the front line. If you are interested in service records, you may like to know that together with the Trotskyist leader Alain Krivine and a few others, I was among the select number to feature on posters, accused of undermining national security, in June 1968, because my name figured as editorial director on numerous publications, each a deeper red than the rest. This ended with *Bastion rouge*, a two-franc broadsheet that precipitated the collapse of a small printer on the rue Cinq-Diamants. Words are sometimes cruel!

Even so, I am sure you will not mind if I do not indulge in the disenchanted cynicism professed by some of my contemporaries. Nor will I succumb to the nostalgia quietly cultivated by others. However, it seems to me necessary to revisit a period – the beginning of the 1960s – whose intellectual excitement it is difficult to imagine amid the torpor of the present. We had the immense good fortune to start out then; that is why I do not envy you having reached twenty after 1980.

Born mostly at the Liberation, we still interest sociologists who are fond of statistics as children of the 'baby boom'. Our numbers will go on disrupting institutions and calculations. The academy in particular has never really recovered from our arrival *en masse* in the lecture theatres. The ancient Sorbonne, whose rituals and teaching methods had scarcely changed since the end of the nineteenth century, found itself literally – physically – inundated in the space of a few years by a new type of student, whom numerous professors, accustomed to lecturing the sons and daughters of the nice bourgeoisie in tranquillity, regarded as savage hordes. But what matters most is that these students had grown up in a different world from that of their parents – a world in which, at the war's close, it had been resolved to reconstruct everything on new foundations. Unawares, we were all imbued with this feeling.

You, for your part, have only ever heard talk of 'crisis'. The great question confronting you concerns the place you will be able to find in this world. How to escape from the general wreckage? Or, at least, how not to stagnate, expelled to the margins of a society that grinds individuals down? The word 'crisis' did not feature in our vocabulary. In our ears it had the ring of a word from the past, a throwback to our parents' world: the interwar period, the 1929 Crash, the rise of Nazism, and the high-pressured political situation that had been their lot during the 1950s, at the start of the Cold War. We entertained no doubts. The question tormenting students in our era involved not their future, but the contribution they could make to building a society where any repetition of the tragedies through which our century had lived would be averted. In effect, we wanted to make a clean sweep of the past. We wanted to succeed where our parents had failed. Hence our zeal for rethinking the world, by making the most of what we had.

Through a reversal that occurred at the end of the following decade, this zeal became suspect. The devastating critique of the 'master thinkers' ushered in the era of the mediocrities who, having renounced the project of changing the world, were content to judge it according to the supposedly eternal divide between Good and Evil. We are still in it, even if the 'ethical' reflection thus rehabilitated has undergone unimaginable developments over the last twenty years.

2

Sixties Militants

First of all, I am going to talk about the rue d'Ulm.[4] Not because the École normale supérieure is the temple of thought – something that was still an article of faith for many at the beginning of the 1960s – but because a good few of the events that marked our history unfolded there. Now, it so happens that from 1965 to 1970 I was a student in the philosophy department. I thus took my place in the small stable of those thoroughbreds who, in order to finish, had to prove themselves by clearing the hurdle of the *agrégation*,[5] after making the grade in the formidable entrance exam. Louis Althusser and Jacques Derrida awaited us.

Althusser was approaching the zenith of his glory in September

---

4 It is Régis Debray who, in his book *Par amour de l'art: une éducation intellectuelle* (Gallimard, Paris 1998), has written most scrupulously about the École normale supérieure of the period – and especially about Althusser – with his typical touch of desperate irony.

5 The *agrégation* is the highest competitive examination for teachers in France. A successful candidate is an *agrégé(e)*. [Trans.]

1965, with the publication of a collection of articles in his famous book *Pour Marx*. Some of us had already read and discussed these texts with passion, in the smoky basement of the Clarté bookshop in the place Paul Painlevé, a favourite meeting-place for left-wing students in Paris. Each issue of the journal *La Pensée*, which had published his initial studies on the young Marx, was impatiently anticipated. The preface to the book, which denounced 'the stubborn, profound absence of any real *theoretical* culture' in the French Communist tradition,[6] and inscribed this work in the conjuncture of de-Stalinization, made an enormous impression on us. In November *Lire le Capital* appeared, product of a seminar organized by the philosopher at the École in the academic year 1964–65 with some of his pupils (Étienne Balibar, Pierre Macherey, Jacques Rancière and Roger Establet).[7]

Such is the oblivion to which he has been brutally consigned that you will have no image of Althusser, who was my friend for over twenty years. The heavy incline of his enormous domed forehead, the bags under his eyes, his sometimes halting gait – these already attested to the atrocious suffering that ravaged his life. His intense blue eyes could be cheerful, sarcastic, arrogant; he would often become abruptly shrouded in the mists of melancholy for long periods of silence. But the pupil I then was did not possess the key to what I have just written. My friends and I discerned in it the stamp of genius. Althusser was the prince of philosophers, the hero of

6 Louis Althusser, *For Marx*, trans. Ben Brewster, Allen Lane, London 1969, p. 23.
7 Abridged 1968 edition published in English as Louis Althusser and Étienne Balibar, *Reading Capital*, trans. Ben Brewster, New Left Books, London 1970. For some amazing first-hand testimony to the atmosphere surrounding this enterprise, readers are referred to the relevant correspondence in Louis Althusser, *Lettres à Franca (1961–1973)*, ed. and introd. François Matheron and Yann Moulier Boutang, Stock/IMEC, Paris 1998.

thought who was defying the Communist Party authorities, the one who was going to save Marx from Marxism and the Marxists.[8]

Beside this *monstre sacré*, Derrida was not yet Derrida. It was in the spring of 1967 that he began his progress towards great notoriety, with the famous communication to the Société française de philosophie on 'La différance' (with an *a*), and the publication of his first three books.[9] His seminar, in which I participated continuously for five years under the gibes of my leftist comrades, remained exclusive. We experienced some great educational moments there. Pacing up and down the room, the dusky little man with dark eyes commented on Husserl with extraordinary meticulousness and practised the 'eidetic reduction' with peerless virtuosity, a packet of Brazza cigarettes in hand.

Neither of these teachers encouraged us to be satisfied at the prospect of the brilliant academic career that had been painted in glowing colours in our preparatory classes. To tell the truth, there was never any question of such a career. At the École we were not concerned with our personal future. We were unaware that such insouciance was a luxury. Politics alone galvanized us. Not, obviously, politics in the sense of ministerial office, which people over at the École nationale d'administration were beginning to dream about. With the exception of our fellow students Alain Juppé

8 Pierre Macherey has admirably conveyed Althusser's glory at the time in his *Histoires de dinosaure. Faire de la philosophie 1965–1997*, Presses Universitaires de France, Paris 1999.

9 *Writing and Difference*, trans. Alan Bass, Routledge & Kegan Paul, London 1978; *Speech and Phenomena and Other Essays on Husserl's Theory of Signs*, trans. David B. Allison, Northwestern University Press, Evanston, IL 1973; *Of Grammatology*, trans. Gayatri Chakravorty Spivak, Johns Hopkins University Press, Baltimore and London 1976. See also Geoffrey Bennington and Jacques Derrida, *Jacques Derrida*, trans. Bennington, University of Chicago Press, Chicago and London 1993.

(cohort of 1964) and Laurent Fabius (1966) – who, as everyone knows, branched off to become successful politicians – we were oblivious of its very existence. Politics we construed, rather, in the epic sense that the accents of de Gaulle could impart to it on occasion; or in the historical sense conferred on it by the grand term 'Resistance' over which our parents' generation had fought. The names of some writers or philosophers, symbols of baseness, circulated among us: Brasillach, Drieu la Rochelle, and so on. Profound disquiet surrounded the *œuvre* of Céline, as well as that of Heidegger, despite Beaufret and Derrida. Others, in contrast, assumed the status of models. There was Jean Cavaillès, philosopher and logician, co-founder of the Resistance movement Libération-Sud, who was taken prisoner several times and escaped, tortured and then shot by the Germans, and buried in the citadel of Arras in February 1944; or his comrade-in-arms and friend, the philosopher and doctor Georges Canguilhem, whose rigorous teaching we were going to discover at the Sorbonne, along with his intransigent and generous personality.[10]

We campaigned against the war in Vietnam waged by the USA. As secondary school pupils, many of us had protested against the 'dirty war' in Algeria at our first meetings. Our first demos were those in the course of which police chief Maurice Papon's men soaked the streets of Paris with blood. In other words, we knew that politics could touch and shatter people's daily lives. Before our very eyes, it still tore families apart. It presented itself to us with an impassioned and brutal appearance, wholly in keeping with the tragedy of history, of which France contained so many echoes and traces during our childhood. Long after the din of 1958 and the sabre-rattling that had accompanied de Gaulle's return to power, the

10 See Georges Canguilhem, *Vie et mort de Jean Cavaillès*, Allia, Paris 1996.

imminence of a fascist 'coup' kept us on the alert. And the gelignite of the OAS in its nights of terror, like the almost daily confrontations in the rue Saint-Jacques, mobilized even the most pacific of us.[11] This was the era when the gabardined troops of Malliarakis, Madelin and Longuet would rhythmically bellow 'Commies back to Moscow', before attacking us in defence of the Occident.[12]

Another impending event galvanized the thinking of the most committed: the end of capitalism announced by Karl Marx. When Jean-Paul Sartre wrote his famous sentence to the effect that Marxism was the 'untranscendable philosophy for our time',[13] he had expressed the deep conviction of many of us. We were not all Communists – I never was – because the shadow of the Soviet Union hung over the French Party. There were unquestionably too many skeletons in the cupboards of the *Internationale*; and that had been the case for so long that you had to stop up your ears and close your eyes to be oblivious of it. But none of us doubted that a radiant future would take shape for humanity, at least if we pulled our weight. Another world was going to emerge, and our mission was to make a contribution to it. For in order to build it, this world had first to be thought through.

11 The Organisation Armée Secrète (1961–63), led by generals Salan and Jouhaux, sought to oppose Algerian independence by terrorist methods after the failure of the military putsch in Algiers.

12 Occident was an extreme right-wing student organization, very active in Paris in the 1960s. Two of its leaders, Alain Madelin and Gérard Longuet, went on to become prominent figures on the mainstream Right in France, while a third – Gilles Malliarakis – founded a neo-fascist group called 'Third Way'. [Trans.]

13 *Critique of Dialectical Reason I: Theory of Practical Ensembles* (1960), trans. Alan Sheridan-Smith, ed. Jonathan Rée, New Left Books, London 1976, p. 822.

In actual fact, those at the École who became militants during the 1960s split into two groups, whose relations were sometimes tempestuous. There were the activists and the theoreticians. The former were considered dedicated militants. This could extend to the adoption of a visionary and voluntary servitude. Tireless distributors of tracts, methodical pacers of staircases, zealous stuffers of letterboxes, the booed heroes of raucous meetings, some of them blossomed under the spittle. I have known *normaliens* in the union common room who exhausted themselves day and night in this way for years on end, to become models of self-abnegation.[14] They later supplied the most solid battalions to the movement dedicated to 'establishing' students in the factories, for the purposes of ideological re-education and political agitation on the Chinese model.[15] Fidgeting at their sides were those who only dreamt of doing battle. Making a virtue of their laziness, they did not await instruction from China before declaring themselves hostile to the 'cult of the book'. A few pioneers took up combat sports; others wielded iron bars. The most frivolous were content to practise permanent eructation, and downed their vodkas in one to the health of Comrade Stalin. In their eyes, genuine science would be proletarian or it would not exist. Accordingly, it was of the utmost urgency to neutralize the mandarins. Zhdanov had some disciples among the *khâgneux* at the Lycée Louis-le-Grand![16]

I owe my decision to write a book on the Lysenko affair partly to

14 A *normalien* (or *normalienne*) is a past or present student of the École normale supérieure. [Trans.]

15 The movement is admirably described by Robert Linhart, who sacrificed himself, in *The Assembly Line* (1978), trans. Margaret Crosland, John Calder, London 1981.

16 Andrei Alexandrovich Zhdanov (1896–1948): member of the Soviet Politburo from 1939, responsible for cultural policy under Stalin. [*Khâgneux* denotes members of the class (the *khâgne*) preparing the entrance examination for the École normale supérieure – Trans.]

the irascible Guy Lardreau and Christian Jambet, at the time implacable leaders of the 'red hawks' at that prestigious institution, after they accused me of succumbing to bourgeois objectivism in my publications on the epistemology of Gaston Bachelard![17] That's the way it was. Out of these drives, whether accepted or sublimated, from these rebellious outbursts against the 'ugly mugs' inhabiting the institutions, the best, like Ollivier Rolin, have today fashioned literature or a scholarly *œuvre*, as have those mentioned above.

The majority, more speculative, were preoccupied above all with theory. This was the great slogan of the epoch, frequently capitalized. An elliptical thesis of Marx's – the eleventh thesis on Feuerbach – became the object of inexhaustible exegeses: 'The philosophers have only *interpreted* the world, in various ways; the point is to change it.'[18] The positivism of the social and human sciences, then undergoing massive expansion, did well out of it. Freed from philosophical tutelage, did not these sciences hold the key to the heralded transformation of the world?

A compulsive desire to consume seized a generation of student militants. It was of the utmost urgency to read Lévi-Strauss, Jakobson and Lacan; the classical political economists; Mauss and Durkheim; the historians of the *Annales* School; and so on. Pierre Bourdieu was already a big success. The book he co-authored with Jean-Claude Passeron in 1964, *Les Héritiers*,[19] spoke to us about ourselves. For a long time to come it marked the thinking of students

---

17 See my *Proletarian Science? The Case of Lysenko*, trans. Ben Brewster, New Left Books, London 1977; and *Marxism and Epistemology: Bachelard, Canguilhem, Foucault*, trans. Ben Brewster, New Left Books, London 1975.

18 Karl Marx, *Early Writings*, ed. Lucio Colletti, trans. Rodney Livingstone and Gregor Benton, Penguin/ *New Left Review*, Harmondsworth 1975, p. 423.

19 *The Inheritors: French Students and their Relation to Culture*, trans. Richard Nice, University of Chicago Press, Chicago and London 1979.

and teachers on what, in Marxist jargon, was conventionally called their 'class position' (to be distinguished from their 'class origin', which for the most part was regrettably bourgeois!). People piled into psychoanalysis lectures. Lacan circulated clandestinely, until the publication of the *Écrits* in 1966.[20] Censier University, which opened its doors then, was the first Parisian stage for this infatuation; at a distance from the old Sorbonne, it was not far from the rue d'Ulm. We scoured courses and seminars without any concern for our career paths, but to satisfy our political appetite for knowledge. We students organized seminars for our own benefit on the philosophy of mathematics, as well as political economy or the dialectics of nature. You will understand why this epoch can be looked back on today as a golden age for publishers and bookshops.

Louis Althusser's stroke of genius consisted in endeavouring to collect the payout in aid of a renovated Marxism. He baptized historical materialism the 'science of history' and, basing himself on Gaston Bachelard, revealed to our astounded eyes the famous 'epistemological break' that definitively separated Marx from his own youth from 1845 onwards! Exploiting the word 'structure', referring to Lévi-Strauss and Lacan, he conveyed the impression that Marxism could benefit from this effervescence and confer a 'revolutionary' political meaning on the new disciplines – without any liability, of course. Moreover, he was personally convinced that if Marxism did not prove itself capable of producing new knowledge of social phenomena, it was going to disappear, to be conclusively transformed into the catechism of a party apparatus. Contrary to his subsequent image, Althusser did not compel universal attention by virtue of his dogmatism, but because he disrupted the vulgate. And

---

20 Abridged English edition published as *Écrits: A Selection*, trans. Alan Sheridan, Tavistock, London 1977.

when he found himself under fire from Communist Party orthodoxy, represented by Roger Garaudy (at the time Politburo member responsible for intellectuals), his glory reached a peak. Even if he banked on a 'return to Marx', it was indeed an 'imaginary Marxism' that he was constructing – as Raymond Aron's formula rightly had it, and as he himself was subsequently at pains to acknowledge.[21]

In referring to a 'recommencement of dialectical materialism',[22] Alain Badiou has captured precisely what it was about this thinking that seduced us. Indeed, far from intoning the consecrated formulas recorded in the innumerable manuals of 'Marxist philosophy', Althusser placed an examination of Marx's philosophy at the centre of his reflection. And unlike so many others in their desperation, he equally refused to identify it with the doctrine expounded in Marx's early writings (*The Holy Family*, the 1844 *Manuscripts*, etc.) – 'humanist' texts which, to us, did not really seem to break with the philosophical practice of 'interpreting the world'. Althusser considered that Marx's philosophy was, in reality, to be found in the 'practical state' in his mature works, but that he had not articulated it explicitly. Through a 'symptomatic reading' of texts, Althusser applied himself to bringing it to light, in order to develop it. His incendiary style and ardour did the rest. The pen of our master quivered with the turbulent alliance he sought to forge between Spinoza and Pascal through the intermediary of Machiavelli.

That said, Althusser did not confine himself to this heterodox return to the founding texts of Marxism. He advanced a non-

---

21 See Aron, *Marxismes imaginaires: d'une sainte famille à l'autre*, Gallimard, Paris 1970; and Althusser, *The Future Lasts a Long Time and The Facts*, ed. Olivier Corpet and Yann Moulier Boutang, trans. Richard Veasey, Chatto & Windus, London 1993, p. 221.

22 Alain Badiou, 'Le (re)commencement du matérialisme dialectique', *Critique*, no. 240, May 1967, pp. 438–67.

Hegelian conception of the social totality, which repudiated the reigning economism; he invited reconsideration of the type of causality governing social phenomena, and opened up original lines of investigation in anthropology and sociology, as well as linguistic theory. Many were the bold researchers, whether his pupils or not, who plunged in enthusiastically.

Today, it is impossible to have any idea of the passions aroused by this enterprise, ranging from sheer adulation to utter detestation. During the 1970s it was routine to invoke or refute Althusser on every subject. From 1965 onwards, 'Althusserianism' became a brand image. Metal-rimmed glasses multiplied, along with proletarian caps, Leninist goatees, and – don't ask me why – corduroy trousers, preferably green. Shame on those who had not read right up to the very last line of *Capital*, in the eight-volume edition published by Éditions Sociales. Woe betide the lazy adepts of selected extracts! We applied ourselves to 'advancing science', to quote Étienne Balibar, who spared no effort and whose modesty and kindness staggered us, given what he had written. The detour might be long, and the apprentice revolutionary often bore a fraternal resemblance to the aspirant mandarin. This occasionally led to memorable meetings, like a row lasting until dawn in the Salle Cavaillès at the École normale about the materialist or non-materialist character of the Lacanian concept *insignifié du signifiant*. On one side were the 'politicos' Robert Linhart and Benny Lévy, [23] adopting the style of state prosecutors – the former jovial, the latter peremptory. On the other were the 'epistemologists' Jacques-Alain Miller, who was preparing

---

23 Robert Linhart: a *normalien* (1963) who played an active role in the creation of the Maoist Union des jeunesses communistes marxistes-léninistes in 1966.

   Benny Lévy: likewise a *normalien* (1965) and the political leader of the post-1968 Maoist organization the Gauche prolétarienne, under the pseudonym Pierre Victor. Subsequently, he acted as Jean-Paul Sartre's secretary.

to become the Son-in-Law by marrying Lacan's daughter, and Jean-Claude Milner, pleading the cause of Science with a starchy rigour![24]

Even so, you shouldn't go believing that the thinking of the period had taken up exclusive residence at 45 rue d'Ulm; or that it can be reduced to scholarly discussions on the interpretation of Marx's texts, illuminated by the experience (painful or exhilarating) of really existing socialism. Intellectual effervescence among the young was universal. With the 22 March Movement, a quite different strain of thought emerged into the open in 1968.

A blue pamphlet had been circulating since November 1966, containing an inflammatory text in the style of a quasi-manifesto, whose tone was wholly original. It had been published at the University of Strasbourg by 'members of the Situationist International and students of Strasbourg'. Its interminable title induced fury in the back rooms of Parisian cafés in the spring of that morose year, 1967: *On the Poverty of Student Life: considered in its economic, political, psychological, sexual and especially intellectual aspects, with a modest proposal for its remedy*. The authors began with this peremptory and astringent declaration: 'It is pretty safe to say that the student is the most universally despised creature in France, apart from the policeman and the priest.'[25] Justifiably so, they added, since students, for all their whining, accepted the material and

24 Jacques-Alain Miller: *normalien* (1962) and pupil of Althusser; active member of the Cercle d'épistémologie at the École normale.

   Jean-Claude Milner: *normalien* (1963) and today Professor of Linguistics at the University of Paris VII. He is currently president of the Collège International de Philosophie.

25 'On the Poverty of Student Life', in Ken Knabb, ed. and trans., *Situationist International: An Anthology*, Bureau of Public Secrets, Berkeley, CA 1981, pp. 319–37 (p. 319).

ideological conditions imposed on them by their family and the university system so that they could become 'lower cadres': pathetic 'compensation', forcing them to flee reality and take refuge in the delights of miserabilism and bohemianism.

Thus berated, French students were enjoined to raise their sights beyond the walls of the institutions training and framing them – even beyond the borders of their own country. The 'revolt of youth against the way of life imposed on it', continued the authors, had begun to develop in Holland (the provos) as well as England (teddy boys) – even in France (hell's angels), but above all in the USA. This rebellion had its emblems, such as motorbikes, electric guitars, clothes, records, and so on. It was not sparing the countries of the bureaucratic East, where a section of youth no longer respectful of the moral order and the family was given over to 'debauchery', despised work, and no longer obeyed the Party police. This rebellion was the germ of a more wide-ranging subversion, an impending 'revolutionary epoch'. Announcing the end of the reign of commodities, the text concluded with some lines whose prophetic style and tone capture the mood of the moment:

The radical critique and free reconstruction of all values and patterns of behavior imposed by alienated reality are its maximum program, and free creativity in the construction of all moments and events of life is the only *poetry* [the proletariat] can acknowledge . . . Proletarian revolutions will be *festivals* or nothing, for festivity is the very keynote of the life they announce. *Play* is the ultimate principle of this festival, and the only rules it can recognize are to live without dead time and enjoy without restraints.[26]

26 Ibid., p. 337.

Even as watered down by Daniel Cohn-Bendit and his comrades at Nanterre University, Situationist thought made its way among youth. The unobtrusive publication in 1967 of Guy Debord's cult book[27] was to reveal the full intellectual measure of an international movement whose début in fact dates back to the end of the 1950s. The name of the author, cloaked in mystery, began to circulate around Nanterre. The whiff of cordite hung over the desolate campus adjoining the shantytown, far from the Parisian elites. These uncompromising agitators defended the 'passionate abundance of life', threatened with extinction under the impact of the 'sanctimonious functionalism' of capitalist society. They inscribed their activity in the revolutionary tradition embodied by the proletariat, while asserting the need to supersede Marxism. If they claimed to derive their inspiration from socialism, they defined it as 'the most thoroughgoing emancipation of the energies and capacities of every individual'. This was miles from the embittered discussions over the dictatorship of the proletariat and democratic centralism that had set Communists and Trotskyists at each other's throats for ages; and a thousand miles away, apparently, from the questions about the scientificity of Marxism raised by Althusser. As for the 'epistemological break', they openly poked fun at it.

The laid-back character of these students, with their sarcasm and elation, their concern to promote a new way of living through daring experimentation, was initially regarded as sheer lunacy by the learned militants of the Latin Quarter. Coarse laughter ensued: the

27 *The Society of the Spectacle*, trans. Donald Nicholson-Smith, Zone Books, New York 1994. A member of the Situationist International, which he co-founded in 1957, and responsible for SI publications, Debord was involved in the various activities of this organization, in particular in Germany, England and Italy. Very active in May 1968, he thereafter acquired a significant influence on the European and American ultra-Left.

Nanterre students were demanding open access to the girls' rooms
in the hall of residence! What mockery from the standpoint of the
higher interests of the revolution. . . . Here moreover, were militants, who were revelling in having daubed 'Never work!' on the
walls of the boulevard Port-Royal in Paris. What an insult to the
workers! They had the audacity to issue the slogan 'Don't say
"Professor" any more. Say: "Clapped-out whore"!' This sounded
wrong to the ears of *normaliens*. Above all, was it not aimed at the
wrong target? A few weeks later, when Nanterre entered Paris courtesy of panicking academic authorities and stumbling political
officials, this invasion installed madness at the Sorbonne, and then at
the Odéon. Let us not forget that it also had the effect of putting the
doctrinaires to rout.

I hope that these brief reflections of a veteran will have helped
you to understand that there never was any real intellectual unanimity among the groups that triggered the demonstrations of May
1968. Moreover, this was borne out in practice throughout the
month, in the courtyard and lecture theatres of the Sorbonne, from
which the Communist students were rapidly expelled, following
PCF leader Georges Marchais's highly regrettable editorial in
L'Humanité denouncing the German anarchist Cohn-Bendit. It was
also noticeable on the famous barricades, from which the majority
of Maoists kept their distance – even though they were regarded by
the press as the most dangerous experts in urban guerrilla warfare.

It was only retrospectively, nearly twenty years later, that some
thinkers in search of notoriety concocted the fiction of such unanimity, the better to channel the ebb of political thinking that began
around 1976 towards their own philosophical positions.

3

A Fiction: '*La Pensée 68*'

In their laboured construction *La Pensée 68*, published in 1985, Luc Ferry and Alain Renaut found themselves stymied by the diverse positions adopted by the protagonists of 1968.[28] Carried away by the urge finally to make a clean sweep for the liberal philosophy of human rights – which, in their view, the French had mistakenly ignored or rejected – the two young academics, otherwise so brilliant, had to produce a fantastic theoretical montage, worthy of a grand *agrégation* lecture. According to them, the key question of May '68 was that of humanism. More precisely, antihumanism, which had affected – or rather, infested – the thinking of the principal French theorists of the 'sixties' (as they put it in English, to be chic). This thinking had supposedly inspired, if not manipulated, the student revolt, and determined its wide-ranging social and intellectual effects.

---

28 Luc Ferry and Alain Renaut, *French Philosophy of the Sixties: An Essay on Antihumanism*, trans. Mary H. S. Cattani, University of Massachusetts Press, Amherst 1990.

In truth, it was not difficult for Ferry and Renaut to demonstrate an identical opposition to humanism in the texts they cited. It was sufficient to review, rubric after rubric, 'French Nietzscheanism' (Foucault and Deleuze), 'French Heideggerianism' (Derrida), and 'French Marxism' (Althusser and Bourdieu). But it remained to be shown that this intellectual current was that of 1968. By their own admission, this was not unproblematic.

Indeed, how is the resolutely humanist tonality of the slogans that fired the demonstrators in May '68 to be explained, if they were inspired by a quite antithetical philosophy? For if the youth on the boulevard Saint-Michel, and those occupying the Sorbonne and the Odéon, did ultimately agree on something, it was on their rejection of the repressive moral order: 'enjoy without restraints!' [*jouir sans entraves*]. They all spat on what they called the 'consumer society', and protested against the alienation of subjects by the system: 'same old routine' [*métro–boulot–dodo*].[29] This, as the two essayists candidly acknowledge, represents a veritable paradox, an enigma. But for these crusaders against 'philosophists', such a paradox is evidently merely apparent. Indeed, on page 67 of their lampoon they reckon to be in a position to crow over their victory: 'One enigma has been removed from the domain of our inquiry, albeit only an apparent one. The "philosophists" of the '68 period inscribe their critiques of the idea of the subject within an intellectual horizon that the principal inspirations of the May movement also evince.'

29 Jean Baudrillard, author of the celebrated *The System of Objects* (1968; trans. James Benedict, Verso, London and New York 1996), and very adept at exploiting the Situationist vein, was to publish a book in 1970 whose opening lines accurately capture the spirit of the period: 'There is all around us today a kind of fantastic conspicuousness of consumption and abundance, constituted by the multiplication of objects, services and material goods, and this represents something of a fundamental mutation in the ecology of the human species' (*The Consumer Society: Myths and Structures*, Sage Publications, London and Thousand Oaks, CA 1998, p. 25).

It is (so they claim) Gilles Lipovetsky's 'subtle analyses'[30] which – a passing courtesy – 'on condition that one has a keener awareness of their limitations', have facilitated this *tour de force*. For they disclose a 'subtle process, where the other face of the affirmation of individuality is the degradation of the ideal of subjectivity'. '*The subject dies with the birth of the individual*,' lament Ferry and Renaut, who strive for its resurrection.[31]

Thus, 'the major representatives of '68 philosophy', 'agents of an individualism they frequently denounced', had supposedly 'made history without knowing the history they were making'.[32] (Note the emphatic Hegelian wink!) Subtlest of the subtle, Ferry and Renaut invite us to turn to the respectable authors who possess the advantage of coherence, and are well versed in moral rearmament of the famous individual-subject: Kant, Fichte, and so on. There you have it.

Alas, this construction makes light of the obvious differences between the authors whose works are subsumed under the category of *la pensée 68*. For example, it is ridiculous implicitly to introduce Gilles Deleuze and Félix Guattari as sons of Lacan, when the old master represents their main target. Yet in their text, *Anti-Œdipe* features, by the same token as the *Écrits*, as a monument of *la pensée 68*, on the grounds that in it one finds 'the figure of the pulverized or disintegrated Ego that appeared on the horizon of the rise of individualism'![33] Our polemicists are untroubled by such details. Their conception of intellectual generations seems to be straight out of the

---

30 *L'ère du vide: essais sur l'individualisme contemporain*, Gallimard, Paris 1983.

31 Ferry and Renaut, *French Philosophy of the Sixties*, pp. 64–6.

32 Ibid., p. 67.

33 Ibid., p. 66. See Deleuze and Guattari, *Anti-Oedipus: Capitalism and Schizophrenia* (1972), trans. Robert Hurley, Mark Seem and Helen R. Lane, Viking Press, New York 1977.

attitude to computer models at IBM: the latest renders the last obsolete – harsh law of the market. Pierre Macherey summarizes the philosophy of this less than scrupulous book very well: 'Get out of the way and give me some room!'[34]

In reality, the events of May '68 left the thinkers 'of the sixties' speechless at the time. And their followers were thrown into enormous confusion. I recall some discreet retreats to the countryside, some hasty departures to Mum and Dad when the petrol began to run out at the pumps. Some of us also remember the peremptory verdict that the most Leninist of the student leaders, reared as they were on antihumanism, publicly delivered on the first night of the barricades in the rue Gay-Lussac: the biggest reactionary demonstration in Paris since 1934! Having rapidly 'rectified' this error, cloistered in the Salle des Résistants of the rue d'Ulm, some of us – and I'm not making this up! – desperately sought to confer an identifiable meaning on the events that were overtaking us by feverishly rifling through Lenin's texts on 'dual power'.[35] We coined slogans infused with all the science at our disposal. We wrote impassioned editorials directed as much against the Communist Party's treason as against 'the anti-working-class Gaullist regime of unemployment and poverty', as a convoluted headline that served as a slogan had it. In addition, we composed revolutionary verses and went to sing them in chorus on what remained of the Parisian cobblestone on the Boulogne (Billancourt) road. But Alain Krivine's Trotskyists had by far the better choir! As for the orgies attracting

34 *Histoires de dinosaure. Faire de la philosophie 1965–1997*, Presses Universitaires de France, Paris 1999, p. 205.
35 See V. I. Lenin, *Collected Works*, vols 24 and 25, Progress Publishers, Moscow 1964.

crowds of an evening to the École des Beaux-Arts, and the joyous verbal spontaneity given free rein at the Odéon, most of the politicos, whether theoreticians or activists, disdained them as displays of petty-bourgeois degeneracy.

Imagine our relief, our happiness, when we saw the workers' strike suddenly unleashed and spreading. The high walls of the occupied factories, the pickets, the red flags. . . . We were on familiar ground once more. In our theoretical rear-view mirror, we saw 1936, 1871, 1848 and 1793 march past in speeded-up motion. We rediscovered France, 'classical country of the class struggle', as the old Marx had written. Some doctrinaires were predicting the Commune for the end of June!

From the start, the May of the mass of young students and workers, who saw no place for themselves in any organization or movement, proved so recalcitrant to the algebra of revolution that political pundits, switching their attention to Herbert Marcuse, declared that it had been inspired by his thought.[36] However, no one in France had read a line of him at the time. I still remember the irritation of a disappointed Jérôme Lindon, owner of Éditions de Minuit, in his office on the rue Bernard-Palissy a few years later brandishing in front of me the pathetic sales figures for their translation of Marcuse.

On the other hand, it is incontestably true that the celebrated ''60s thinkers' reacted to the events by reorienting their intellectual approach. The question they asked themselves, in complete conformity with their original ambition, concerned the status of their theoretical work *vis-à-vis* the social changes that were under way.

36 *One-Dimensional Man: Studies in the Ideology of Advanced Industrial Society* (Beacon Press, Boston, MA 1964) was a universal reference point for student radicals in Germany and the USA.

How could they get some intellectual purchase on this strange movement whose explosion had taken everyone by surprise?

Ferry and Renaut maliciously recall that in 1968 Jacques Derrida gave a lecture in the USA on 'The Ends of Man', taking the opportunity to salute the movement of Parisian students. The lecture was indeed given in New York in October at an international colloquium on 'Philosophy and Anthropology', and subsequently published in *Marges de la philosophie* in 1972. Derrida dates the composition of his text from April 1968; he then adds:

> It will be recalled that these were the weeks of the opening of the Vietnam peace talks and of the assassination of Martin Luther King. A bit later, when I was typing this text, the universities of Paris were invaded by the forces of order – and for the first time at the request of a rector – and then reoccupied by the students in the upheaval you are familiar with. This historical and political horizon would call for a long analysis. I have simply found it necessary to mark, date, and make known to you the historical circumstances in which I prepared this communication. These circumstances appear to me to belong, by all rights, to the field and the problematic of our colloquium.[37]

What a godsend this remark is for Ferry and Renaut's thesis! But that is to forget the philosopher's very reserved attitude during the events themselves. Contrary to what they suggest, May '68 can by

37 *Margins of Philosophy*, trans. Alan Bass, University of Chicago Press, Chicago 1982, pp. 109–36 (p. 114).

no means be regarded as a product of 'deconstruction'. In actual fact, the notion that made Derrida's fortune, especially in the USA, was diffused post-May.

From April onwards, a serious bout of depression had seen Althusser rushed into a wing of the Eau-Vive hospital on the edge of the Sénart forest, where he was to find himself once more twelve years later, following the murder with which everyone is familiar. Back at the rue d'Ulm at the end of June, in response to the events – what he called the 'tremor' – he set about taking the break with the 'theoreticism' of his earlier work a stage further. In June 1970 he published in *La Pensée* his famous article on the 'Ideological State Apparatuses', essentially devoted to schools and the family.[38] It was presented as 'notes towards an investigation' of the two institutions most visibly shaken by the May events. Althusser would not stop calling for those 'concrete analyses of concrete situations' to which, before departing the scene, he still hoped to devote a new institution with the unlikely name of CEMPIT – a project that remained at the planning stage.[39] In line with the lecture he had given to the Société française de philosophie in February 1968, in the heart of an over-heated Sorbonne, when he had turned up in a cap and called his colleagues 'graduated flunkeys', scandalizing Jean Wahl,[40] he would henceforth define philosophy as 'in the last instance, class struggle in theory', not as the 'theory of theoretical practice'. This comprehensive re-examination led to the publication in 1974, in a

38 'Ideology and Ideological State Apparatuses: Notes towards an Investigation', trans. Ben Brewster, in Louis Althusser, *Essays on Ideology*, Verso, London 1984, pp. 1–60.

39 Between 1978 and 1980 Althusser multiplied his contacts with a view to creating a 'Centre d'études marxistes politiques internationales'.

40 'Lenin and Philosophy', trans. Ben Brewster, in Louis Althusser, *Philosophy and the Spontaneous Philosophy of the Scientists & Other Essays*, ed. Gregory Elliott, trans. Ben Brewster *et al.*, Verso, London and New York 1990, pp. 167–202 (p. 173).

short-lived new collection from Hachette, of what he saw fit to call his *Éléments d'autocritique*, with a taste for parody that was adjudged all the more incongruous in so far as – with a good many ulterior motives – he dedicated his book to Waldeck Rochet, former PCF general secretary.[41] He would no longer speak of 'Marxist philosophy', but of the 'Marxist practice of philosophy' – a distinction with a difference.

Let us now turn to Gilles Deleuze, since he features prominently on Ferry and Renaut's list. As I have said, he wrote and published *Anti-Œdipe* with Félix Guattari in 1972. But far from being perceived as an offshoot of theoretical antihumanism, this book seemed at the time to be the manifesto of a philosophy celebrating, *contra* Freud and his established interpreters, the anarchic freedom of the desire expressed with extraordinary vitality during the wild days and nights of May. Its success – which, by the way, was instantaneous – collided with a united front of Marxist and Lacanian 'antihumanists'. Élisabeth Roudinesco – who, at the time, occupied with exceptional pugnacity the junction of Althusserianism and the École freudienne – did not mince her words.

As we shall see, however, Michel Foucault is arguably the figure who best illustrates the reorientation to which I referred, and who unquestionably played a crucial part in determining its fate.

Examination of his trajectory will only serve to confirm my statement: a *pensée 68* is nowhere to be found, whether before, during, or after the month of May. It is only by retrospective artifice that Luc

41 'Elements of Self-Criticism', in Louis Althusser, *Essays in Self-Criticism*, trans. Grahame Lock, New Left Books, London 1976, pp. 101–61. The *Analyse* collection from Hachette included two other publications: Renée Balibar's important books on *Le Français national* and *Les Français fictifs*.

Ferry and Alain Renaut have thought it possible to identify a common essence consisting in 'antihumanism' and then, joined by others, to denounce it as fundamentally 'Nietzschean': a judgement that is also wanting in accuracy.

4

Michel Foucault's Power

We first learnt of Foucault through an imposing work, rapidly unavailable in its original version, published by Plon in 1961.[42] This person, to whom we could not as yet put a face, already possessed an *aura*. It was known that he had taught abroad for a lengthy spell, which at the time was very rare and even seemed rather suspect. In his case rumour also had it that he flaunted his homosexuality! Had he not held a post in Scandinavia and another in Tunisia? Ribald winks from titillated academics indicated that they had, if not direct information, then notions about the customs of these countries.

I even had the surprise of hearing one of my teachers opine that this man must himself have been mad to write a book on such a subject! This was my first encounter with academic malice, the sheer meanness that wreaks havoc in institutions. But, by contrast, what a

---

42 *Folie et déraison. Histoire de la folie à l'âge classique*, Plon, Paris 1961; abridged 1964 edition trans. Richard Howard as *Madness and Civilization: A History of Insanity in the Age of Reason*, Tavistock, London 1967.

joy the book was! We discovered a philosopher who, in sumptuous style, could produce powerful historical analyses, and vouchsafed us a more open outlook on the world we inhabited.

Yes, Foucault: in the first instance the brilliance of his prose and, above all, a new way of working ('a new archivist', as Deleuze would later put it) which, despite the sarcasm, calumny and back-biting, rapidly gained a following. His work will, without doubt, remain that of the French philosopher of the period who inspired, and continues to inspire, the largest number of original works the world over. *Naissance de la clinique*, a book published in 1963 in the *Galien* collection directed by Georges Canguilhem at Presses Universitaires de France, gave us a new sample of this novel way of handling the great philosophical questions.[43] His historical inquiries, which dazzled us thanks to his talent for depiction, forced us to recognize the depths of our ignorance. This was a healthy humilia-tion. Industrious *agrégés*, we had studied Plato, Aristotle, Descartes and Kant; we had the classics at our fingertips. But we had not read Lamarck, or Cuvier, or Maupertuis's *Vénus physique*, or Xavier Bichat's *Recherches physiologiques*.[44] Intoxicated with delight, we dis-covered that a life of scholarly labour could also help us to understand the basic mechanisms of our societies, and elucidate the hidden presuppositions of the classical philosophical works. We were being invited to grasp the genesis of the thought systems that

---

43 *The Birth of the Clinic: An Archaeology of Medical Perception*, trans. A. M. Sheridan, Tavistock, London 1973.

44 In 1744 Pierre-Louis Moreau de Maupertuis (1698–1759) wrote a *Dissertation physique à l'occasion du nègre blanc*, which he reworked in 1746 under the title *Vénus physique*.

In 1800, the doctor and anatomist Marie-François-Xavier Bichat (1771–1802) published his *Recherches physiologiques sur la vie et la mort*, in which he defined life as 'the totality of forces that resist death'. In some magnificent pages of *The Birth of the Clinic* (pp. 144–5), Foucault defines Bichat's 'vitalism' as a 'mortalism'.

tended to impose themselves on us with all the force of self-evident
truths or the authority of positive knowledge.

You can understand why I react strongly when any old denigrator
of the so-called 'philosophies of suspicion' comes along to pour scorn
on Foucault's *œuvre*. With all due respect to Jean Baudrillard, we shall
not be able to 'forget Foucault'.[45] And it must be added that – rightly
or wrongly, and notwithstanding his references to Nietzsche – we did
not draw from his work a lesson in nihilism. We found there decisive
grounds for combining intellectual fervour with political passion. It
is true that a few years later Foucault did not conceal his opposition
to Althusser's theses on the state, and that he curtly rejected any
analysis of Stalinism in terms of a 'deviation' from the Marxist theory
and practice of the class struggle.[46] He had voiced these criticisms in
veiled terms in *Surveiller et punir*,[47] and was to repeat them loud and
clear in several interviews with journalists at the end of the 1970s.
But what struck us at the time was, on the contrary, what they had in
common. Together, they were encouraging us not to rest content
with the emotional and moral grounds for our political commit-
ments. By their example they enjoined us to think through the
reasons for them. Indeed, Foucault made a point of directly relating
his historical studies to the questions that engaged our thinking.

When *Les Mots et les choses* was published in 1966,[48] Foucault's face
emerged from obscurity. The glamour he acquired never deserted

45 See Baudrillard, *Forget Foucault* (1977), Semiotext(e), New York 1987.

46 See, in particular, Louis Althusser, 'Unfinished History', trans. Grahame Lock, in
    Dominique Lecourt, *Proletarian Science? The Case of Lysenko*, trans. Ben Brewster,
    New Left Books, London 1977, pp. 7–16.

47 *Discipline and Punish: The Birth of the Prison* (1975), trans. Alan Sheridan, Allen
    Lane, London 1977.

48 *The Order of Things: An Archaeology of the Human Sciences*, Tavistock, London 1970.

him. For all that its subtitle ('An Archaeology of the Human Sciences') referred back to that of *Naissance de la clinique* ('An Archaeology of Medical Perception'), this book displayed much greater intellectual ambition. Foucault stamped his anti-evolutionist position in the history of ideas with the term 'episteme'. Against every species of continuism he proposed to use this word, of Platonic provenance, to designate 'configurations of knowledge' as so many successive great subterranean layers, governed by specific structural laws. This thesis was to be taken up and revised in *L'archéologie du savoir*, a methodological work that advanced a general theory of 'discursive practices'. [49] As for the skill with which Foucault organized their succession and analysed each of them in detail, it still compels admiration today. For all the quibbles, and despite the particular errors of detail identified in his analyses of political economy, linguistics, or natural history, the overall impression was compelling.[50]

Yet, as the creators of *La Pensée 68* observe, it is perhaps above all the concluding considerations on the figure of 'Man' that turned this general survey into a reference point, and secured its author's fame at once. For although Foucault did not use the phrase, he had well and truly proclaimed the death of man, in hypothetical fashion. Man, he wrote, was merely 'an invention of recent date', an integral part of a given episteme – precisely that of the age of the 'human sciences' – whose base, in his view, was visibly in the process of

---

49 *The Archaeology of Knowledge* (1969), trans. A. M. Sheridan Smith, Tavistock, London 1972.

50 The PCF, of which Foucault had briefly been a member in the 1950s, put its specialists to work in its reviews. Each set about his quibbling, but none of them ventured to confront the work in its entirety, or the problematic employed. Michel Foucault confided to me that he had been very bitter about it at the time. However, the laughter with which he made a point of punctuating this confidence gave me to understand that he had scarcely entertained any illusions.

fissuring under the triple impact of anthropology, linguistics and psychoanalysis. Were its collapse to ensue, he concluded, 'then one can certainly wager that man would be erased, like a face drawn in sand at the edge of the sea'.[51]

However, if Foucault's thinking played a role – albeit marginal – in the May '68 movement, it was through the impact of *Histoire de la folie*, as well as *Naissance de la clinique*, in psychiatric institutions and hospitals rather than via the antihumanist theses propounded and systematized in *Les Mots et les choses*.

Incidentally, Foucault made his views on May '68 very clear: 'During that May,' he told an interviewer, 'as happened in the period of the Algerian War, I was not in France: I was still a bit displaced, marginal.' In post in Tunisia at the time, he had witnessed serious student riots in March and the wave of repression unleashed in response. He had given the movement discreet but effective support, remembered by everyone over there. Upon his return to France in November–December, he was (he states) 'quite surprised – and rather disappointed – when I compared the situation to what I had seen in Tunisia'. The political experience of French youth lacked the intensity that 'direct, existential, physical commitment' had imparted to the young Tunisians. The memory of this disappointment did not prevent Foucault from affirming that 'without May of '68, I would never have done the things I'm doing today; such investigations as those on the prison, sexuality, etc., would be unthinkable'.[52]

---

51 *The Order of Things*, p. 387.
52 Michel Foucault, *Remarks on Marx: Conversations with Duccio Trombadori* (1981), trans. R. James Goldstein and James Cascaito, Semiotext(e), New York 1991, pp. 132, 138, 137, 140.

The book Foucault published in 1975, *Surveiller et punir*, was posited in continuity with his earlier work. To make the link between it and his previous investigations quite clear, he subtitled it 'The Birth of the Prison'. Henceforth Foucault intended to take up, explicitly and methodically, the connection that had been made between his theoretical work and the protest movement. He had written the bulk of his first two great books in the tranquillity of libraries. Subsequently, he had discovered their delayed effects in the relevant circles. He would write *Surveiller et punir* in direct contact with a prisoners' movement, which he had set up in the framework of a militancy intended to challenge not only the mechanisms of the prison system, but also reformist policies that did not question the *political* function of institutions radically enough. Foucault chaired the Groupe d'information sur les prisons (GIP) with Jean-Marie Domenach and Pierre Vidal-Naquet.

Praising his colleague at the Collège de France in *Le Monde* the day after his death, Pierre Bourdieu credited his 'urge to break . . . with the totalizing ambition of what he called the "universal intellectual", often identified with the philosophical project, while avoiding the alternative of saying nothing about everything and everything about nothing'. The sociologist recalled the expression Foucault had coined to designate his own conception of commitment: the 'specific intellectual', or a thinker who agreed to renounce 'the right to speak as an authority on truth and justice' and the status of 'moral and political conscience'.[53]

In the dossiers they regularly devote to French intellectuals, journalists who clearly identify an old chestnut here note this desire. They contrast it with the figure of the intellectual idealized in France

53 'Le plaisir du savoir', *Le Monde*, 27 June 1984.

since the Dreyfus affair and Émile Zola's *J'accuse*, of which Jean-Paul Sartre supposedly represents the final avatar.

'Specific intellectuals' do not claim any authority to pontificate in terms of Good and Evil on the great events that perturb the planet. They invest their skills in a given social practice, and submit them to the test of a struggle for emancipation with the social agents themselves. In dialogue with Gilles Deleuze, in the issue of the review *L'Arc* devoted to Deleuze in 1972, Foucault summarized the situation of the intellectual as regards politics, up until 'the most recent upheaval', in the following terms: '[t]he intellectual spoke the truth to those who had yet to see it, in the name of those who were forbidden to speak the truth: he was conscience, consciousness, and eloquence.' Today, however, '[t]he intellectual's role is . . . rather . . . to struggle against the forms of power that transform him into its object and instrument in the sphere of "knowledge," "truth," "consciousness," and "discourse."'[54] In writing *Histoire de la sexualité*,[55] to which he devoted what were to be the last years of his life, the philosopher in one sense proved faithful to this conception.

In May 1981, a few days after François Mitterrand's election to the presidency, there was an interview with Foucault by Didier Eribon in *Libération*. There, in the shape of a warning to the parties of the Left now in power, Foucault voiced his reservations about the role of the intellectual in the impending social changes:

His role, since he works specifically in the realm of thought,

---

54 'Intellectuals and Power', in Foucault, *Language, Counter-Memory, Practice: Selected Essays and Interviews*, ed. Donald F. Bouchard, trans. Bouchard and Sherry Simon, Cornell University Press, Ithaca, NY 1977, pp. 205–17 (pp. 207–8).

55 *The History of Sexuality*, trans. Robert Hurley: vol. I, *An Introduction* (1976), Allen Lane, London 1979; vol. II, *The Use of Pleasure* (1984), Viking, London 1986; vol. III, *The Care of the Self* (1984), Viking, London 1986.

is to see how far the liberation of thought can make those transformations urgent enough for people to want to carry them out and difficult enough to carry out for them to be profoundly rooted in reality. It is a question of making conflicts more visible, of making them more essential than mere confrontations of interests or mere institutional immobility. Out of these conflicts, these confrontations, a new power relation must emerge, whose first, temporary expression will be a reform. If at the base there has not been the work of thought upon itself and if, in fact, modes of thought, that is to say modes of action, have not been altered, whatever the project for reform, we know that it will be swamped, digested by modes of behavior and institutions that will always be the same.[56]

The importance Foucault attributed to history assumes its full significance in this context. He counterposed a 'new type' of relationship between philosophy and history to the stance traditionally adopted by philosophers, who tended rather to look down on the historian's craft, regarding it as material on which their reflection would confer a meaning and truth it did not in itself possess: 'No longer a reflection *on* history, but rather a reflection *in* history. A way of confronting thinking with the test of historical work; and also a way of putting historical work to the test of a transformation of conceptual and theoretical frameworks.'[57] The genuine symbiosis

---

56 'Practicing Criticism', in Foucault, *Politics, Philosophy, Culture: Interviews and Other Writings 1977–1984*, ed. Lawrence D. Kritzman, trans. Alan Sheridan *et al.*, Routledge, New York and London 1988, pp. 152–6 (pp. 155–6).

57 'A propos des faiseurs d'histoire', interview with Didier Eribon in *Libération*, 21 January 1983; reprinted in Foucault, *Dits et écrits, 1954–1988*, vol. 4, Gallimard, Paris 1994, pp. 412–15 (p. 413).

achieved between his inquiries and the works of the historian Paul Veyne illustrates this position of principle.[58]

Given all this, you will understand our astonishment and consternation at the positions the philosopher had unexpectedly taken in the interim in favour of the 1978 Iranian Revolution. How could the same person who had fashioned the concept of the specific intellectual end up in a grand hotel in Tehran singing the praises of Ayatollah Khomeini – 'the holy man exiled in Paris' – and extolling the merits of the Islamist uprising in hyperbolical terms, when he himself conceded that he possessed only an incomplete and fragmentary knowledge of the history of the country, its culture and religion? On 26 November 1978 he wrote in the *Corriere della sera*:

> It is an insurrection of people with their bare hands who want to lift the tremendous burden that weighs on us all, but especially on them, these ploughmen of oil, these peasants on the borders of empires: the weight of the whole world order. This is perhaps the first great uprising against the planet's systems, the most modern form of rebellion and the wildest.

Worse: he added, loftily: 'The embarrassment of the politicians is understandable.'[59]

Several other texts, written in the same style at the same time,

---

58 See Paul Veyne, *Comment on écrit l'histoire*, Seuil, Paris 1971. The 1978 reprint contains the text 'Foucault révolutionne l'histoire' as a postface.

59 'Le chef mythique de la révolte de l'Iran', reprinted in Foucault, *Dits et écrits, 1954–1988*, vol. 3, Gallimard, Paris 1994, pp. 713–16 (p. 716).

reveal him, in turn, acting the part he had gibed at a short time before: the role of conscience and eloquence. It is barely noticeable that this conscience is no longer supposed to be moral, but political. Furthermore, Foucault justifies himself in the introductory paragraph to the series of articles in which the lines above appeared. This justification consists in a phrase – 'reportage of ideas' – characterized as the principle according to which 'analysis of what people think will be linked to an analysis of what happens'. He then specifies that '[i]ntellectuals will work with journalists at the point where ideas and events intersect'.[60] Apart from Foucault's reflections on Iran, the Italian daily was to publish in this same series a text by André Glucksmann on the Vietnamese 'boat people' and a study of the USA by Alain Finkielkraut.

A strange fate for the 'specific intellectual': to find himself 'reporting ideas'. . . .

In a famous lecture at the Collège de France a few years later, partially published under the title 'Qu-est-ce que les Lumières?',

---

60 'Les "reportages" d'idées', in ibid., pp. 706–7 (p. 707). Embarrassed and appalled by the tragic mistake he had made, Foucault barely forgave those who took it up publicly. He went so far as to refuse to reply in Le Matin to the critiques addressed to him by M. Debray-Ritzen and then by Jacques and Claudie Broyelle, who had no hesitation in summoning him 'to explain himself'. The argument he initially offered to justify this refusal is enough to make the mind boggle: 'I shall not reply to either of them, because I have never engaged in a polemic in my life. And I don't intend to start now' (letter to Le Matin, 26 March 1979, reprinted in Dits et écrits, vol. 3, p. 762). Yet who could have forgotten, for example, his very public sharp polemic with Jacques Derrida on the subject of Descartes (see 'My Body, this Paper, this Fire' [1971], trans. Geoffrey Bennington, Oxford Literary Review, vol. IV, no. 1, Autumn 1979, pp. 5–29)? And some of us had seen him cross swords with François Dagognet on the subject of Cuvier. The least one can say is that he could be scathing in his comments; and that he apparently took pleasure in it.

Foucault would not hesitate to load the responsibility for this stance on to Kant. The philosopher of Königsberg had supposedly formulated the question of modernity: 'What is my present? What is the meaning of this present? And what am I doing when I speak of this present?'[61] Hence his definition of the Enlightenment: it involved the first epoch that named itself, that formulated its own motto, its own precept.

A few years later, this illustrious ancestry would enable Jürgen Habermas to enlist Foucault in his own struggle for the completion of the 'project of modernity'.[62] But above all, for the time being it 'covered' a practice that facilitated an amalgamation between the approach of the philosopher and that of the journalist.

In this instance, Foucault was not breaking new ground. A philosopher who is indeed forgotten today had preceded him: Maurice Clavel. The influence exercised by this intellectual during the ten years that followed May '68 should not be underestimated. Liberator of Chartres and mystical Gaullist; a Catholic who could not stop talking about his conversion, but was in revolt against the modernism of the Church; booming philosophy teacher and quick-tempered columnist on the *Nouvel Observateur* (he well understood the significance of controlling its TV column); generally awkward cuss, [63] Clavel had characterized his own activity as 'transcendental journalism'. He professed an intense veneration for Foucault, seeing

---

61 'The Art of Telling the Truth', in Foucault, *Politics, Philosophy, Culture*, pp. 86–95 (p. 89).

62 See Jürgen Habermas, *The Philosophical Discourse of Modernity: Twelve Lectures* (1985), trans. Frederick Lawrence, Polity Press, Cambridge 1987.

63 Clavel marked the history of French TV one evening in December 1971, when he left the set during a live broadcast of the programme 'À armes égales', while shouting at the organizers of the debate that pitted him against the Mayor of Tours, Jean Royer, known for his ultra-conservatism on moral matters, a resounding 'Messrs Censors, good night!'.

in him a new Kant. For Clavel, *Les Mots et les choses* was the twentieth century's *Critique of Pure Reason*. The conception of the historical
a priori governing the formation of objects of knowledge renewed
transcendental philosophy, as he stated straight away in his somewhat
grandiloquent manner.

Michel Foucault, who had subsequently seen him often thanks to
their mutual Maoist friends, eulogized his admirer in *Le Nouvel
Observateur* on 30 April 1979, following Clavel's sudden death:

> In our century of exhausted promises he had a unique way of
> waiting. He was only a 'prophet' to those who did not under-
> stand. He was not awaiting the final end, catastrophe,
> deliverance, or whatever. He 'awaited' intransitively. Out of his
> certainty he had fashioned an ability purely to wait. The least
> historical attitude imaginable? At any rate, this is what made him
> thrill to every event in history, whether near or far, huge or tiny.
> Waiting was his way of receiving everything the world could
> bring him, so as simultaneously to welcome and destroy it.[64]

As so often when speaking of one of his friends, Foucault no doubt
revealed something of himself here.

Even so, it is a short step from transcendental journalist to journalist plain and simple. In Iran, Foucault took it. It is only one more
step from plain journalist to journalist as victim of the transcendental illusion. Others were not slow in taking it.

Some younger figures who had behind them neither the *œuvre* of
a Foucault or a Sartre, nor the past of a Clavel, have in truth rushed
headlong into it. They made current events their concern straight

---

64 'Vivre autrement le temps', *Le Nouvel Observateur*, 30 April–6 May 1979; reprint-
    ed in *Dits et écrits*, vol. 3, p. 788.

away, as a result of which they were to parade themselves as 'modern thinkers'. Henceforth they would write in 'emergency' mode. The opinion columns and diaries of the dailies and weeklies were opened to André Glucksmann, Bernard-Henri Lévy, and then others like Jean Baudrillard and, later, Luc Ferry. These thinkers continue to 'thrill' at the turn of events on which they comment – invariably in unison, in bass tones.

5

The Burial of Leftism

André Glucksmann affixed the date 1 July 1968 to the opuscule he published during the third quarter of that memorable year under the title *Stratégie et révolution en France*. In these pages the author of *Discours de la guerre* (1967) continued his commentary on Clausewitz and geopolitics. Converted to Maoism, however, he produced a veritable political report, castigating 'parliamentary cretinism' and extolling naked violence before an imaginary central committee. His analysis can be summed up in a sentence: 'Beneath the ballot papers survives the revolutionary situation disclosed in May.'[65] The publisher moved things up a notch on the back cover: 'The new opposition forces, faced with the freeze-up of the dual European order of West and East, foreshadow the constellation that makes France the continent's centre of gravity, one of the keys to the world.'

65 'Strategy and Revolution in France in 1968', *New Left Review*, no. 52, November/December 1968, pp. 67–121 (p. 83). A chapter of *Discours de la guerre* was translated in *New Left Review*, no. 49, May/June 1968, pp. 41–57.

At the same time, Serge July and Alain Geismar wrote and published a book with the unambiguous title *Vers la guerre civile*. The following diagnosis was offered there: 'May '68 has turned French society right side up again. It has restored revolution and class struggle to the centre of all strategy.' The prognosis followed: 'Without wishing to play the prophet, the horizon for '70 or '72 in France is revolution.'[66] In 1972 precisely, as if on cue, a special issue of Sartre's *Les Temps Modernes* appeared, 'entirely conceived and produced under the supervision of Maoist militants grouped around *La Cause du peuple*', as the editorial committee informed readers. It was entitled *Nouveau fascisme, nouvelle démocratie*.[67] Alongside a contribution by Geismar, it was notable for a very long article by Glucksmann, 'Fascismes: l'ancien et le nouveau', which persisted in error and invited readers 'to hear the sound of jackboots in France in 1972'! Under Glucksmann's pen, as talented as ever, poor old President Pompidou became a 'Napoleon of the new fascism'.

I do not cite these declarations and analyses out of derision or morose delight. As I reread them today, what strikes me is the self-evidence that the logic of their reasoning and their conclusions seem to possess for the authors. The quiet self-confidence with which they order a 'struggle against the police', or 'confrontation with the other systems of the state machine', is stunning. They were, so to speak, setting off for civil war with a flower in their rifle barrels! Glucksmann's prophecies turned out to be highly imprudent, for the year 1972 was marked instead by the funeral of Pierre Overney, a twenty-three-year-old militant of the Gauche Prolétarienne killed by a security guard on 25 February, as he handed out leaflets in front of the Zola gate of the Renault factory

66 Alain Geismar and Serge July, *Vers la guerre civile*, Lattès, Paris 1969, p. 16.
67 *Les Temps Modernes*, no. 310 bis, May 1972.

at Boulogne-Billancourt. The long funeral procession that accompanied his remains from the place Clichy to Père-Lachaise cemetery – an enormous crowd, martial and chilling, stretching seven kilometres – marked the burial of the May of the *groupuscules*. Sartre and Foucault flanked the coffin. It was the idea of revolution that began to be interred in France that day.

André Glucksmann himself would take on the task of throwing the last spadeful of earth on the coffin five years later, in *Les maîtres penseurs*.[68] Issued between covers modelled on the *série noire*, this work represented the sequel to *La Cuisinière et le mangeur d'hommes* (1975), which had signalled the author's volte-face and contributed to maximizing the impact of Alexander Solzhenitsyn's recently translated *Gulag Archipelago* in the French intellectual world. It also helped to substantiate the idea that the militant youth of the 1960s had engaged in political activity out of simple fascination with the societal models offered by 'really existing socialism' in the Soviet Union, Cuba, or China. This was profoundly mistaken. Even if China – the country most implicated – had focused all the hopes of some people, it was only by contrast with the disgust that gripped them when they were confronted with the fate of the Soviet Union.[69] A few notorious Maolaters, and two or three fearsome

68 *The Master Thinkers*, trans. Brian Pearce, Harvester, Brighton 1980.

69 The anthropologist Emmanuel Terray has magnificently described what China, and especially the Cultural Revolution, represented for leftist militants in *Le troisième jour du communisme* (Actes Sud, Arles 1992, pp. 17–23). He writes: 'When the Cultural Revolution was launched, most people's reaction was one of amazement: Mao, head of the largest Communist party in the world, with all the connotations that entails – "democratic centralism", omnipotence of the Party, socialist order, iron discipline, etc. – supported students in revolt and summoned the masses to rise up against "headquarters". Chinese youth was enjoined to rebel against party cadres and leaders at every level' (p. 19).

It was in 1977 that Éditions du Seuil published Jacques and Claudie Broyelle's book *Deuxième retour de Chine*, which conducts the same reversal of position as

Lin Piao fans,[70] cannot mask the real motives for this commitment during the 1960s, whose specifically French and generously internationalist historical roots I have recalled. What is valid for Maoists obviously also applies to Trotskyists of all persuasions, and even numerous Communists, who remained militants in their workplaces and neighbourhoods despite what they knew of the Soviet Union.

Be that as it may, Glucksmann found himself enlisted in the crusade of the 'New Philosophers', signalled by *La Barbarie à visage humain* in the strained, slightly forced style characteristic of its author. The young Bernard-Henri Lévy was a brilliant figure, who (I can attest) was never himself a Marxist or a Maoist. Prior to this, he had not been involved in anything except the creation of a daily paper of 'the optimistic Left', *L'imprévu*. It ran to only a few issues, written mostly by him and a few of his fellow ex-students. Here is a sample of the prose of *La Barbarie à visage humain*, which caused a sensation at the time, but today (let us admit) is difficult to read. To begin with, Lévy comments on his approach, which aims to work back from the critique of Marxism to an interrogation of the Enlightenment:

I know the problem is difficult, and posing the question so harshly leads directly to vertigo in the face of the intolerable and the impossible. At this point, as you may have guessed, what is at stake is the basis of our illusions, the hard core of

Glucksmann (*China: A Second Look*, trans. Sarah Mathews, Harvester, Hassocks 1980). Claudie Broyelle had published a work of Maolatry, *La Moitié du ciel*, in 1973 with Denoël-Gonthier (*Women's Liberation in China*, Harvester, Hassocks 1977).

70 Lin Piao (1908–71) was one of the military leaders of the Long March in 1935 and of the Civil War in 1946–49. Minister of Defence from 1959, he played an important role during the Cultural Revolution.

optimism. And the landmarks are few on this path, past the wretched guard of honour that history provides for happiness.

Hence this purple passage:

> No doubt that's why I suddenly feel tempted to call for help, to gather around me that small band of heralds, the exemplary deserters who, in the solitude of madness, at the threshold of death, their bodies riddled with stars and their faces streaming with tears, send us a sign from afar. Only these disturbing presences have dared to tell the agonizingly comic tale of the 'will to live,' they alone have been able to speak of the inexhaustible horror of the pure and simple social bond.[71]

A turgidity typical of the epoch? No doubt. But there is more to it than the style. In sum, a simple theme is posted: we were mistaken. Marxists (or allegedly such), we agreed to be complicit with unspeakable crimes of whose full enormity we can no longer be ignorant.[72] Redeem us!, entreats the rue des Saints-Pères.[73] Françoise Verny, the book's editor and herself a repentant Communist, a specialist in contrition, took charge of the media orchestration.

In his text, Lévy gave Gilles Deleuze a hard time. This is the scene in the opening pages of the lampoon:

> We know them well, these happy warriors, apostles of drift

71 Bernard-Henri Lévy, *Barbarism with a Human Face*, trans. George Holoch, Harper & Row, New York 1979, pp. 19–20.

72 See especially André Glucksmann, *La Cuisinière et le mangeur d'hommes: essai sur l'État, le marxisme, les camps de concentration*, Seuil, Paris 1975.

73 61 rue des Saints-Pères is the address of Éditions Grasset in Paris. [Trans.]

and celebrators of diversity, anti-Marxist in the extreme and joyful iconoclasts. These dancers of the latest fashion are coming, they're already here, painted and spangled with a thousand flames of unleashed desire, champions of immediate 'liberation'. These sailors of the modern ship of fools have their helmsmen, Saint Gilles and Saint Félix, shepherds of the flock and authors of *Anti-Oedipus*.

This goes on for several pages, leading to a conclusion doubtless of such import that it is duly underscored in italics: '*Deleuze and Guattari are Marxist philosophers.*'[74]

Stung, the co-author of *Anti-Œdipe* at once came up with a ferocious response in an interview in *Le Monde*.[75] 'New philosophers'? Their thinking utilized heavy concepts, 'as heavy as hollow teeth' (law, power, master, world, rebellion, faith, etc.); and proceeded by grotesque amalgams and peremptory dualisms: the law and the rebel, power and the angel, and so on. What they expounded was not the content of their thought, given that this was nonexistent. The sole object of their discourse was the subject of its enunciation: 'I, who am lucid and courageous; I, who belong to the lost generation; we, who were there in May '68 . . . we, who won't be duped again.'

As for the political mechanics of their success, Deleuze dismantled its logic by relating it to the prospect of the possible – if not certain – victory of the Union of the Left in the legislative elections of 1978. You may remember the wave of panic that swept the respectable bourgeoisie on the evening of 10 May 1981: naive or

74 *Barbarism with a Human Face*, pp. 6, 9.
75 Reprinted as 'À propos des nouveaux philosophes et d'un problème plus général', as a supplement to *Minuit*, no. 24, 5 June 1977.

devious, their 'hostage' or their accomplice depending on your convictions, newly elected President Mitterrand was going to appoint Communist ministers to his government! It was a case of run for your life, for it was to be expected that Soviet tanks would make straight for Paris the following day. Well, the fear of the propertied was that much greater in 1978, because the Communist Party had not yet been licked. What is more, President Valéry Giscard d'Estaing rashly declared himself ready to take a back seat, if not withdraw, in the event of electoral defeat. There was talk of Rambouillet or Fontainebleau, no doubt because the name of Versailles was unmentionable. At any rate, the idea of cohabitation did not find favour with the President. So the New Philosophers arrived at just the right time. 'Resentment about '68 is all they have to sell,' wrote Deleuze, and he continued:

> In this sense, whatever their position as regards the elections, they are certainly on the electoral register. From this point everything is grist to their mill – Marxism, Maoism, socialism, and so on – not because real struggles have led to the emergence of new enemies, new problems and new means, but because THE revolution must be declared always and everywhere impossible.

In writing these lines, Gilles Deleuze must have had Glucksmann's book in mind. The key formula of *Les maîtres penseurs* – alleged to epitomize the 'circle' in which the 'four aces' (Fichte, Hegel, Marx, Nietzsche) have compelled our thought to turn for a century and a half – is stated thus: 'to conceive is to dominate'. This is the translation of a sentence Glucksmann writes in German: *begreifen ist beherrschen*. At the cost of a discreet intellectual fraud, he has no qualms about presenting it as the heart of Hegelian logic, and thus as the matrix of totalitarian monstrosities.[76] His book is addressed to French intellectuals. It exhorts them never again to be Marxists of any stamp, and to renounce the urge to be revolutionary. And Glucksmann makes the enormous groan of the torture victims reverberate so as to project his own voice further. But if 'to theorize is to terrorize', according to another of his well-minted maxims, the operation of intimidation and deterrence is jacked up a rung. What is the philosopher's task to be if he abstains from theoretical activity as if it were the innermost peril harboured by his thought? It will remain for him to be . . . stirred. We have come full circle.

Clavel heaped praise on Glucksmann, and it was Michel Foucault who introduced *Les maîtres penseurs* to readers of *Le Nouvel Observateur* in May 1977 in extravagant fashion.[77] He celebrated the book's 'éclat', 'its beauty, its fits of rage, its thick clouds and its laughter'. He had no misgivings about concluding as follows:

76 In a pamphlet composed in the most stereotyped language imaginable, and published by François Maspero in 1978 as *Dissidence ou révolution?* (see Appendix, below), I dismantled Glucksmann's *modus operandi*. He attributes the formula to Hegel, and does not hesitate to state that it is the cornerstone of his doctrine: '"To think, to conceive, is to dominate" (*Begreifen ist beherrschen*) was the happy thought on which he built up his science. (If you remove the word "concept" from the *Great Logic*, the text drains away)' (*The Master Thinkers*, p. 112). Yet, Glucksmann knows as well as I do in which text Hegel had occasion to employ this formula, in the shape of an aphorism: in a draft of *The Spirit of Christianity and its Fate* – an early work where Hegel sees in it a summary of Jewish thought! As Dominique Janicaud and Jean Wahl – the very commentators to whom Glucksmann refers in a note – explain very well, Hegel was able to constitute his own system only by abandoning this formula and *rejecting* its philosophical implications. Glucksmann – who, in fact, is not unaware of this – writes: 'At first, Hegel recoiled from the idea in horror, proclaiming it to be "Jewish". Then he got used to it.'

77 'La grande colère des faits', *Le Nouvel Observateur*, no. 652, 9–15 May, pp. 84–6; reprinted in Foucault, *Dits et écrits, 1954–1988*, vol. 3, Gallimard, Paris 1994, pp. 277–81 (p. 281).

Les maîtres penseurs is like some of the great books of philosophy (Wagner, Nietzsche), a theatrical piece in which two plays are strangely combined on the same stage: *La mort de Danton* and *Woyzeck*. Glucksmann does not invoke Dionysus beneath Apollo afresh. Into the heart of the most elevated philosophical discourse he suddenly introduces these deserters, these victims, these indomitable elements, these dissidents with their heads held high – in short, those 'bloody heads' and other 'white shapes' that Hegel wanted to erase from the 'Night of the World'.

6

Gilles Deleuze's Battle

An interview with Bernard-Henri Lévy, published in *Le Nouvel Observateur* two months later, clarifies one of the main reasons for this enthusiasm. Its occasion was the publication of Foucault's book *La Volonté de savoir*.[78] Asked about the originality of the analyses he proposes of the mechanisms of power, Foucault equally lays into the Marxist vulgate, which views them exclusively through the optic of the state, and the 'leftist doxa', with its anti-repressive refrain. When he recalls that '[a]ll modern thought, like all politics, has been dominated by [the] question of revolution', Lévy asks him: 'Do you continue, as far as you are concerned, to raise this question of revolution and reflect upon it? Does it remain, in your eyes, the question *par excellence*?' Answer: 'You know very well: the very desirability of the revolution is the problem today.' Lévy presses the point: 'Do you want the revolution? Do you want something more

78 *The History of Sexuality*, vol. I: *An Introduction* (1976), trans. Robert Hurley, Allen Lane, London 1979.

than the simple ethical duty to struggle here and now, at the side of one or another group of mental patients and prisoners, oppressed and miserable?' Foucault replies: 'I have no answer. But I believe that to engage in politics – aside from party politics – is to try to know with the greatest possible honesty whether or not the revolution is desirable. It is in exploring this terrible molehill that politics runs the dangers of caving in.' And he spells it out: 'We are perhaps living the end of politics.'[79]

As you may know, Foucault and Deleuze publicly exchanged glowing mutual tributes (Foucault: 'the century will be Deleuzian'; Deleuze on the work of his friend: 'one of the greatest philosophies of the twentieth century'). Glucksmann and Lévy drove a wedge between them, no doubt because their imprecations against the state and on behalf of the 'plebs' coincided with the main lessons drawn by the author of *Surveiller et punir* from the failure of his Maoist friends, as from his passage through the ranks of the Communist Party many years earlier.

Every conscientious philosophy student had read Gilles Deleuze's scholarly and profound works on Hume, Bergson and Kant. His study of Nietzsche, published by Presses Universitaires de France in 1962,[80] had, strictly speaking, launched the career of what Ferry and Renaut call French Nietzscheanism. Nor have students at the École normale forgotten the extraordinary sessions of his course on Spinoza, given at Althusser's invitation, in the studious silence of the Salle des Actes at the rue d'Ulm. The essence of it was published in book form as

79 'The End of the Monarchy of Sex', trans. Dudley M. Marchi, in *Foucault Live: Collected Interviews, 1961–1984*, ed. Sylvère Lotringer, Semiotext(e), New York 1989, pp. 214–25 (p. 223).
80 *Nietzsche and Philosophy*, trans. Hugh Tomlinson, Athlone Press, London 1983.

Spinoza et le problème de l'expression.[81] We admired the amazing scholar, the dandy with long fingernails who bewitched us with his metallic voice, and treated as a philosopher, at once scathing and precious, the classical texts into which he breathed new life. We could not get over seeing him slip off his jacket one day and open his shirt collar. A mocking Georges Canguilhem had shown me the slovenly-looking photo of Deleuze on the cover of the issue of *L'Arc* devoted to him: 'no more stiff collars for the Bergsonians', he exclaimed, in a burst of laughter! Nevertheless, we continued to regard Deleuze as less 'political' than Foucault. Spiteful gossip insinuated a relation between the leftward inflection of his writings and his nomination to the experimental university of Vincennes. There was talk of opportunism. Retrospectively, it can be said that he ultimately proved a better analyst of the situation than the more engaged of his colleagues.

The 'more general problem' Deleuze formulated in connection with the New Philosophers was not lacking in shrewdness. He poked fun at the highly comical results obtained by the obscure figures of François Aubral and Xavier Delcourt, authors of a book 'against the New Philosophy' that had the effect of endowing it with the concrete substance of a school of thought.[82] No, Deleuze was to retort: whatever the poverty of the schools, the New Philosophers could not be said to form one. Their real novelty consisted not in their thought, but in the fact that 'they have introduced literary and philosophical marketing into France'. This marketing followed two principles. The first was that people should talk about a book, or be made to say about it, more than the book itself had to say. The second was that the same book or product

---

81 *Expressionism in Philosophy: Spinoza* (1968), trans. Martin Jouglin, Zone Books, New York 1992.

82 *Contre la nouvelle philosophie*, Gallimard, Paris 1977. The same mistake is made by Günther Schiwy, *Les nouveaux philosophes*, Denoël-Gonthier, Paris 1979.

should have several different versions, catering to all tastes: a pious version, an atheistic version, a Heideggerian version, a leftist version, a centrist version, even a Chiracian version, a neo-fascist version, a qualified 'Union of the Left' version, and so on. Deleuze anticipated that this mode of existence of texts was destined to have profound effects on thought: 'Intellectuals and writers, even artists, are thus invited to become journalists if they wish to conform to the new standards. This is a new type of thought: interview-thought, discussion-thought, one-minute-thought.'[83] Deleuze went so far as to imagine a time when people would not write articles on books any more but, rather, write books in order to get people to write articles! And soon – who knows? – books on articles to elicit further articles. He doubtless had no idea just how right he was.

Subsequently, he, like us, had all the time in the world to observe our philosophers become integrated into the media spectacle and 'create events' around their own persons. From Bucharest to Sarajevo, from Berlin to Algiers, from obscene New Year's dinners to costly and dubious para-diplomatic trips, they have proceeded to take up with the protagonists of the bloodiest conflicts, and offer their support to particular figures – Alija Izetbegovic in Bosnia, for example – going so far as to justify the policies and exactions of such and such a clan (e.g. the military in power in Algeria).

In May 1994, a 'Sarajevo list' was formed around Bernard-Henri Lévy, André Glucksmann and Marek Halter; it threatened to stand at the European elections, so as to pressurize the government into responding to a 'duty to intervene' also promoted by Bernard

---

83 'À propos des nouveaux philosophes et d'un problème plus général', supplement to *Minuit*, no. 24, 5 June 1977.

Kouchner on the Socialist list.[84] At his own risk, it is Lévy who has pushed the logic that inspired this media strategy furthest. Why not hold the camera himself? This yielded *Bosna!* Next, why not personally direct some famous actors in a screenplay written by himself? This was the mistake of the film *Le Jour et la nuit*.

---

84 Jean-Pierre Chevènement was one of the few French politicians vehemently to reject this notion and the practices it legitimates in *Le Vert et le noir: intégrisme, pétrole, dollar*, Grasset, Paris 1995.

7

The Liberal Transmutation of the French Libertarian

The May of the 22 March Movement, anti-authoritarian or libertarian in its essence, rallying rebellious youth around the double-bind slogan according to which 'it is forbidden to forbid', remains enigmatic if one keeps one's eyes glued to the Latin Quarter in Paris. The publication in a single volume of the twelve issues of the review *Internationale Situationniste* (1958–69) indicates that this movement, which took everyone by surprise, had a long past behind it.[85] It derived from extended reflection on the evolution of Western societies, especially in the light of the practical critiques to which American youth were subjecting it as they grappled with the Vietnam War, explosions of institutionalized or rampant racism, the malaise induced by the concrete jungle, and the moral con-

---

85 *Internationale Situationniste, 1958–1969 (édition augmentée)*, Fayard, Paris 1997. The first two editions of the review were published respectively in 1970 by Van Gennep (Amsterdam) and 1975 by Éditions Champ Libre (Paris). The 1997 edition reprints the original texts, together with an introduction and some previously unpublished material, notably texts by Gil J. Wolman and Guy Debord.

formism of a culture whose puritanism was disintegrating on all fronts.

Moreover, the success of the 'cartel of media intervention'[86] that was the New Philosophers is unintelligible if one sticks exclusively to the strategies deliberated at length, and implemented with determination, in Saint-Germain-des-Prés, notwithstanding the fire-power of a few publishers.

In 1970, Jean-Marie Benoist – a dashing *normalien* who at the time was cultural attaché at the French Embassy in London, and who four years later was to become a lecturer in Claude Lévi-Strauss's research laboratory at the Collège de France – had published a book entitled *Marx est mort*, which Gallimard immediately released in a paperback series. However, it acquired great notoriety only when the American magazine *Time* borrowed its title for the front cover of its 5 September 1977 issue, which introduced the French New Philosophers to readers. With this spectacular gesture the editors were expressing their divine surprise at seeing anti-Marxism blossom in France – this time not from the pens of old reactionaries bereft of an audience, but from those of bright young things who obviously had a future ahead of them.

Whether deliberately or not, the arguments mounted by Glucksmann and his friends chimed perfectly with the American ideals of free enterprise and individualism for which the magazine founded by Henry R. Luce and Britton Hadden had always liked to think itself the spokesman. With hindsight we can better appreciate the great game that then ensued. The New Philosophers presented themselves as defenders of the West against Eastern totalitarianism. Under the semi-indulgent, semi-ironic gaze of Raymond Aron, they

86 See Gilles Châtelet, *Vivre et penser comme des porcs. De l'incitation à l'envie et à l'ennui dans les démocraties-marchés*, Exils, Paris 1998.

adopted concepts and arguments for which the liberal Right had vainly sought acceptance since the Liberation, in a country where ideological hegemony was divided between Gaullists and Communists. In the Anglo-Saxon countries the opposition between totalitarianism and democracy, which our philosophers affected to have discovered, was a veritable cliché. Since Bertrand Russell and Karl Popper, criticism of the philosophical bases (Platonic and Hegelian) of totalitarianism had formed part of schoolwork.[87]

In France, readers' attention was focused on the question of the Soviet Union, amid anxiety about the kind of state that would come into operation were the Left to attain power. Glucksmann's formulas rang out: 'Today, if your heart escapes the state's clutches, you will understand Solzhenitsyn.' In *Les maîtres penseurs*: 'I think, therefore the State is'; or 'Science of the State, science of the Revolution, science of setting to work – three variants of a single body of knowledge.'[88] The term 'dissidence', seized on by intellectuals in the countries under Soviet domination to denote their resistance to bureaucratic oppression, was construed by Glucksmann as a 'radical refusal of the State'.

To Jacques Attali, who denounced him shortly afterwards as the ideologue of a 'French New Right', Glucksmann objected that right-wing thought venerated what he, on the contrary, was holding up to ridicule: the state, order, elites, and so on. Was this the deviousness of an ex-student of the École polytechnique who was not unaware of what the term 'New Right' covered? The acronym of the Groupe de

---

87 See especially Popper, *The Open Society and its Enemies*, 2 vols, Routledge & Kegan Paul, London 1945 (translated into French in 1979); and Victor Goldschmidt's powerful *Platonisme et pensée contemporaine* (Aubier-Montaigne, Paris 1970), as well as Dominique Lecourt, *L'ordre et les jeux: le positivisme logique en question* (Grasset, Paris 1981).

88 *The Master Thinkers*, trans. Brian Pearce, Harvester, Brighton 1980, p. 149.

recherche et d'étude sur la civilisation européenne (GRECE), a body set up in 1968, was becoming familiar. The New Right, of which it formed the backbone, propagated its views through the journals *Éléments* and *Nouvelle École*, which advocated a racial and genetic conception of human societies;[89] and the renovation of pre-Christian ideas, zealously promoted by Alain de Benoist, was to strike a certain chord in intellectual circles.[90] Was it a case of cunning on Glucksmann's part, or a lack of discernment? Raymond Aron's pupil must have known very well that right-wing thought – at least in its liberal version – was not as favourably disposed to the state, to order, or even to elites, as he claimed. Even so, transatlantic liberals were not mistaken. Henceforth their language was spoken in France; a path was cleared for their ideas. Well-positioned, the anti-totalitarians-turned-neo-libertarians were set to end up as neo-liberals! This would make it possible to solder together, in one and the same ideology, repentant members of the *groupuscules* and Situationists converted to the defence of their private lives and moderate enjoyment of their individual creature comforts.

When Guy Debord proceeded to the dissolution of the Situationist International in 1972, he had offered by way of explanation an excellent portrait, in his clinical style, of what was to be the new way of

89 See Jean-François Sirinelli, ed., *Histoire des droites en France*, vol. 2, Gallimard, Paris 1992, pp. 201–7. In January 1980 the review *Critique* devoted an issue (vol. 36, no. 392) to the politico-philosophical year under the title 'Le comble du vide'. It contained a scathing article by Yves Michaud, 'Dernier avatar de la frénésie du nouveau: "la nouvelle" droite', on the collective volume *Renaissance de l'Occident*, published by Plon the previous year, and Alain de Benoist's *Les Idées à l'endroit* (Libres Hallier, Paris 1979).

90 See Anne-Marie Duranton-Crabol, *Visages de la nouvelle droite: le GRECE et son histoire*, Presses de la Fondation Nationale des Sciences Politiques, Paris 1988.

life and thinking in the Western countries in the decades to come. If you open the volume entitled *The Veritable Split in the International*, you are in for a surprise. Debord begins by recalling the remarkable destiny of the theses he had defended since the late 1950s. Universally ignored in the cultural and political world for a good decade, they had demonstrated an extraordinary capacity for mobilization in May 1968, especially in France. Triumphal and parodic, Debord reported victory: 'for whoever can "hear the grass grow", [this victory] is . . . *indisputable*'.[91] As a result, however, his organization had found itself besieged by admirers. Debord derisively dubbed them 'pro-situs', just to put them in their place – that is to say, outside the movement. With them, he added, Situationism was in danger of degenerating into a petty ideology of the executives, an ideology akin to that of 'a laughable western "socialist" party [that] proposes blithely to "change life"'.[92]

Debord does not skimp on the irony when sketching the portrait of the 'pro-situ':

> The pro-situ, as he will never fear to say, lives off passions, dialogues with transparency, radically reconstructs the festival and remakes love, in the same way that the executive finds at the grower's the little wine that he then bottles himself, or touches down at Katmandu. For the pro-situ as for the executive, the present and the future are solely occupied by consumption become revolutionary. . . .

Thesis 43 begins with words that combine gloomy nostalgia with

91 Situationist International, *The Veritable Split in the International*, Chronos Publications, London 1990, p. 36.
92 Ibid., p. 58. [The reference is to the programme of the refounded French Socialist Party – Trans.]

acute foreboding: 'We were there to combat the spectacle, not to govern it.' It had therefore proved imperative to subject the SI itself to the critique it had so appropriately mounted against the 'old world', and to proceed with it as it had endeavoured to do with that world: '*breaking* [it]'. The italics are Debord's, and he offers his readers an unsparing analysis of the ideology of the upwardly mobile middle classes in its post-'68 version.[93]

After 1981, the middle classes did indeed get carried away with 'modernity' in its anti-repressive, libertarian form, but also, very rapidly, in an ultra-liberal guise. On the one hand, people liked to think themselves 'cool', even 'Zen'; they started addressing each other as *tu* and (like good Americans) calling each other by their first names. School became a 'life space' where the main thing now was not to traumatize children. Any idea of competition between them was declared 'reactionary'; to some, even grading seemed improper. On the other hand, these years witnessed the flourishing of a bellicose idiom, with the spread of a corresponding arsenal of practices: success, and then the law of the jungle, were lauded. An imagery of tigers and killers invaded people's psyches, while the casualties found themselves consigned to social security. The hazards of parliamentary and presidential election results contributed some decisive episodes to this national schizophrenia. In a spirit of every man for himself, people found themselves on a 'quest for meaning'.[94]

93 Ibid., pp. 58, 65, 73.
94 The private French TV channel TF1, which symbolizes American-style dumbing-down, adopted the philosophical slogan 'quest for meaning' (Luc Ferry) as a marketing ploy. [In the final paragraph of the chapter the author is alluding to the fact that the principal meaning of *quête* in contemporary French is 'collection', as in taking a collection in church or making a collection for charity – Trans.]

Michel Houellebecq's carnal and karmic 'elementary particles' loomed on the horizon of this world of disenchanted errancy.[95] If this novel is so shocking today, it is perhaps because it is a faithful enough reflection of the fate of that ideology of the executives whose rise Debord had long anticipated. The mirror should not be smashed just because the image proves shabby and, in some respects, downright odious. For my part, I read it as a ferocious parody of that hilarious 'quest for meaning' to which our thinkers, with touching unanimity, desperately seek to bring the lustre of an answer that would possess the dignity of the great sacred texts. Let us concede that this quest merited a minor literary effort, since it seems that housewives under fifty have themselves been touched by the 'grace' of TF1. Clearly, Michel Houellebecq loathes them. But it is the game they collude with – the famous 'quest' – that he principally holds up to ridicule.

Have you reflected on this noble word 'quest', so prized today? Rarely used in our language outside sacristies and the world of chair attendants and patronesses, it carries with it an imposing set of references that account for its fortune. Since Chrétien de Troyes (c.1135–c.1183), in French the 'quest' has been for the Grail. It is not some vulgar search but promises, rather, to be a mystical adventure. Our philosophers on a 'quest for meaning' adopt the posture of terrestrial knights acceding to celestial knighthood. The term 'quest' brings in tow the emerald, the sword, the Round Table, and so on – so many sacred hues, imbuing the most rationalist of discourses with an air of mystery. To you this has a trendy, gently New Age tonality which is well worth holding up to ridicule, given the swindles it sanctions.

95 *Les Particules élémentaires*, Flammarion, Paris 1998; trans. Frank Wynne as *Atomised*, Heinemann, London 2000.

8

Death and Resurrection of the Intellectual

In 1983, Max Gallo was not yet devoting his energies from his office in the place du Panthéon to the novelistic celebration of the great men in our history. He occupied the post of government spokesman – a thankless task, to say the least. In this capacity he took the initiative of arraigning the intellectuals in *Le Monde* on 26 July. He queried their reticence towards the Socialist government, which had just made its 'switch to austerity', following the phase of reflation through consumption and nationalization. 'What switch? What austerity?', François Mitterrand had the nerve to demand in a memorable television interview.

'Where are today's Gides, Malraux, Alains, Langevins?' Gallo hurled at the assembled company. A stream of replies followed. 'We won't be had again,' rejoined older intellectuals. 'No, we won't be Mitterrand's Aragons,' echoed their younger colleagues, who had read the illustrious poet's odes to Stalin. This generation 'moralizes, judges, sniggers', exclaimed Gallo, who deviously recalled the Coluche episode: 'Some of this generation, a minority, supported a clown, so derisory did elections and politics seem to it.'[96] Some prominent older figures, like Vladimir Jankélévitch or Henri Guillemin, did profess warm support for the Left, but without mincing matters. What emerges most clearly from this incredible brouhaha, with its talk of discord, rupture, distance and, above all, silence, is that the eminent contributors to Le Monde had now adopted the stance of spectators on politics. The urgent summons to them to participate actively in the modernization of the country left them cold.

Underlying this refusal was a fundamental disagreement. Since 1977, left-wing French intellectuals, relayed by the media, had convinced themselves in the wake of the New Philosophers that the main enemy was represented not by the Right, but by pro-Sovietism. Emmanuel Le Roy-Ladurie expressed this point in choice terms in 1980:

It seemed to me that the opposition between totalitarianism and freedom was ultimately more important than the old Left–Right opposition. As regards the Europe in which I live, Nazism having been crushed militarily and fascism scarcely representing a threat except in some people's rhetoric, the main danger comes from the structures put in place since 1945.[97]

96 Gallo's article was published as a 'viewpoint' under the title 'Les intellectuels, la politique et la modernité', in Le Monde, 26 July 1983, and formed part of a series entitled 'Le silence des intellectuels'. [In 1981, supported by such intellectuals as Deleuze and Guattari, the clown Coluche sought to contest the presidential election. Having failed to obtain the five hundred signatures of elected representatives required to stand, he was compelled to withdraw – Trans.]

97 Le Point, 1 February 1982, p. 78.

In these circumstances, how could people have confidence in a President elected courtesy of the votes of a Communist electorate, especially when the very strong links between the French Party and Moscow were well known? On 1 February 1982, *Le Point* had some fun: 'Hard times for left intellectuals', it proclaimed. They had not wanted Mitterrand to win; they had not seen it coming; they lacked the wherewithal to analyse it: 'Wintertime for sacred cows'.

A significant event immediately after the elections had meanwhile deepened the distrust between our thinkers and the political authorities: their lack of support for the Solidarity movement of the Gdansk workers in Poland, for which Foreign Minister Claude Cheysson angrily took responsibility ('What are you going to do? – 'Nothing, obviously!'). This was to trigger a battle of petitions, traditionally the highest form assumed by political struggle among French intellectuals. Culture Minister Jack Lang sacrificed himself to limit the damage.

Guy Sorman took advantage of the opportunity offered by Max Gallo to intervene in the debate and amuse himself. Known at the time as the author of *La Révolution conservatrice américaine*, just published, Sorman was very pleased that the Socialist dignitary had clearly spotted the danger Reaganism represented for the Left ('the political space vacated for historical reasons by the Left intelligentsia is occupied by the conservative wave'). The sardonic Sorman mocked: 'From a simplistic cowboy Reagan has become the Devil for a certain Left because, over and above his anecdotal character, he crystallizes a comprehensive ideological system that is actually the counter-example to the socialist model.' The future adviser to Gaullist premier Alain Juppé lauded the alliance between populism, anti-statism and free enterprise in the framework of the new American liberalism. Not without malice, he noted that none of these themes was in fact absent from the Left's discourse. But keeping a straight face, he affected to regret that 'the Socialists do not accept its consistency'. He set about the French intellectual or political Right because it remained 'even more statist than the tradition of the Left, which has at least from time immemorial nourished a faint current of libertarianism and self-management'. By way of conclusion, Sorman cruelly predicted that if socialism carried on distancing itself from statism, 'the debate between left- and right-wing intellectuals is going to bear wholly on the appropriation of this new liberalism'.[98]

This prediction depended for its fulfilment on left-wing intellectuals continuing to identify themselves as intellectuals, which was precisely what they did not do.

Evidence of this is a text that has remained famous, published in the context of the same debate by Jean-François Lyotard on 25 August 1983, under the title 'Tombeau de l'intellectuel'. The author of *La Condition postmoderne*[99] tacitly adopts the Foucauldian critique of the universal intellectual and trumpets that intellectuals no longer exist, at least in the sense of 'thinkers who identify themselves with a subject endowed with a universal value so as to describe and analyse a situation or condition from this point of view and prescribe what ought to be done in order for this subject to realize itself, or at least in order for its realization to progress'. As a consequence of the collapse of the Soviet Union, which has discredited the last of the universal subjects (Marx's proletariat), 'there is no universal subject-victim, appearing in reality, in whose name thought could draw up an indictment that would be at the same time a "conception of the world"'. From Sartre to Péguy, and then from Zola to Voltaire, the

98 *Le Monde*, 2 August 1983.
99 *The Postmodern Condition: A Report on Knowledge* (1979), trans. Geoff Bennington and Brian Massumi, Manchester University Press, Manchester 1984.

argument rebounds against the Enlightenment, 'which has animated liberal politics for a century'. Lyotard sniggers and pronounces judgement: 'It has become obsolete.' On this point Lyotard found himself in agreement with the New Philosophers. But ought we to be distressed at the wreckage? On the contrary, we should rejoice in it: 'The decline, perhaps the ruin, of the universal idea can free thought and life from totalizing obsessions.' The programme that emerges is stated rather brutally, since it involves 'distinguish[ing] intelligence from the paranoia that gave rise to "modernity"'.[100]

You know the rest: the stage show that is postmodernity, which has had an uninterrupted run for some years now and enjoyed particular success in the USA. The Sokal affair revealed to the French public at large the institutional power acquired by the 'pomos' in numerous universities and some prestigious publications.[101] In fact, it was a case of 'return to sender', for it was over there that the very term 'postmodern' had begun to circulate in the lacerated world of the urbanists.

I have sketched an analysis of this history elsewhere.[102] Van der Rohe, spiritual heir to modernist architecture, suffered the initial onslaughts in 1975. From architecture the movement spread to painting, with the first works by David Salle and Eric Fischl. And the

---

100 'Tomb of the Intellectual', in Lyotard, *Political Writings*, trans. Bill Readings and Kevin Paul Geiman, UCL Press, London 1993, pp. 3–7 (pp. 3, 6–7).

101 See Yves Jeanneret, *L'affaire Sokal ou la querelle des impostures*, Presses Universitaires de France, Paris 1998. The author clearly demonstrates the amalgams effected under the cover of this rubric, from Bruno Latour to Derrida via Lacan!

102 See Dominique Lecourt, *Contre la peur: de la science à l'éthique, une aventure infinie*, Presses Universitaires de France, Paris 1999, and specifically the chapter on 'La querelle de la modernité', pp. 111–46.

1980 Venice Biennale marked the official inception of the postmodernist movement in Europe, with the blessing of the Italian architect and art critic Paolo Portoghesi. Artists thus found themselves licensed to draw freely on the treasures of the tradition and engage in the practice of mélange, collage, placage, juxtaposition in fragmentary style. But it was Jean-François Lyotard who distilled the philosophical bases of the movement. His book *La Condition postmoderne* celebrated the catastrophic end of modernity as an unprecedented opportunity for thinkers to emancipate themselves from the 'tradition of the new', which valorized the present at the expense of the past. The equal dignity of all styles would henceforth be affirmed.

Gilles Lipovetsky's book *L'ère du vide*, which did so much to light the way for Ferry and Renaut, belongs to this movement. 'No political ideology', he wrote, 'is any longer capable of inflaming crowds. Postmodern society possesses neither idols nor taboos, neither a glorious self-image nor a historical project with the capacity to mobilize people. The void henceforth governs us, but a void devoid of the tragic or the apocalyptic.'[103] Lipovetsky also set the perky tone for what was to be the postmodernist ethic: hedonism,[104] which was to cease being the privilege of the intellectual and artistic elite, and penetrate the masses.

Against the mounting tide of technophobia, in the prose of these philosophers the postmodern spirit readily turned technophiliac. Jean-François Lyotard, for example, offered a personal subsidy in

103 Gilles Lipovetsky, *L'ère du vide: essais sur l'individualisme contemporain*, Gallimard, Paris 1983.

104 This ancient moral system – which makes pleasure the highest value of human existence, and was severely criticized by all moralists of Kantian descent – was to find renewed success during the 1980s in the works of Michel Onfray (see Chapter 10 below).

order to conceive and curate the exhibition 'Immatériaux' at the Centre Georges Pompidou in 1985.[105] Its lesson was clear: the new information and communication technologies contribute powerfully to the creation of a network society – decentred, no longer pyramid-shaped, traversed by innumerable unstable flows – in which the individual could conduct himself in conformity with a more or less jubilant nomadism. Lyotard thus made himself the apostle of a kind of joyous nihilism that dances on the ruins of the great conceptual contributions of modernity: Marxism, Hegelianism, rationalism, structuralism. According to Gianni Vattimo, eulogist of 'weak ontology',[106] the world does not progress, as is incorrectly believed, via sequences of events and supersessions, but by 'weakening and fading' in the context of a radical absence of meaning. You know the refrain: let us bid farewell to unitary, totalizing reason, which is always inherently totalitarian; let us renounce the deplorable idea of universal happiness, offspring of the detestable idea of progress! Let us abandon ourselves to erring, 'the only wealth, the only being that is given to us'. Chic anarchist music for the jet set!

It was in the very civilized form of personal stereos and Nike trainers that nomadism found itself at the end of the 1990s the object of a veritable cult from the pen of Jacques Attali, who was to be wickedly recalled to his pipe and slippers by Gilles Châtelet:

105 'Immatériaux, dramaturgie d'un siècle qui vient', exhibition mounted at the Centre Pompidou, 28 March–15 July 1985, to foreground this question: What good is the development of science and technology if it does not help humanity to emancipate itself from poverty, despotism and ignorance? See the volume *Modernes et après: les immatériaux* (Autrement, Paris 1985), published in conjunction with the exhibition. Lyotard's texts bear the trace of the polemics triggered by the exhibition, notably from the sharp pen of Michel Cournot.

106 *The End of Modernity: Nihilism and Hermeneutics in Post-Modern Culture* (1985), trans. Jon R. Snyder, Polity, Cambridge 1988. The Italian philosopher ascribes being solely to the event: a weak ontology.

'Attali believes he can make out a multitude of young knights laden with more and more "intelligent" nomad-objects,' writes the mathematician-pamphleteer, who objects that 'their life won't be so amusing', since they 'will often be bulimic, constipated, and always "stressed", stunned by tests and connected up to pitiless thermostats, always compelled to answer their own ultimatums: "Mirror, mirror on the wall! Am I in good shape? Do I conform? Answer quickly! You know that's what I'm paid for!".'[107]

Neither Guy Sorman nor Max Gallo had an opportunity to see their respective appeals heard or wishes granted, for others on the Left – and not the least among them – had proceeded in the intervening years to bury the engaged intellectual, albeit in a very different perspective from the champions of 'postmodernity'. In May 1980, introducing a new review with a prosperous future ahead of it – Le Débat – Pierre Nora wrote: 'The time of the intellectual as oracle is up. . . . However great his prestige, he is no longer sacerdotal. The intellectual has been largely secularized; his prophetism has undergone a change of style. Scientific investment has immersed him in a wide network of research teams and funds.'[108] Within this wide network the Fondation Saint-Simon, set up in 1982, would make it possible to tighten links around the historian François Furet of the École des hautes études en sciences sociales, with Roger Fauroux, former chairman of Saint-Gobain Pont-à-Mousson, and the ex-CFDT activist Pierre Rosanvallon.[109]

107 *Vivre et penser comme des porcs. De l'incitation à l'envie et à l'ennui dans les démocraties-marchés*, Exils, Paris 1998, p. 104.

108 *Le Débat*, no. 1, May 1980.

109 CFDT: the Confédération Française Démocratique du Travail, one of the three principal French trade-union federations. [Trans.]

Another former member of this union federation, Jacques Julliard, having published in the *Politiques* series at Seuil militant texts from all tendencies in the revolutionary tradition in the early 1970s, released a collective work entitled *Regards froids sur la Chine* in 1976. Issued the very year of Mao's death, it had given the first signal of the French intellectuals' break with Maoism.[110] In 1986 he was to write these lines, presenting the 'retreat of the intellectuals' as a resurrection: 'An intellectual community is in the process of being constituted in this country on the fringe of politics, an intellectual community with its own distinctive rules and system of values, which no longer merely reproduces that of the political parties.'[111]

It seems to me that Jacques Julliard could only have been referring to himself, since he was thereafter most often to be seen, beneath his unchanging pensive photo, distributing good and bad marks to political actors from his column in *Le Nouvel Observateur*. He brings to the task all the authority conferred by his status as a historian, and an especial ardour when it comes to denouncing the mistakes of the Left – invariably taxed with, or suspected of, archaism.[112] But in heralding a new type of intellectual, one year after the publication of *La Pensée 68*, the author maybe had in mind the new generation that was asserting itself in the circumstances we have noted.

---

110 See Michel Winock, *Le Siècle des intellectuels*, Seuil, Paris 1997, pp. 575–616.

111 *Le Nouvel Observateur*, 8–14 August 1986.

112 In his book *La Faute aux élites*, published by Gallimard in 1997, we find him reflecting on 'the inversion of roles in industrial disputes' in connection with the social movement of 1995: 'It is as if wage-earners had become the resolute defenders of archaic forms of capitalism against its modern forms. . . . The backwardness of the workers in comparison with employers as regards their perception of the future is not unusual.'

9

Good, Evil and Wisdom

Ask a recognized French philosopher what preoccupies him nowadays. Address a 'French thinker' as seen on TV – who, like his cousin the 'French doctor', is an export product. He will immediately plump for Evil: the Evil that attests to a native wickedness in man; the Evil Kant called 'radical' because it corrupts the foundation of all maxims.[113] He will exhort you to remain on guard and defend yourself against its onslaughts, to resist its incomparable powers of seduction.

Once again, it was André Glucksmann who led the way. Identifying this Evil with the historical reality of the Gulag, and thus with the totalitarian state, he imputed it to the intellectual currents that had brought forth this monster: Marxism, socialism, and – one thing leading to another – progressivism and rationalism. In *Les maîtres penseurs*, Glucksmann introduced another figure of such

---

113 Immanuel Kant, *Religion within the Boundaries of Mere Reason and Other Writings*, ed. and trans. Allen Wood and George di Giovanni, Cambridge University Press, Cambridge 1998, p. 59.

radical evil alongside the Gulag: Auschwitz. Auschwitz was to take precedence in his thought, as is evident from what he wrote in an opinion column in *Le Monde* on 1 December 1983, in the midst of the crisis over Pershing missiles,[114] under the title 'What is an intellectual?'. Glucksmann recaps, and then sets about 'Green pacifists and European Christians': 'They occupy the position allotted by Pascal to the "pious", who bathe in virtue and display "more zeal than knowledge".' 'What knowledge do they lack?', he asks: 'Knowledge of the inhumanity impending in and around us, which, in the century of Auschwitz and Kolyma, cannot be reduced to Western nuclear technology.' The rhetoric has not changed: the dead in their millions are summoned to testify to the correctness of the argument. It is as if, since his first book on Hiroshima, the thinking of this philosopher

114 The Williamsburg Summit of the heads of the seven leading industrialized countries ended on 30 May 1983. A new version of the logic of 'confrontation' between the two 'superpowers' was clamorously asserted by it. An economic declaration was issued announcing, in the mechanistic terminology beloved of experts, 'recovery', and advocating 'convergence' of the Western economies, in the framework defined by the Reagan administration: the struggle against inflation and liberalization of world trade within GATT. The so-called 'developing' countries would have to submit to the dictates of the IMF, which saw its means expanded. Notwithstanding French reservations, another declaration was appended that was unusual from such an authority. It affirmed the determination to maintain 'a sufficient military force to deter any attack'. Economic confrontation and military deterrence were flaunted in tandem: 'peaceful coexistence' and 'Cold War' thus came to be dialectically identified. The Williamsburg document contained echoes of the very tough negotiations under way with the Soviets at Geneva on the deployment of 'Euromissiles' – negotiations that precipitated enormous columns of 'pacifists' on to the streets in Germany and several other European countries. The shadow of a new world war lurked. The destruction in midair, above Sakhalin Island, of a South Korean Boeing 747 carrying 269 people by Soviet fighters on 2 September 1983 pertained to this logic: fear breeds suspicion. And for servicemen, suspicion is a reason to act without delay.

could support itself only if it is perched on piles of corpses. From his angle of vision, Auschwitz and Kolyma – it's all the same.

Yet it would not be long before Glucksmann accorded genocide a unique status. Indeed, he was to advance a philosophical argument to the effect that it involves an *unthinkable* event, confronted with which all thought should have learnt to admit defeat. Humanity could be defined by the crime of which it had proved capable: rendering itself culpable *vis-à-vis* itself. All the philosophical questions that have since fed the enormous ethical literature on the Shoah start out from this argument: by virtue of the systematic character of its implementation, and because it was directed against a people as such, the extermination of the Jews confronts human thought with an irreducible mystery. According to the logic of this reasoning, any thought that claims to understand or explain the event immediately sets about reducing it, thereby making itself complicit with it.[115] The same logic also has it that all thought is brought back to this essential 'unthinkability', which disclosed itself to humanity with the intervention of Hitler and the Nazis. Accordingly, thinking would resume exclusively on the basis of the evil of which it has shown itself capable, and of which humanity proved guilty in unveiling its inhuman aspect.

As a result, history in its entirety is put in a new perspective. Totalitarianism emerges as 'the politics of organized evil',[116] neutralizing any moral appreciation of human actions and giving free rein to the dehumanization which, in civilized countries, manifests itself in the form of barbarism. Jean-François Lyotard offered his

---

115 This logic is pushed to an extreme in a mediocre book by Éliette Abécassis, *Petite métaphysique du meurtre*, Presses Universitaires de France, Paris 1998. After a furious tirade against historians as such, the author does not hesitate to advocate the *lex talionis* as an ideal of justice for modern democracies.

116 Ibid., p. 68.

own version of this logic of the 'unthinkable'. In *Heidegger et les juifs* (1988)[117] he conceives the Holocaust as the consummation of a forgetting on which Greek and Roman thought was stubbornly set: that of a native impotence of human thought to which Judaism precisely bears witness, by way of the infinite debt the Jewish people invite humanity to recognize towards the Other.[118]

For all that, should we give in to intimidation? Can we withhold assent to the rationalization of this religious intellectual stance, without thereby aligning ourselves with the executioners? I consider it all the more necessary in so far as the 'Auschwitz' argument is not only fallacious, concealing a dogmatic allegiance beneath the semblance of philosophy, but politically dangerous. Indeed, I am not the first to observe that it is easy to conclude, from the fact that an event is unthinkable, that it is impossible.[119] It is then very difficult to prevent negationists from adding that if it is not possible, it is most certainly not real. Rather than stamping human thought with impotence in principle, the better to bring to bear on it the suspicion that as a result it is always on the verge of engendering monsters, is it not,

---

117 *Heidegger and 'The Jews'*, trans. Andreas Michel and Mark Roberts, University of Minnesota Press, Minneapolis 1990.

118 See Jacques Rancière, *Disagreement: Politics and Philosophy* (1995), trans. Julie Rose, University of Minnesota Press, Minneapolis 1999. The author, who offers a superb commentary on this text, supplies the key to the ethical discourse that rapidly developed: 'Ethics is thinking that hyperbolizes the *thought* content of the crime to restore thought to the memory of its native impotence. But ethics is also thinking that tars all thought and all politics with its own impotence, by making itself the custodian of the thought of a catastrophe from which no ethics, in any case, was able to protect us' (p. 135).

119 See ibid., p. 133, where the weakness of the argument from the 'unthinkable' in the face of negationists is exposed: 'There is absolutely nothing outside what is thinkable in the monstrousness of the Holocaust; nothing that goes beyond the combined capabilities of cruelty and cowardice when these benefit from all the means at the disposal of modern states.'

rather, imperative to think, not the metaphysical essence, but the historical determinants of the extermination of the Jews during World War II? Auschwitz happened. How was it possible? And what led to this potential horror becoming a reality? Can we identify potentialities in our own reality that might, in one way or another, induce a similar horror? Obviously, it is not easy to answer these questions. But I think it is a serious matter to reject them on the grounds that Auschwitz was an event whose uniqueness conclusively defeats all rational thought.

Twenty years after *Les maîtres penseurs*, André Glucksmann continues on his way. His book very simply entitled *Le Bien et le Mal* articulates and exemplifies his general conception of philosophy.[120] The philosopher, he writes, 'judges the course of the world, venturing opinions on current events'. Presumption or humility? The intellectual 'affects to think out loud, on behalf of everyone'. And if this intellectual 'is mistaken, like everyone else', it is inasmuch as he tries, at his own risk, to disclose 'the subterranean and obscure drives that haunt the public at large'. The most powerful and constant of these drives consists in not wanting to face up to the existence of Evil. The whole history of the West, and especially German Idealism, can be explained by the incorrigible optimism for which this refusal is the covert motive. Every theodicy supposedly presents itself as a veiled admission of the existence of Evil. From Plato to Leibniz and then Hegel, the philosophy has been fomented that gave birth to Auschwitz as well as the Gulag, to the damaging effects of asbestos or the threat of mad cow disease. Doubtless for the benefit of the general public to whom he addresses himself, Glucksmann adds this piece of information: 'Even if it appears fashionable and tabled by current events, the question of Evil is not a

120 *Le Bien et le Mal: lettres immorales d'Allemagne et de France*, Robert Laffont, Paris 1997.

new one.' Hence this new slogan, from a thinker who has certainly
not been niggardly with them: 'Against the spontaneous
Hegelianism that rules on the front page of newspapers . . . , let us
become classical once again.' Let us rediscover Racine. We shall
relearn from him that it is in the black night of the human soul that
the truth of our being lies. Let us re-read Voltaire, who, in inviting
us to follow Candide from one disaster to another, 'invented television'! This is called taking one's readers for imbeciles. . . .

But here once again is Luc Ferry, this time in a duet with André
Comte-Sponville, on the occasion of a work presented by the
authors – in all modesty – as the outcome of twenty-five years'
individual labour and twenty-five centuries of philosophy.[121] What
we are given to read derives from a sort of correspondence (Dear
Luc, Dear André) which sets out from the firm shared conviction
that 'life is too short, too precious, and too difficult to resign oneself to living it in any old manner. And too interesting not to take the
time to reflect on it and discuss it.' The initial contribution of the
author of *L'homme-Dieu*, a work already intended (according to its
subtitle) to teach us the meaning of life, integrates the journalistic
into the epistolary genre: 'Images of Rwanda, seen in a foreign
country. Worse than any that could be shown in France. Children
cut up with a machete while still alive – just like that, for pleasure.'
To explain Dear Luc's terror in the face of these images, I should
explain that Dear André had earlier advanced this daringly paradoxical definition: 'The sacred is that which can be profaned.' His

---

121 'It will be appreciated that it involves something quite different from an occa-
    sional book. For both authors twenty-five years' labour led to it and twenty-five
    centuries of philosophy': André Comte-Sponville and Luc Ferry, *La Sagesse des
    modernes: dix questions pour notre temps*, Robert Laffont, Paris 1998, p. 10.

interlocutor is in complete agreement: 'The sacred is a limit that could not be breached (even though it obviously always can be) without entering into the sphere of *absolute* evil.' Hence the question: 'This relation to the sacred, to the absolute – is it merely an illusion?' And the unequivocal response: 'My firm belief is that it is not.'

Luc Ferry has not taken the trouble to return to Rwanda, as any ex-New Philosopher would have done under the gaze of an obliging or hired camera. So no more transcendental journalism! Today the philosopher will confine himself to commenting on images viewed on television – which does not matter, since it is manifestly not Rwanda that interests him. Why these massacres? Not a word. Whence derives the ethnic hatred that is said to prevail between Hutus and Tutsis? And why should it explode now?[122] Not even the names of the protagonists appear. Where Glucksmann would have taken the opportunity to indulge in his meta-geopolitical passion, Ferry is satisfied with this touch: 'Children cut up with a machete while still alive – just like that, for pleasure.' As if it was in fact just 'like that, for pleasure'! Images are what retain his attention and what he retains. Moreover, it is their affective content that focuses his attention. Hence this necessary specification: they were 'seen abroad', so that he is in a position to add that they were 'worse than any that could be shown in France'. Enhancing the horror of the image by means of the unbridled imagination, the transcendental journalist here cedes to the multimedia moralist. The scene could have occurred in Cambodia or Afghanistan, in the USA or Vaulx-en-Velin. The only thing that counts is the evidence of evil in the shape of mutilated bodies. In other words, for him the human drama has

---

122 Readers seeking an analysis of this history will find it in Dominique Franche's *Rwanda, généalogie d'un génocide*, Mille et une nuits, Paris 1997.

interest only as a spontaneous illustration of a perennial theme contained in the philosophy syllabus. The children of Rwanda are thus reduced to the mere opportunity – a shade unexpected, even a little incongruous, let us admit – to undertake a dissertation of the most academic kind . . . on materialism! And for Luc Ferry to explain to us that the Buddhist East, Epicurus, Spinoza and Marx certainly comprise a respectable tradition, but one that he rejects, precisely so that he can condemn absolutely acts as horrific as those he has just reported! For his part, he aligns himself with the Christian West, Descartes, Kant, and Husserl's phenomenology.[123]

As for the 'ethical' question, from Glucksmann to Ferry the argument remains the same. The multimedia moralist explains that it is the propensity not merely 'to do evil' but to make it a project which, 'alas, indeed seems to be the peculiarity of man'. This gratuitous pleasure in doing evil, 'when it is pointless and not inscribed in any natural logic', paradoxically serves better than any altruistic behaviour to demonstrate human beings' freedom *vis-à-vis* natural determinisms. This propensity, this malicious delight, attests to the demonic surplus that inhabits us. It supplies the key to the sacred. For it is this surplus, this 'non-natural' element, its very essence, which it allegedly 'transposes' in the shape of sacred reality.

Is Ferry as innovative as he claims with his 'transcendental humanism', or his solemn 'transcendence in immanence' – which, Comte-Sponville goes so far as to suggest, will remain attached to the name of his friend just as the 'a priori forms of the sensibility' are to Kant's? You will permit me to enter some doubts. For ultimately, his intellectual schema appears to derive directly from the first philosopher to construct his doctrine around the idea of 'Man–God': Ludwig Feuerbach (1804–72). Bizarrely, Luc Ferry

123 *La Sagesse des modernes*, p. 21.

does not even mention among his influences the name of this dissident disciple of Hegel, who so influenced the thinking of the young Marx and the 'Left Hegelians'.[124] In *The Essence of Christianity* (1841), the work on which his reputation is based, Feuerbach pronounced himself unsatisfied with a negative critique of the Christian religion. Quite the reverse, he declared: he intended to extract its vital element, as expressed in such terms as 'love', 'imagination', or 'heart'. Through an audacious genetic analysis he made God appear as the essence of man or, more precisely, the human species. In this being, each of us modern individuals could discover the truth that 'man is the supreme being for man', at least if he ceased 'thinking of God as an extra- and superhuman reality on to whom he could project all his aspirations'. In reality, concluded Feuerbach, the mysteries of Christian theology came within the purview of anthropology: 'The beginning, middle and end of religion is Man.'[125]

In his debate with Comte-Sponville, Ferry gallantly issues this slogan of typically Feuerbachian tonality: 'To my mind, the great philosophical task of today consists in this: following the advances of humanism, and while preserving them, we need to reappropriate

---

124 In 1960 Louis Althusser published a translation of Feuerbach's *Manifestes philosophiques* in the *Épiméthée* series from Presses Universitaires de France, directed at the time by Jean Hippolyte. His immediate politico-philosophical aim was to set the cat among the pigeons in Marxist orthodoxy, which claimed that the Marx–Hegel relationship was summed up in the materialist inversion of the idealist Hegelian dialectic. If any system of thought wanted to operate this inversion, it was quite expressly Feuerbach's, from which Marx, with great difficulty, had to detach himself.

125 *The Essence of Christianity*, trans. George Eliot, Harper & Row, New York 1957, p. 184. *The Essence of Christianity*, which was first translated into French by Joseph Roy in 1864, was retranslated by a pupil of Althusser's, Jean-Pierre Osier, and published in 1968 in the *Théorie* collection directed by the philosopher at Maspero.

the truth of religious discourse.'[126] And – again like Feuerbach – he immediately invokes love as a sentiment 'totally immanent to itself and, at the same time, totally transcendent, completely egotistical and completely altruistic'. But it is Husserl whom Ferry opts to cite on this theme:

> Ultimately, it is clearly love that incarnates the highest figure of that plural structure which, following Husserl, I designate here as transcendence in immanence. Patently, it is what saves us, to the extent that we are capable of it. I mean that in the last instance it is what gives our lives meaning.

That for a Christian this transcendence is founded on the existence of a God who is indeed 'real' requires 'no comment' as far as he is concerned.

André Comte-Sponville, author of the celebrated *Petit traité des grandes vertus*, situates himself on the same terrain. You will perhaps object that he defends the materialist position rejected by Ferry. You would not be wrong. Indeed, immanence is the only thing Comte-Sponville ever talks about. He mocks the transcendence so dear to his partner and applies himself to demonstrating that materialism – at least, if it is not construed in the vulgar sense as a philosophy of the stomach, wallet and sex – presents itself as a 'theoretical antihumanism' – an Althusserian formula – which issues, without the slightest paradox, in a practical humanism: a benign enough humanism that does not disdain on occasion

126 *La Sagesse des modernes*, p. 52.

to adopt the gentle expression of the Dalai Lama. Yet the kind of argument he employs is not fundamentally different from that of his interlocutor.

Comte-Sponville in his turn summons the unhappy children of Rwanda on behalf of his cause, and just that little bit more abstractly still – we forget that we're even talking about Rwanda! You would think that the Rwandan image of horror had become the mandatory illustration of philosophical reasoning for contemporary thought. 'When I say that I would not in any circumstances cut a child to pieces, in what respect is this illusory?', the virtuous André solemnly inquires of himself. He is worried – seriously worried, it seems – that a materialist, being unable to attribute an absolute universal value to any moral imperative, might also condemn the pretensions of moralists who submit to it as 'illusory'. Rest assured – the answer arrives forthwith: 'On the contrary, I have every reason to believe that it is true. But this truth concerns solely oneself, or a particular individual, not the absolute.' The author does not shrink from classical philosophical means in order to secure his position: 'What is a truth? It is what describes the real adequately.' He thus deploys nothing less, in passing, than the Thomist definition of the truth to support his stance, leading us to expect a definition of the real. Alas, we are in for a disappointment. What follows is utterly empty: 'The only reality here is that Luc, myself, and all of us do not in any circumstances want to torture a child!'[127]

In fact, we note that this abstract morality can generate 'thought-experiments' that verge on the ridiculous. It abandons concrete cases, including those each of us is called on to confront in the course of our lives. It diverts thinking from the most urgent task, which consists in analysing the material and spiritual forces that

127 Ibid., p. 54.

determine our evaluations. In lieu of this labour on the self – which makes it possible to wrest, often with great difficulty, the requisite distance from the obviousness of our beliefs and allegiances for the exercise of a certain freedom – these moralists offer us general formulas of astonishing vacuity. As François Dagognet writes, with a certain sense of parody: 'We are all persuaded that good must triumph over evil: the whole question is to know what this good consists in and what it requires of us – unless we call "good" what we desire, in which case we reckon to "possess" the good at the very moment it eludes us.'[128]

On this last point, the discussion by the authors of *Sagesse* reaches its apex: Ferry appears to be of the opinion that we desire the Good because it is the Good (in the sense that it is not Evil); while Comte-Sponville maintains that the Good is good solely because we desire it! They invoke the great names of Kant and Spinoza – but in vain. For when moral argument is conducted in this fashion, we are condemned to countersigning the aporias of common sense. The lustre conferred by a suitable rhetoric will never help anyone to understand what it is correct to do, or not to do, in some determinate situation.

The rhetoric of our two sages then runs out of control around the word 'sacred'. They realize it and desist, at the cost of some jokes that must certainly have made them laugh ('*sacré* Luc!', '*sacré* André!'). Let us pardon their childishness, for the sacred belongs to the climate of the age. In a book likewise written – as if fortuitously – in epistolary mode, and published at the same time as *Sagesse*, Catherine Clément and Julia Kristeva attempt to appropriate the theme for women – or, to be more precise, 'the feminine'.

---

128 *Une nouvelle morale: travail, famille, nation*, Les empêcheurs de penser en rond, Paris 1998, p. 20.

The text has its attractions. Indeed, these writers travel a great deal, so that we are given some piquant psychological remarks and picturesque descriptions of a religious ethnology as wild as it is comparative. Moreover, as each of them is more intelligent than the other, and anxious to let it be known, we are swept along on a scholarly tour of the most diverse cultures. We discover those that are marked by the monotheistic religions, those that carry the trace of 'Buddhism, Confucianism, Taoism, and the animist religions of Africa and elsewhere'. Dear Julia prophesies:

> The sacred is unquestionably experienced in private. It has even seemed to us to be what confers meaning on the most intimate of the singularities, at the point where the body and thought, biology and memory, life and meaning meet – in men as in women. Women *perhaps* being located at this point in a more dramatic, more symptomatic, more imponderable fashion, in times to come.

But why this emphatic 'perhaps', which seems to qualify the prophecy? Answer: 'I deliberately say "perhaps", for one is always surprised, and often even happily so, by the "feminine" in men as well.' Duly noted, writes her correspondent, who finds the last word there.[129]

In *L'homme-Dieu*, Luc Ferry had expanded the notion of the sacred to the point of making it into an omnipotent historical category. I quote: 'For millennia the sense of the sacred had inspired all spheres of human culture, from art to politics, from mythology to ethics. Illusory, perhaps, but imposing.'[130] For Catherine Clément and Julia

---

129 *Le Féminin et le sacré*, Stock, Paris 1998, p. 287.
130 *L'homme-Dieu ou le Sens de la vie*, Grasset, Paris 1996, pp. 16–17.

Kristeva it is space, rather than time, that evinces the power of the sacred. Masculine or feminine, in time or space, the sacred plays the same role in the argument. It serves to confirm the idea that the famous 'disenchantment of the world', which supposedly occurred in the West, has led us to deny the universally attested existence of a 'sense of the sacred'. It is now urgent to reappropriate it. Such, indeed, is the task for the future: 'to recognize the sacred in man'[131] – which obviously applies to woman as well.

Before so liberally attributing such a 'sense of the sacred' to humanity, however, are there not good reasons first of all to ponder the meaning of this notion? Far from being eternal, the category of the 'sacred', such as we spontaneously contrast it with the 'profane', was in fact invented very recently – in the early years of the twentieth century, when Émile Durkheim published *Les Formes élémentaires de la vie religieuse* (1912),[132] and Rudolf Otto a famous work entitled *Das Heilige* (1917).[133] These books have inspired the two major currents in the historiography of religion.[134] The first comprises the 'immanentist' historians, who regard religious facts as assimilable to the same type of explanation as the set of phenomena studied by the social and human sciences. The second inspires those who regard such facts as intrinsically different from other facts, because they

131 Ibid., p. 42.
132 *The Elementary Forms of the Religious Life: A Study in Religious Sociology*, trans. Joseph Ward, Allen & Unwin, London 1915.
133 Rudolf Otto (1869–1937): German philosopher and historian of religion, who applied phenomenological analysis to religious sentiment. His *The Idea of the Holy* (trans. John W. Harvey, 2nd edn, Oxford University Press, London and New York 1950) was translated into French in 1948.
134 As Daniel Dubuisson has demonstrated in his magnificent book *L'Occident et la religion. Mythes, science et idéologie*, Éditions Complexe, Brussels 1998.

refer to a distinct order of reality. But ultimately, the opposition between 'immanentists' and 'transcendentalists' proves secondary. The essential thing is that 'religious facts' exist and that they are observable, identifiable as such, throughout human history. What, however, of the conception of religion that has governed the characterization of these 'facts'? Let us read Otto: it is clearly a Christian conception – the particular conception that prevailed in the Lutheran current of the Reformation, placing emphasis upon inner feelings, on the faith that would inevitably be born out of the experience of transcendence.[135] By what right do we universalize this conception? Can the 'facts' assembled under the heading of 'Greek religion' really be conceived in these terms? Or Roman religion? Or Aztec rites and beliefs? Buddhism? There are excellent reasons to doubt it. What, then, is the purpose of such universalization? Otto – who at least does not conceal his hand – answers as follows: in the end, it involves a celebration of the superiority of Christianity, such as he practises it, over all other religions!

It is now good form to deplore the fact that the philosophers of the 1960s abandoned the terrain of ethical reflection out of an exclusive concern with the political dimension of human action. At the Sorbonne, for example, Vladimir Jankélévitch[136] remained

---

135 Otto's *œuvre* has its place in a lineage in which the names of Johann G. Herder (1744–1803) and Friedrich D. E. Schleiermacher (1768–1834) stand out. But we should not neglect to add that of Benjamin Constant (1767–1830).

136 Vladimir Jankélévitch (1903–85): mobilized in 1939 while a senior lecturer at Toulouse University, he was wounded the following year and then dismissed from his duties under the exceptional laws of the Vichy regime. He joined the Resistance, and at the Liberation organized the musical programmes on Toulouse-Pyrénées broadcasting. In 1949 he published a *Traité des vertus* whose

one of the few to carry on teaching moral philosophy in this period of extreme politicization of philosophy students. If his audience never waned, this was due above all to the charisma of his person, his talent as a teacher, and ultimately to his political commitment.

Here I must once again invoke the role of Michel Foucault. Contrary to what has been claimed, he had by no means abandoned the terrain of ethics, but had in reality undertaken to open up a path for inventive thinking in it. It will be remembered that following the polemics provoked by *La Volonté de savoir*, which was presented as the first volume of a *Histoire de la sexualité*, he published nothing for eight long years. It was only on the eve of his death in 1984 that he decided to publish the volumes that make it possible to see in what direction – partially unanticipated – he had pursued his project. Several of the interviews he gave on this occasion place morality at the centre of his thinking.

Already exhausted by illness, he replied in *Les Nouvelles* to questions posed by Gilles Bardebette and André Scala. The weekly chose 'Le retour de la morale' as the title for the interview. Foucault first of all explained his new style, which was significantly balder than that of his earlier great books. This restraint stemmed from the object he had selected: a history of the subject, focused on the 'individual conduct' that he had left to one side in studies like *Histoire de la folie* or *Surveiller et punir*. In this new object, he added enigmatically, he had discovered a sort of 'guiding thread which didn't need to be justified by resorting to rhetorical methods by which one

moral problematic remained at the heart of his thought. He held the chair in moral philosophy at the Sorbonne from 1951 to 1978. A collection of his texts, entitled *Philosophie morale*, was published by Flammarion in 1998.

could avoid one of the three fundamental domains of experience' (alongside truth and power).[137]

Foucault turned next to the reasons for his prolonged silence – what some have called his 'intellectual crisis'. Having set out on the same footing as in his previous inquiries, *en route* he had come up against a very important question: 'Why have we made a moral experience of sexuality?' Hence his sudden immersion in Greek antiquity: in order to highlight what he called 'an appropriation of morality through the theory of the subject . . . beginning with Christianity'.[138] The style had possibly changed since the previous books, but the analyses offered us in both *L'usage des plaisirs* and *Le Souci de soi* handle as much historical material, exhume some equally ignored texts, and paint canvases of similarly vast proportions. In another interview, given at Berkeley in April 1983 to Hubert L. Dreyfus and Paul Rabinow, Foucault had distilled the most general import of the conception of the work that had imposed itself on him over the years: 'In my view the work that needs to be done is a work of problematization and incessant reproblematization. What blocks thought is implicitly or explicitly accepting a form of problematization, and then seeking a solution that could be substituted for that problematization.' And he added:

> If the labour of thought possesses a meaning, it consists in tackling the way in which human beings problematize their behaviour at its source. . . . The labour of thought does not consist in denouncing the evil supposedly concealed in

137 'Le retour de la morale', *Les Nouvelles*, 28 June–5 July 1984, pp. 36–41; trans. John Johnston as 'The Return of Morality', in Sylvère Lotringer, ed., *Foucault Live: Collected Interviews, 1961–1984*, Semiotext(e), New York 1989, pp. 465–73 (p. 466).

138 Ibid., pp. 472–3.

everything that exists, but in sensing the danger that lurks in everything customary, and in rendering everything that is solid problematic.[139]

Foucault himself emphasized that this reflection, of a strongly Nietzschean cast, itself veiled a morality organized around a certain notion of 'style of existence'; this doubtless dispels the enigma of the alteration in his prose style. We are all familiar with the maxim he evolved in his last texts: 'to make of one's life a work of art'. But it is not a question of some simple aestheticizing view of existence, formulated by a moralist judging the course of the world from the summits of his own experience and reading. The words that carry weight in his text are the ones leading up to this oracular phrase. Grouped around the verb 'problematize', they invite thought to be dynamic; they encourage us to conceive thinking as a movement that is always resumed against that which, in thought, stubbornly and insidiously obstructs it. These words include an explicit challenge to Freudian concepts, as well as the more or less Stoic, Christian or Kantian categories that constitute the dominant morality in the West.

I recommend that, in counterpoint, you read the final chapter of André Comte-Sponville's *Petit traité*. There you will find a good hundred pages, written in a lively and lucid style, devoted wholly to love. For Comte-Sponville love involves the highest virtue, as is immediately apparent: 'We have need of morality only for want of love, let us reiterate it; and that is why we need morality so much! It is love that is in command, but love is lacking: love commands in

---

139 'À propos de la généalogie de l'éthique: un aperçu du travail en cours', in Foucault, *Dits et écrits, 1954–1988*, vol. 4, Gallimard, Paris 1994, pp. 609–31 (p. 612). [The earlier English version of this interview, available in *The Foucault Reader*, ed. Paul Rabinow, Penguin, Harmondsworth 1986, pp. 340–72, does not contain these passages – Trans.]

its absence, and through this very absence.'[140] Very good, you may say. But what is love? Answer: 'It is the good itself.'[141] Understand that if you can. . . . And sexuality? Very straightforward: 'Even if it is born out of sexuality, as Freud maintains and as I readily believe, love cannot be reduced to it, and goes beyond our minor or major erotic pleasures.' Moreover: 'Our life in its entirety, private or public, familial or professional, is valuable solely in proportion to the love that we bring to, or find in it.' In other words – and to sum up – love is an excellent sentiment. Highly recommended. But just try sorting your life out on the basis of such empty counsel!

In *L'homme-Dieu*, Luc Ferry takes up this page to make a link with Camus and mark the sign of a transcendence: 'Morality is useful, even necessary. But it remains of the negative order of prohibition.' He will therefore relax his rigid standards. The supreme positive value is love. Camus wrote: 'I love my mother more than justice.' Ferry comments: 'As a general rule, there is no need to tell a mother that she should feed her child.' Proof that it is indeed a matter of transcendence. Yet there is no God to impose his law from without. Accordingly, what we have is a transcendence per-taining to the 'order of meaning'. A few pages later, Ferry believes he can enlist Emmanuel Lévinas in the cause of this 'secular spiritu-ality': 'Henceforth it is profane love that is going to confer its most evident significance on the existence of individuals.'[142] But this love, naturally, will be construed aside from any history of sexuality. Why bother with Freud – albeit only to criticize him – when 'it is no doubt Plato who gives us the essentials on Eros. Freud will merely

---

140 *Petit traité des grandes vertus*, Presses Universitaires de France, Paris 1995, p. 294.
141 Ibid., p. 292.
142 *L'homme-Dieu*, p. 52. For a counterpoint, see Benny Lévy, *Visage continu: la pensée du retour chez Emmanuel Lévinas*, Verdier, Paris 1998.

repeat him twenty-three centuries later: exalted in the passion of lovers, sexual desire is lack. It calls for the *consumption* of the other.' (The word is emphasized by the author, who derives from it a brief, cannibalistic variation on Eros and Thanatos.)

Poor Eros! Our moralists get along extremely well at its expense. It already cuts a sorry figure beside *Philia*, the friendship extolled by Aristotle, which in their eyes possesses the merit of revolving around a presence, not an absence. It appears derisory opposite *Agapē*, the love commended by Christ in the Gospels: 'Love that is disinterested, gratuitous, even without justification', extending to the whole of humanity over and above any presence. We shall have occasion to return to the heady lure of love that has gripped our two friends. Meanwhile, here is a further sample, taken from Comte-Sponville, who certainly never tires of gratifying us: 'Why would we be selfish if we did not love ourselves? Why would we work if it wasn't out of love of money, creature comforts, or work itself? Why philosophize, if not for the love of wisdom?' And for Luc to exclaim in turn: 'For anyone who loves their children, it is impossible to remain wholly indifferent to the misfortune that befalls their *fellow creatures*, even at the opposite ends of the earth.'[143] Strange reasoning that would oblige modern humanity, with implacable strictness, to procreate out of humanism, just as any old parishioner once had to out of religious piety.

The intellectual posture here is one of exhortation. It aims to incite adherence to values that are not in the least 'problematized' but, rather, exhibited, illustrated, and lauded. When reference is made to the works of historians, anthropologists or sociologists – invariably very much at arm's length – it is by way of raw material,

---

143 *L'homme-Dieu*, p. 163.

to justify a philosophical thesis that is supposed to confer on them their true meaning.[144] Thus our mediocrities 'spontaneously' rediscover the philosophical practice rejected by Michel Foucault when he embarked on his first work.

Certainly, not everything is political in the sense understood by the intellectual terrorists of the leftist sects post-May, who subjected their followers to an intolerable emotional blackmail. And one cannot, as some did, reduce moral questions to the moods of petty bourgeois devoted, out of idleness, to the suspect cult of their own ego. But all such questions are addressed to a unique, concrete being, who maintains relations with other unique beings in a given society. That these relations happen to be socially structured by institutions that embody the existing morality; that these institutions give them purchase by working the imaginary of each and every one of us – this is what we can all learn if we engage in critical analysis of the conditions determining the singular modalities of our development as subjects. These conditions involve the intervention of the institutions, beliefs and practices that are inseparable from them.

The research programme formulated, launched and illustrated by Foucault in the final volumes of *Histoire de la sexualité* continues to inspire important works, whether on the medicalization of human existence or the advent of a society dominated by a potent and

---

144 It is thus that in *L'homme-Dieu* Ferry makes copious use of Philippe Ariès (*Essais sur l'histoire de la mort en Occident*, Seuil, Paris 1975), as well as Denis de Rougemont (*Passion and Society*, trans. Montgomery Belgion, Faber & Faber, London 1956), Edward Shorter (*The Making of the Modern Family*, Basic Books, New York 1975), and Niklas Luhman (*Love as Passion: The Codification of Intimacy*, trans. Jeremy Gaines and Doris L. Jones, Polity, Cambridge 1986).

diffuse bio-power. The principle of this programme consists in the thesis that the idea of a 'moral subject' is a historical construct whose first elements were put in place in classical philosophy – particularly that of late Stoicism. Foucault suggests that these elements were adopted in the new form of thinking represented by Christianity, whose penitential offices inspired in each believer a methodical attention to the self, an exacting vigilance towards the self on the part of the self. The fact that this subject has subsequently been reconstructed several times explains how the prescriptions, prohibitions or counsels figuring in ancient morality, even when they are adopted to the letter in the modern world – sometimes in open conflict with Christian values – in fact play a very different role in the individual's relationship with itself and others. Must Foucault's analyses be examined and emended? Obviously. But at least they are presented as analyses designed to make us think, not as the justification of an ethic to be adhered to.

10

The Heady Lures of Love

The 'return of morality', which set in in the early 1980s, unquestionably corresponds to the retreat of the political vision of the world that had crystallized around the idea of revolution. This simple observation, however, is insufficient to explain the contemporary powers of attraction of ethical thought. It did not prevail by default. It responded, and continues to respond, in paradoxical fashion to one of the major social upheavals induced by May '68. I want to discuss the novel place that sex and its pleasures occupy in our societies.

An indication – albeit rather discreet – of this upheaval can be found in the 1966 Situationist pamphlet *On the Poverty of Student Life*. Among the sarcasms aimed at the mass of students, the authors wrote: '[they are] so "unconventional" that thirty years after Wilhelm Reich, that excellent educator of youth, [they continue] to follow the most traditional forms of amorous-erotic behavior, reproducing the general relations of class society in [their] intersexual relations.'[145] Two works by the 'excellent educator' were cited in a note to the text: *The Sexual Struggle of Youth* (1932) and *The Function of the Orgasm* (1942–45).

The first of these texts was to be newly translated by Jean-Marie Brohm, who introduced it to French readers in 1972 in the *Petite Collection Maspero* – the portable library of every good young leftist militant. The translator endorsed its 'critique of the repression of pleasure, of the inculpation of happiness, of the ideology of procreation and the bourgeois family'. In his 1932 Preface the author himself had waxed highly indignant: 'The sexual misery of contemporary youth is immense. The greater part of its sex life goes on beneath the surface and does not manage to express itself openly.' Hence his radical plea: 'Youth has more than a mere right to "information"; it fully possesses a right to sexuality. It has been deprived of this right.'[146]

It is true that these lines seem to have been written for people of my generation. They describe, with force and precision, an essential aspect of the situation we experienced. The extraordinary cult of sexuality prevalent since then must not be allowed to obscure the institutional and moral constraints facing us. For the record, I will recall a factual detail: the Neuwirth Law, authorizing the public marketing of the contraceptive pill, dates only from 14 December 1967,

---

145 'On the Poverty of Student Life', in *Situationist International: An Anthology*, ed. and trans. Ken Knabb, Bureau of Public Secrets, Berkeley, CA 1981, pp. 319–37 (p. 323).

   Wilhelm Reich (1897–1957): American doctor and psychoanalyst of Austrian extraction. Throughout his life, Reich was impelled by the search for a monistic, biophysical energetics as the key to phenomena as diverse as sexual physiology, cancer and cosmic energy. Following a speedy trial, the federal American authorities condemned him to two years in prison. His works and scientific equipment were burnt! He was imprisoned on 12 March 1957 in Danbury penitentiary and then, following a report that pronounced him a paranoiac, in Lewisburg, where he died on 3 November 1957.

146 *La Lutte sexuelle des jeunes*, Maspero, Paris 1972, p. 31.

and it awaited statutory implementation for a long time. A further eight years passed before the Veil Law decriminalized abortion.[147] Another fact: my generation attained its majority at the age of twenty-one; the law reducing it to eighteen was passed only in 1974, during the modernizing phase of Valéry Giscard d'Estaing's presidency.[148] And since we are dealing with dates and institutions, I will further note that it has been rather too quickly forgotten that coeducation in the state school system was progressively introduced only after 1968. As for homosexuality, it had been declared a 'social scourge' by honourable parliamentarians. The sex life of adolescents was supervised, to say the least. Fear and shame weighed heavily upon it.

The erotic slogans of May '68 ('enjoy without restraints') thus by no means represented the poetic whim of young bourgeois playing the provocateur to shock their parents. The 'restraints' in question were very concrete realities. But the most intolerable thing, without a doubt, was the hypocrisy prevalent in this domain. Jean-Claude Guillebaud is right to recall that the parents of the 'baby boom' belonged to a generation, born in the 1920s, which had carried aloft the banner of 'natalist ideology, the cult of the family, and a puritanical strictness about sexuality'.[149] I will not mention here the multiple proceedings started against Jean-Jacques Pauvert for publishing works that offended moral decency: let us nevertheless salute the courage of this man, so long maligned. I simply recall that on 10 January 1957, the Seventeenth District Court in Paris condemned him for an edition of the works of the Marquis de Sade, and ordered

147 The definitive enactment of the legislation on voluntary abortion, legalizing it during the first ten weeks of pregnancy, dates from 20 December 1974.

148 On 28 June 1974, at the end of the parliamentary session, the law on majority at eighteen was passed, as was the law liberalizing contraception.

149 *La Tyrannie du plaisir,* Seuil, Paris 1998, p. 291.

'the confiscation and destruction of the works seized'.[150] A decade later, on 1 April 1966, a ban was imposed on *La Religieuse* – Jacques Rivette's film based on his reading of Diderot.

You will object that such was the lot of all our contemporaries; that American youth, for example, suffered much more intense puritanical repression. There is some truth in this. The Beat generation was to testify to it with unequalled virulence; and in England the Rolling Stones would sing 'I can't get no satisfaction' until they were blue in the face!

In France, however, the issue had taken a particular twist on account of the rivalry between Church and state over the institution of marriage, which had been evident since the 1930s. The Catholic Church had decided to promote married life as a centrepiece of the religious existence of the faithful. There thus developed among young Christian couples what Althusser called the 'aggressive exhibitionism' of an 'intimate public behaviour'.[151]

Personally, I have retained a very precise memory of this 'conjugal obscenity'. During my primary-school years, for complicated family reasons, I found myself a pupil of the Jesuits at the Collège Saint-Louis de Gonzague. My mother, a divorcee, worked so hard that numerous well-off families of my classmates generously welcomed me in. From frequenting the Catholic milieu, I know that it is utterly false to claim, as was subsequently done, that questions about sex were not confronted in it. The post-'68 discourse on taboos and prohibitions always seemed very misleading to me. On the contrary, after centuries of hypocritical prudishness, Catholics

---

150 See Michel Delon's introduction in *Sade: Œuvres*, Bibliothèque de la Pléiade/Gallimard, Paris 1990, p. ix.

151 'On Conjugal Obscenity', in Louis Althusser, *The Spectre of Hegel: Early Writings*, ed. François Matheron, trans. G. M. Goshgarian, Verso, London and New York 1997, pp. 231–40 (pp. 233–4).

spoke freely about sex, even if they did so in a manner peculiar to them: as of a natural reality that must be inscribed in the reality of the Christian life of couples.

In fact, the halting speech of the parents, as well as the remarks borrowed from the unfortunate chaplains who strove to advertise their liberty, sounded terribly false to the ears of children like us, who were on the lookout. Well might the Catholic couple tirelessly engage in a discourse about itself that was designed to pass off as *natural* the fact of conferring a supernatural meaning upon 'nature'; it was not difficult to spot the artifice. Far from attesting to their liberty, the authorized forms of release from repression in which they engaged disclosed a servitude still more burdensome, and perhaps more grievous, than that of our grandparents, who at least did not tell themselves stories or inflict them on us.

In secular milieux, some indulged in a veritable ideological auction in response to this policy of the Church, whose offensive character they appreciated. The most retrograde version was probably the one offered by the Communist Party. Thus it was that in these progressivist times Jeannette Vermeersch, redoubtable wife of General Secretary Maurice Thorez, was to be heard vaunting the familial virtues of the proletariat and denouncing the hypocrisy of the 'morally degenerate' bourgeoisie; while Politburo member Jacques Duclos violently attacked 'queers', condemned as mentally ill and urgently in need of medical treatment or re-education.

Parallel to these repressive discourses, the discourse employed by the most enlightened of genuine progressivists was likewise built on a naturalist conception of the sexual function. The couple, if not the family, supposedly had nothing to hide once sex, freed from its guilt, found a way of blossoming there – not in a supernatural sense, but in the very prosaic sense of the psychic equilibrium of individuals, considered from a hygienic or medical standpoint. In sum, as between Catholics and laity, it was each to their own nature: nature in the Divine plan of creation and procreation for the former; nature in the biological interaction of the vital functions for the latter – but nature all round.

The key to the enigma about our generation that continues to intrigue demographers – the sudden and vertiginous decline in marriage from 1964 onwards – is doubtless to be found here.[152] We refused the hypocrisy of our parents. We condemned their so-called liberation as illusory. Hence also, no doubt, the aggressiveness of youth, who (as is well known) proved no less rebellious at the family dining table than on the Parisian cobblestones. Gide's exclamation – 'Family, I hate you!' – became our universal slogan. Our liberation would not be a pale imitation conducted within a prim-and-proper marriage: it would be a genuine emancipation! We were going to cast off all 'restraints'.

The reverberation of Reich's text on the sexual struggle of youth is therefore readily explicable. We discovered a thinker who did not contrive to present a social form – the couple, the family – as natural. The only nature he invoked was that of sexual pleasure, around which the words of our teachers skirted with varying degrees of candour and perversity – or, perhaps, perverse candour.

The other side of the coin – the trap we did not spot – consisted

152 See Jean-Claude Guillebaud, *La Tyrannie du plaisir*, p. 269: 'Today, demographers still ponder the powerful signal given by all Western countries in 1964–65. The statistical cataclysm it indicated amazes sociologists. Simultaneously, all the demographic parameters were suddenly reversed: a drop in fertility and marriage rates; lengthening duration of single life for women; a stunning increase in the divorce rate; a reduction in the number of children per family, etc.'

in the fact that Reich and his emulators were once again employing the discourse of nature as regards pleasure. This time we were roused to indignation on behalf of 'authentic nature'![153] On the lecture benches of the old faculties people rejoiced in speaking at last about masturbation, fellatio, and everything we wanted to know about sex but were afraid to ask. On this score the students and teachers at Vincennes University, established by Education Minister Edgar Faure's legislation after May, made it a point of honour fully to redeem its title as an experimental university. Some of them were even to be seen going so far as to practise naturism at the Fête de *l'Humanité* on the large lawn at Courneuve, under the dumbfounded gaze of PCF leader Georges Marchais!

But nature is a fiction, empty in itself. The title of the second book by Reich to which *On the Poverty of Student Life* refers perfectly indicates the content with which people rushed to fill it. *The Function of the Orgasm* betrays a resolutely biologistic inspiration, even if the biology of the 'orgone' – the allegedly measurable, mysterious substance of pleasure – proves to be largely fantastical. In the introduction to this book, Reich summarizes the general spirit of his theory of sexual economy as follows:

Psychic health depends upon orgastic potency, i.e., upon the degree to which one can surrender to and experience the climax of excitation in the natural sexual act. It is founded upon the healthy character attitude of the individual's capacity for love. Psychic illnesses are the result of a disturbance of the natural ability to love. In the case of orgastic impotence, from which the overwhelming majority of people suffer, damming-

---

153 See the Quebec film *La vraie nature de Bernadette*, which enjoyed considerable success at the beginning of the 1970s.

up of biological energy occurs and becomes the source of irrational actions.

And he adds, in consequence: 'The essential requirement to cure
psychic disturbances is the re-establishment of the natural capacity
for love. It is dependent upon social as well as psychic conditions.'[154]

The biological functionalism that took hold the pleasures of
sex, under cover of these revolutionary references and the intensive
sexological propaganda subsequently deployed, has played a decisive
role in the medicalization of existence, which began to develop in
the course of the 1980s.

In *La Volonté de savoir*, published in 1976, Michel Foucault pierced
the illusion fostered by the post-1968 discourse of sexual liberation
with some shafts of irony. Reread the opening lines of the book: 'For
a long time, the story goes, we supported a Victorian regime, and
we continue to be dominated by it today. Thus the image of the
imperial prude is emblazoned on our restrained, mute, and hypocritical sexuality.' Such is the 'repressive hypothesis' to which the
best minds had yielded. Foucault adds: 'This discourse on modern
sexual repression holds up well, owing no doubt to how easy it is to
uphold.' To this illusion he counterposes the history of a West not
preoccupied with silencing sex, but determined to make it speak.
From confessors to psychoanalysts ('ears for hire'), our civilization
has never stopped seeking to 'put sex into discourse', in order to
construct a knowledge of it: a knowledge much more essential for
the exercise of power over individuals than prohibition, censorship,
or denial. And Foucault ventures the idea that the critical discourse
directed against repression is 'in fact part of the same historical

154 *The Function of the Orgasm: Sex-Economic Problems of Biological Energy*, trans. Vincent
R. Carfagno, Souvenir Press, London 1983, p. 6.

network as the thing it denounces (and doubtless misrepresents) by calling it "repression"'.[155]

Eight years later, with the publication of the subsequent volumes of *The History of Sexuality*, the argument had hardened. Protesting against the 'monarchy of sex', calling for sex to be put back 'in its place' in our conception of existence, Foucault condemned the intellectual abdication performed by our age when it elevates sexuality into the nucleus of human existence, and sensual pleasure into the supreme value because it is inscribed in nature.

His position emerges with especial clarity in the 1977 interview with Bernard-Henri Lévy, whose strategic importance in his political thought has already been stressed. Here Foucault manipulates the Reichian idiom of sexual misery. The philosopher agrees with his interlocutor when he poses the objection: '[s]ome would answer that, despite such discourse, repression and sexual misery still exist'. Yes, they do indeed exist. But the interesting thing, Foucault says, is to 'analyse the forms and conditions of misery'. Establishing an analogy with Marx's works on working-class misery, he adds that his research will consist in seeking 'to understand which are the positive mechanisms that, producing sexuality in such or such a fashion, result in misery'.

Foucault then indicates the path that he is currently taking, going beyond Reich and no longer resting content to invoke some fundamental prohibition attendant upon an economic situation ('work, don't make love'). The famous misery is in the first instance that of childhood and adolescence. It had an objective: 'It was to constitute, through childhood sexuality suddenly become important and mysterious, a network of power over children.'

155 *The History of Sexuality*, vol. I: *An Introduction*, trans. Robert Hurley, Allen Lane, London 1979, pp. 3, 5, 10.

While it is true that Foucault could subsequently be caught taking some liberties with this programme, he would never waver on the essential point: the discourse of 'sexual liberation' always seemed to him a snare, whose effect was merely to reinforce an apparatus of power exercised over individuals from infancy. What a formidable instrument of control they were, these words that tempt you with a smile: '"You have a sexuality, this sexuality is both frustrated and mute, hypocritical prohibitions repress it. So come to us, show us, confide in us your unhappy secrets."'[156]

It was doubtless somewhat imprudent to rely on a book by Hervé Guibert to diagnose an '"anti-sex" challenge', and herald a movement that would fight its way back from '"always more sex"' and '"always more truth in sex"': a movement that would result in 'the end of the monarchy of sex' – hence a revolution! – and open the way to 'other forms of pleasure, of relationships, coexistences, attachments, loves, intensities'.[157] But how can one not subscribe to the diagnosis: the monarchy of sex is not freedom? Commercialized by cinema, television and the video industry, it has, on the contrary, proved an insidious form of servitude: the servitude of an imposed and dictated sexual freedom. Should we not attribute to its performance imperatives a role in the violent outbursts that betray the personal malaise of contemporary youth, fed a non-stop diet of sexual injunctions from their earliest years? Does not the media eroticization of couples contribute to shattering the family?

Teachers know very well that the rebelliousness – whether joyful, aggressive, or pathetic – displayed by a number of their pupils, and

156 'The End of the Monarchy of Sex', trans. Dudley M. Marchi, in Sylvère Lotringer, ed., *Foucault Live: Collected Interviews, 1961–1984*, Semiotext(e), New York 1989, pp. 214–25 (pp. 215–16).

157 Ibid., pp. 218–19. See Hervé Guibert, *La Mort propagande*, Régine Déforges, Paris 1977.

their unamenability to the rules of communal living and the norms of personal life, have something vaguely to do with this 'monarchy of sex', which has since degenerated into the 'tyranny of sexuality' via an exasperation of desire.

Following in the footsteps of such a master, are our mettlesome contemporary philosophers going to embark on the difficult path of analysing what is in play in this historical development? No. When it comes to sex, sexuality, or pleasure, their hortatory style borders on sermonizing: for them we must have done with the 'false subversions' of the 1960s. The objective is wisdom, as evinced by Luc Ferry's picture of what he calls 'the dialectic of love life'.[158]

He begins by posing a classic question: 'Are the feelings inspired by passion such as to found enduring relationships? Are they not by their very nature so unstable that nothing solid can be built on them?' As required by their rhetorical character, the first question is answered in the negative; the second in the affirmative. Happiness is definitely not to be sought there: 'People already sensed it in Plato's time, and nothing occurs today to contradict him.' Let us overlook the anachronism whereby the modern notion of passion is attributed to Plato (albeit in the form of a 'presentiment'); what follows is instructive. The reader is subjected to a discourse on temptation! It begins with a bitter reflection on the 'erosion of desire' and a few lines later rejoins the Devil, in the guise of the famous serpent. After an obligatory passage via Tristan and Don Juan, antithetical figures of altruism and egotism, we arrive at this axiom: 'To survive, passion requires a perfect equality between lover and beloved.'

158 *L'homme-Dieu ou le Sens de la vie*, Grasset, Paris 1996, p. 149.

Doubtless through free association on the phrase 'perfect equality', Ferry permits himself to write that it involves, 'so to speak', 'the fundamental law of a physics which, for all that it is a physics of the heart, is no less constraining than that of bodies'. What follows, however, discloses neither the other laws of this physics, nor its problems, nor its concepts. Instead, the text approximates to rules for supervision of the conscience: Be wise, young people! Do not let yourselves be carried along by your inflamed senses. You will know only disappointment or bitterness. Examine what you have experienced. Refrain from building on sand. Master sexual excitement, and discover the true love that is borne from soul to soul.

André Comte-Sponville, for his part, defends a hedonism – a philosophical attitude more favourably disposed to pleasure. But his is a moderate hedonism, one tempered by an awareness of the tragic character of existence. If he claims to draw inspiration from Epicurus, he emends his Epicureanism by means of Montaigne, under the authority of his master Alain. 'Over the pleasures', he writes, 'I will not linger. It would be indiscreet, and completely pointless, to go into too much detail about my own. Everyone knows enough about them. The body is a good judge – and the only one. Eating is good; drinking is good; making love is good.' This is no longer modesty; it borders on prudishness. Yet here is the audacity it conceals: 'Who desires death when he has a hard-on?' asks Comte-Sponville. Is it some lack of experience? In any event, rest assured, gentle folk: a sage of this stamp will not indulge in extravagances. He does not imagine that there is more than a vague assonance between hanging and coming. If I understand him correctly, the main point lies in the conclusion: 'Hedonism is not nihilism.' And in conformity with a cast of mind that enjoys abrupt volte-faces, he adds: 'The taste for death persists, even in desire itself. But it is perhaps less universally perceived than the stronger, more immediate, and more intoxicating taste for pleasure.'[159]

But as this taste undoubtedly persists, we must recognize that we cannot be satisfied with the pleasure of the senses; and that *Philia* is more valuable than *Eros*, and prepares for *Agapē*. As I told you at the outset, young people, the choice is yours. You are modern and wish to be wise? *Agapē* for all is indicated. Austerity and moderation: spiritualized hedonism or tempered hedonism!

This wisdom, this sweet reason, and this mercy provoke violent opposition from Michel Onfray – another kind of philosopher, who has made the question of sensual pleasure a speciality. Even so, does his thought unfold on a different plane from that of his opponents? The plane, for example, on which de Sade or Bataille is located? Not a bit of it. In Onfray we will not find the least invitation to rethink the notion of nature, of rules, norms and discipline, constantly manipulated by his comrades – without ever problematizing them, needless to say. We will merely read a new 'supervision of conscience', exercised in the direction of a more or less joyful invitation to debauchery. And we will be sensitive to the style of a thinker who has reached the conclusion that there is 'no philosophy without the autobiographical novel that makes it possible'.[160] Indeed, exhibiting an unbridled hedonism and zealously manipulating the erotic metaphor (thunderbolt, volcano, and so on), this eternal youth does not permit us to ignore anything of the life of his ancestors and parents, his museum trips, his indigestions and copulations. According to him, is not hedonism, like anarchism in politics, 'a vital option, dictated by a body that remembers'?

One word recurs endlessly from the pen of this rebel, to the

159 *Impromptus*, Presses Universitaires de France, Paris 1996, pp. 62–3.
160 *Politique du rebelle. Traité de résistance et d'insoumission*, Grasset, Paris 1997.

point of constituting a veritable jingle: 'jubilant'. I have no doubt
that a film or TV producer could be interested in the novel whose
episodes he unfolds from book to book. As a title for the series I suggest *Jubilator*. With the second volume of the *Journal hédoniste* we
reach *Jubilator II*.[161] Here he indulges in an extravagant eulogy of
Raoul Vaneigem, author of the *Traité de savoir vivre à l'usage des jeunes
générations*, published in 1967 – one of the Situationist texts that
marked the 1960s.[162] It is called 'Celebration of tear gas'. The chapter opens – like others – with an indictment of 'the philosophical
fellow travellers of Christianity who gambol between the Legion of
Honour and cardinal virtues, advisory committees to right-wing
ministers and celebration of a Catholicism repainted in the insipid
colours of Kantian secularism'.[163] The 'autobiographical novel' is
manifestly also a *roman à clef*. In contrast, Vaneigem finds himself
truly beatified: great historian of 'margins and shadowy figures',[164]
the Belgian thinker supposedly demonstrates that 'the dominant
ideology feeds on the orthodoxies promoted by them with the
intention of celebrating the death drives and containing or destroy-
ing proliferating vital energies'. Jubilator II advances: 'There is
enough dynamite stored up there to mine the Christian edifice in its
entirety.'[165]

We are given to understand that 'when he takes off his historian's
hat, Raoul Vaneigem can be a philosopher-imprecator, and make the

---

161 *Le Désir d'être un volcan: journal d'un hédoniste*, Grasset, Paris 1996; *Les Vertus de la
foudre: journal hédoniste II*, Grasset, Paris 1998.

162 *The Revolution of Everyday Life*, trans. Donald Nicholson-Smith, Left Bank Books
and Rebel Press, n.p. 1983.

163 *Journal hédoniste II*, p. 144.

164 Onfray has in mind Vaneigem's *Résistance au christianisme: les hérésies, des origines
au XVIIIᵉ siècle* (Fayard, Paris 1993) and *Les Hérésies* (Presses Universitaires de
France, Paris 1994).

165 *Le Désir d'être un volcan*, p. 148.

epoch his preferred object'. Then 'he risks concepts that make cynics laugh, and have the scent of tear gas once more.' Unwitting hedonist, he would argue, for example, that the will to power and the will to pleasure must be made to coincide – 'the totality', concludes Onfray, 'furthering the ends of jubilation multiplied tenfold'.

Philosophy teacher in a *lycée*, so he writes, out of contempt for academic titles and procedures, Jubilator II rejoices at Vaneigem's 'imprecations' against teaching establishments: 'In these places of death are extolled the structure over the pupil; the curriculum over creativity; training over education; servitude over freedom; boredom over jubilation; obedience over autonomy; the soul over the body.' Poor pupils! They must greatly enjoy seeing a teacher round off his philippic with this appeal: 'May the time of rag-day processions and refreshing uproar come!'[166]

'Well, there we are!', as they say in Normandy, out of contempt for sermonizers. . . .

Our thinkers argue? They at least concur in playing life instructors – even when, as self-declared anarchists, they would wish to recognize no Gods or Masters!

166 Ibid., p. 152.

11

Machiavelli in Carpet Slippers

'Rehabilitate politics': such is the universal slogan among our philosophers in these times of grey managerialism and generalized racketeering. This is a very reasonable programme. Yet the task does not appear to be an easy one, since in the eyes of Comte-Sponville, as of so many of his disabused contemporaries, 'no politics is really best'.

From Marxism Comte-Sponville retains the primacy of the economy, but construed in the most 'economistic' sense. 'Our fellow citizens', he notes, 'have the feeling, perhaps rightly, that the most important issues are no longer played out on the political stage.' This stage supposedly brings the egotisms of the individuals who subscribe to the social contract face to face; indeed, 'the regulation of egotisms is the great affair of politics, or rather, is politics itself'.[167]

---

167 André Comte-Sponville and Luc Ferry, *La Sagesse des modernes: dix questions pour notre temps*, Robert Laffont, Paris 1998, p. 466: 'This is what politics extends and adapts.'

Dear André calls on Epicurus, Rousseau, Hobbes and Spinoza to help him reach the following conclusion:

> Rehabilitate politics? This will not happen if we do not know how to explain to our contemporaries that politics is there for them, not against them; to improve their quality of life and that of their children, to protect them against poverty and violence, to impart or restore power to them – in short, *to defend their interests*.[168]

In truth, this is a curious rehabilitation, since it actually ratifies the classical Anglo-Saxon theory of the 'mutual adjustment' of interests and, in conclusion, presents 'what we in France call "the Republic" as the instrument for reconciling these interests' – which is precisely what it has never intended to be.[169]

With Ferry, the rehabilitation scarcely seems better initiated since, according to him, 'everyone has understood it, albeit reluctantly: with the end of communism it is the fantasy of "another politics" in general that has collapsed'.[170] Let us therefore revert to greater modesty: let us register the fact that since 1968 the meaning of our lives has taken refuge in the private sphere of existence. The bewitching sentiment that reigns there is *philia*, the modern love which, in the framework of the family, is directed at the presence of the other. This love opens up our hearts to universal sympathy. Hence this sentence: 'As long as politics continues to underestimate the importance of the story of modern love, it will not understand the extraordinary potential for solidarity, for

168 Ibid., p. 469; original emphasis.
169 See Claude Nicolet, *L'idée républicaine en France (1789–1924). Essai d'histoire critique*, Gallimard, Paris 1982.
170 *La Sagesse des modernes*, p. 476.

sympathy, contained in the private sphere; as long as it does not root itself in that, nothing in politics will excite enthusiasm.'[171] Consequently, the author advocates a 'politics of love', a 'politics of sentiment', intended to accommodate the famous 'grand designs' that we lack: Don't be fobbed off with empty words! Don't ever again succumb to some mythology of the radiant future. In the first instance, love your wife and children; love of humanity will be vouchsafed you in addition. By Ferry's own admission, there is only a 'difference of intonation' between Comte-Sponville's vision and his own.

This proximity is marked by a joint celebration of humanitarian action – obviously not for itself, with its problems, ambiguities, tragedies and impasses, but because it seems to embody the general philosophical theses on man they both propose. For the one, the victim to whom aid is brought reminds us that man is a living, suffering, mortal being, with a capacity for cruelty and cowardice, but also for experiencing compassion when confronted with the sufferings of fellow creatures, and for displaying mercy in the face of base human deeds. For the other, by the emotion it inspires the victim reveals the sacredness we all recognize in every human being – the sacredness that constitutes the 'positive' horizon of any morality.

But, you will ask, whence derives the philosophical renown of humanitarianism, which for decades attracted nothing but sarcasm from political militants deriding philanthropy and charity? Each of us remembers well-chosen words directed against the naivety, even the secret perfidy, of actions that aimed to remedy the most crying ills of the capitalist system, and especially its imperialist methods.

171 Luc Ferry, *L'homme-Dieu ou le Sens de la vie*, Grasset, Paris 1996, p. 225.

Without a doubt, 1978 was decisive. That year an image caught people's imagination. On the steps of the Élysée Palace, following a meeting with Valéry Giscard d'Estaing, André Glucksmann held the arms of Raymond Aron on his right and Jean-Paul Sartre on his left: a potent symbol, to use the subsequent overwrought idiom of the *énarques* in power.[172] More potent, perhaps, than was realized at the time. For it did not just involve a kind of public reconciliation between the two veteran rivals of the French intelligentsia, through the intermediary of a philosopher who had been a pupil of the one and a fellow traveller of the other. The trio had in fact just solicited the aid of the President of the Republic for the operation 'A boat for Vietnam', mounted by Bernard Kouchner. Humanitarian action was making its official entry into French politics at the very top. And what an emotional charge it had for everyone! Support for the struggle of the Vietnamese people against American imperialism had been the initiation into politics for so many young militants; and prior to 1968 it had represented the terrain of a confrontation between the Communists of the Comité Vietnam National – 'Peace in Vietnam!' – and the leftists of the Comités Vietnam de base – 'Victory to the NLF!' – which had contributed significantly to the formation of all concerned.

This solidarity was no longer required. Worse, people were beginning to ask out loud about the destiny of servitude that was said to be in store for this 'liberated' people. But nothing was very clear. The Élysée trio was conveying this message: now is no longer the time for political analysis and action; let us aid the victims without pondering the responsibility of the various parties in the human disaster that is unfolding.

---

172 An *énarque* is a past or present student of the École nationale d'administration. [Trans.]

The reverberations of 'humanitarianism' have gone on increasing in the subsequent twenty years. The universal clamour that has since accompanied certain major actions, for better or worse, must not be allowed to conceal the long history of which the 'French doctors' were, in reality, the heirs. All those who have studied this history have identified several 'ages' in it.[173] In 1863 the first 'Comité international de secours aux militaires blessés' was founded by Henri Dunant (1828–1910), a Swiss citizen who had witnessed with horror the agony of tens of thousands of wounded soldiers on the battlefield of Solferino. Shortly thereafter, he would create the Red Cross, the first private organization with a specifically humanitarian mandate. The original Geneva Convention was signed at the same time.

Some difficulty was experienced in conceptually grasping the notion of a 'sanctuary' on the field of military operations, as well as the distinction between combatants and non-combatants, which is very arbitrary in certain circumstances. People soon began to query the perverse effects of arrangements which, in restoring the wounded to strength, contributed to prolonging the hostilities, which in consequence became increasingly murderous. But at least the philosophical grounds on which these first agents of humanitarianism based themselves were explicit and coherent, borrowed from the fathers of international law, the natural law theorists foremost among whom was the Dutch jurist Grotius (1583–1645).[174]

---

173 See Rony Brauman, *Humanitaire le dilemme* (Éditions Textuel, Paris 1996), as well as Alain Destexhe's *L'humanitaire impossible ou deux siècles d'ambiguité* (Armand Colin, Paris 1993) and Luc Boltanski's *La Souffrance à distance. Morale humanitaire, médias et politique* (Métaillié, Paris 1993).

174 Hugo de Groot (known as Grotius), *De Jure Belli ac Pacis* (1625). In English, see Grotius, *Prolegomena to the Law of War and Peace*, Liberal Arts Press, New York 1957.

It is quite otherwise with what Rony Brauman calls the 'second birth' of humanitarianism, which accompanied the emergence of the Third World during decolonization and 'peaceful coexistence' – that is, acute competition between East and West. The war in Biafra was the occasion of the first media famine, and gave rise to the first great humanitarian operation – hence ten years prior to 'A boat for Vietnam'.[175]

That this type of international intervention can be effective, and – assuming good logistics and great devotion – save human lives by the thousands in an emergency, is a fact. Proof of this was produced in Biafra. But it is equally a fact that humanitarian action rapidly becomes open to manipulation by the political forces operating on the ground. The French Red Cross had a bitter experience of this in Biafra. The same Rony Brauman has written some pages of an astringent lucidity on the derailment that occurred. French doctors

> believed in all good faith that they were witness to a genocide and did not realize that they were making themselves spokesmen for the propaganda of the secessionist leaders. In this they were like the Irish missionaries and British NGOs, who were the first to violate Nigerian sovereignty in order to transport aid directly via the military supply flights of Biafra.[176]

Similar derailments have regularly taken place when intervention has occurred on a terrain of open conflict. This was especially the case in Bosnia, where a 'politics of the ambulance' was neatly integrated into the strategy of a triumphant fascism.

175 'Republic of Biafra' was the name taken by the region of south-east Nigeria, inhabited mainly by Ibro, when it entered into armed secession from 1967 to 1970.

176 *Humanitaire le dilemme*, p. 22.

That the quintessential medium of humanitarian action – television – has played a key role in the successes, as well as the derailments, is a universally acknowledged fact. TV, vehicle of emotion, imposes the naked image of calamity in the shape of tortured or famished bodies. This image, often presented as 'intolerable', stirs the heart, arouses indignation, and excites compassion.

In thus stirring profound drives and constitutive fantasies in television viewers (aggression, mutilation of the body, death, the tortured life of an emaciated child, etc.), without rooting these images in concrete reflection on any singular history, and without offering viewers the perspective of a rational understanding, it is not human 'fraternity' or 'solidarity' that is solicited and reinforced, but utter sentimentalism that is exploited, as in any old American B-movie. The world becomes a pitiable tele-spectacle rendering those who allow themselves to be caught up in it hysterical, and consigning those who refuse to go along with the game to a brutal indifference.

Thus conveyed in images, humanitarian action is of interest to all political authorities, who are tempted to reduce it to a simple but effective tool of communication. Far from inciting citizens to think – that is to say, analyse the causes of the human dramas it exposes in supplying aid – it has the inverse effect of 'placing all cases of distress on an equivalent plane of significance' (Brauman) by naturalizing them: famines, floods, epidemics, pogroms or ethnic cleansing. The morality of emergency does not permit us – and cannot permit itself – to discriminate as to their human significance between the suffering of a child agonizing amid the ruins and that of a child dying under the blows of an executioner. Questions of responsibility are, by definition, alien to it.

Hence the unease felt at the strange expression 'humanitarian crisis', which emerged in the course of the 1990s and structured the moving discourse of the international organizations in Rwanda. A crisis certainly calls for measures that pertain to humanitarian action, but can never itself be said to be 'humanitarian'. When it does not refer to a straightforward natural catastrophe (but do such things, devoid of any human involvement, any longer exist?), it always involves a complex of determinate economic, political, ideological and military causes. This phrase, which focuses attention on the effects of the crisis, sounds in truth like a veritable ban on analysing the process from which the situations in need of remedy derive.

The hazards of humanitarian action, and the concrete context in which it must be conducted, represent so powerful a constraint for the doctors who devote their energies to it that, spotting the trap, they sometimes end up declining to intervene or packing up and leaving, death in their soul. Our moralists pay no heed to this; they are glued to the spectacle. And in the exploits of 'French doctors' they merely seek arguments to illustrate and reinforce the personal version of humanism to which each intends to affix his name.

In sum, we have a morality of pity on the one hand, an ethic of respect on the other, both of them topped off by a minor metaphysics of love. Or – to put it another way – a spirituality of 'de-speration'[177] that squints insistently at a certain Buddhism; and a Christian spirituality secularized by a humanization of the Divine that ultimately possesses meaning solely via the deification of the human licensed by it.

Combined with the technocratic conception of politics that tends to prevail on a planetary scale, humanitarian action can conduce to a situation in which our world ends up accepting the destitution of the majority, with a good moral conscience, as a fatality. Rony

177 André Comte-Sponville, *Traité du désespoir et de la béatitude*, vol. I: *Le Mythe d'Icare*; vol. II: *Vivre*, Presses Universitaires de France, Paris 1984–88.

Brauman bluntly sketches such a perspective, when he ironically foreshadows 'a dream-world in which a handful of social workers would confer their blessings on a mass of grateful wretches'.[178] The law of the jungle would prevail between 'rational agents' – calculating tigers or wolves unleashed for ferocious competition in the global market; the principle of compassion – or, if you prefer, the law of love – would inspire 'compassionate agents' in their action to rectify the human damage induced thereby.

This is why there are grounds for concern when we see our philosophers appealing to the humanitarian conception of suffering humanity to secure the subordination of politics to ethics, in the name of human rights.

You will retort that there is nothing reprehensible about wanting to moralize politics. And you will stress that it is in fact through a lack of ideals that contemporary politicians have allowed their art to degenerate into a sheer technique of deceit for the benefit of the most powerful – that is, the wealthiest. I reply at once that, in my experience, any politics pursued in the name of morality is pregnant with tyranny as soon as it is conducted in the name of a cut-and-dried division between Good and Evil. Recent years have furnished at least two sinister examples of this. The first is that of the ayatollahs in Iran raging against the moral corruption of the Pahlavi dynasty at home and the American 'great Satan' abroad. I will not linger over this, since it could be objected that this morality was very particular in so far as it is theologically grounded in the Absolute. The second example is more compelling. It involves the Gulf War, prosecuted by the international community against Iraq under the

178 *Humanitaire le dilemme*, p. 56.

banner of Human Rights. Everyone remembers the incredible bellicose displays by some of our transcendental journalists demanding in such terms that Iraq be crushed. We know what it revolved around: oil interests. Note that this does not mean that war should have been avoided. This is open to debate from a political point of view. But today it seems clear that invoking the moral themes of 'human rights' in order to prosecute it allowed Saddam Hussein, a dictator from a secular party hitherto pampered by the West, to rally his fellow citizens around him in the name of Islam, and to enslave them that little bit more in a country flattened under the bombing.

Thus there is good reason for distinguishing between different orders of reality: the order of ethics and that of politics. To do politics cannot be to combat Evil (remember, too, Reagan designating Brezhnev's Soviet Union the 'Evil Empire', before Tehran took its place!); it is to act on a highly complex system of relations of force in a way that is conducive, or otherwise, to popular emancipation.

Such, incidentally – or so it seems to me – was the political logic that inspired the drafters of the Universal Declaration of Human Rights in 1948. The very considerable philosophical value of this text derives from the intellectual *dynamic* animating it, as disclosed in the first two articles. The drafters in fact made a point of linking to the affirmation of the freedom of all human beings, and their equality in dignity and rights, the formulation of a duty to act. Article 1 of the Declaration, adopted by the General Assembly of the United Nations in Paris on 10 December 1948, states: 'All human beings are born free and equal in dignity and rights. They are endowed with reason and conscience and should act towards one another in a spirit of brotherhood.' From the outset, what represents the greatest threat to democratic regimes is condemned: the passivity, or apathy, of their citizens. This passivity has its economic causes and psychological springs. Today, it is powerfully organized on a planetary scale. It rapidly becomes tantamount to renunciation, and obedience then becomes servitude. In 1948 it was impossible to forget that such passivity can amount to consent to the worst atrocities. Everyone recalled that only a few years before, numerous citizens in the great democracies had proved capable of acquiescing out of cowardice, and because they did not want to know, to what – since 8 August 1945 – have been called crimes against humanity. Arguably, this summons to concrete action by every one of us to assert freedom and equality ultimately represents the very spirit of the Declaration.

Indeed, this orientation is confirmed by the next article: 'Everyone is entitled to all the rights and freedoms set forth in this Declaration'. In moving from 'all' to 'everyone', the Declaration confers its meaning on the enumeration of rights that occupies the next twenty-five articles. Every human being is summoned to a struggle against the forces opposed to their assertion. Each of the situations evoked represents a concrete case where grounds then existed for initiating this struggle; the list could be updated today.

Accordingly, the Declaration must not be read as a simple inventory or corpus of inviolable rights. Its logic is that of a mobilization around rights and freedoms, whose concrete assertion represents at one and the same time a duty for everyone and an ideal for all. It involves pushing back the forces opposed to the realization of those rights, and abolishing the obstacles to the deployment of those freedoms.

This logic emerges as a dynamic of emancipation on behalf of a *politics* aimed at 'the free and full development of [the individual's] personality', according to the terms of Article 29. But it is here that full significance must be given to the 'spirit of brotherhood' which, according to the text, should inspire action posited as duty. This allusion signifies that the individual, whose 'free and full development' one wants to further, is in no way identifiable with the monadic reality cultivated by modern individualism: the egotistical, possessive individual who believes that he is able to realize his own freedom only by trampling over that of his competitors. This is why the Declaration is addressed instead to individuals who know that they can realize themselves only by combining with their own 'full development' that of their fellows – with whom, whether they like it or not, they happen to be interdependent. And in this sense it is opposed to every form of human servitude, including that imposed by individuals on themselves when they believe it is possible to isolate their being in order to affirm their freedom against others – others who are, nevertheless, their human brothers and sisters.

The Declaration thus condemns the mutual mistrust that is impairing human relations ever more gravely in our world. The text does not merely invite us to maintain or consolidate rights supposed to attach to the being of a human subject who is reputed identical in all places and times. It enjoins the assertion in action of 'all the rights and freedoms' required for the existence of democratic societies. The conception of democracy advanced certainly remains rather imprecise, but it goes beyond the content of Article 21 (access to public service, exercise of universal suffrage, and so on). Without distorting it, one could translate it into quasi-Spinozist terms: democracy emerges as the regime that facilitates the optimal balance between the preservation of individuals and the existence of the state, because it prompts a mutual enhancement of the capacity for existence of the individual and of the community to which he or she is joined as a citizen.

This interpretation, however, must not be allowed to mask the serious ambiguities attaching to the use of the word 'democracy' today. It has ended up being identified purely and simply with one of its forms – parliamentary democracy – whereas, in its concept, democracy must always be reinvented. Its institutional existence assumes that everyone strives with others to maintain and intensify the dynamic that allows individuals to concert their energies collectively, in order to give shape and power to the body politic. This requires a collective effort: a political dynamic of thought, or analysis, of the processes of accumulation and redistribution of powers and rights between citizens and the state.

But what most assuredly arrests this dynamic is the status of supreme value attributed in the West to the word 'democracy', which is presented there as an article of faith and scarcely any longer as an occasion for reflection on the concrete forms in which the 'demos' exercises its putative sovereignty. It is as if the more democracy is heaped with praise, the less open to investigation are its principles and mechanisms.

This is particularly so in our country, for strange as it may seem, until the reversal of opinion at the end of the 1970s, the word did not form part of the standard lexicon in French political discourse. Marxists, who continued to militate for the dictatorship of the proletariat, missed no opportunity to criticize the classical idea of it as formal and its contemporary manifestations as – in the final analysis – designed to mystify the exploited masses. Communists counterposed to bourgeois democracy the 'new democracy' which, in the countries under Soviet domination, took the allegedly provisional form of 'people's democracies'. For a long time the German Democratic Republic was considered its flagship!

Gaullists, for their part, evinced only mistrust for this word, with its odour of America. They preferred the term 'Republic', which had the advantage of referring to glorious historical episodes when France had shown the way to other peoples: it echoed their own struggle in the Resistance to restore the republican form of state against Vichy, and bore the stamp of a desire for national independence attached to the image of the soldiers of Year II.

Finally – for reasons related in the first instance to the policy of the Church – in France there was never a political party that officially claimed to have its roots in Christian Democracy. The party that came closest – the Mouvement Républicain Populaire (MRP) – likewise preferred to play on the republican reference.[179]

President Giscard d'Estaing broke new ground, causing surprise when, at the beginning of his term, he published an opuscule entitled *Démocratie française*. Democracy suddenly became the supreme political value in our republic. Who today would dare not to declare themselves a democrat? If some democratic regime, like the USA itself,[180] calls on occasion for severe criticism – apathy, corruption, manipulative puritanism – it is always levelled in the name of a more pure, ideal conception of democracy. Access to democracy is readily regarded as the end of history – at least by those who have not renounced the idea that history could proceed in the direction of human progress.

The ascent of the idea of democracy in the scale of values recognized by political thought has occurred at the cost of an uninterrupted confrontation with so-called totalitarianism, then with the 'terrorist threat', and now finally with the menace of Islamist fanaticism.[181]

179 The MRP, created in 1944, was a political party that brought Christian democrats together. It scored a big electoral success in 1945, becoming the premier party in France, but was abandoned by a section of its electorate with the formation of the Gaullist Rassemblement du Peuple Français in 1947. It participated in most of the governments of the Fourth Republic, and supported General de Gaulle in 1958. See, in particular, Jean-François Sirinelli, ed., *Histoire des droites en France*, Gallimard, Paris 1992.

180 See Denis Lacorne, *L'invention de la république: le modèle américain* (Hachette/Pluriel, Paris 1991) and *La Crise de l'identité américaine: du melting pot au multiculturalisme* (Fayard, Paris 1997); André Kaspi, Jean-Claude Bertrand and Jean Heffer, *La Civilisation américaine* (Presses Universitaires de France, Paris 1993).

Resorting to paradox, Luc Ferry makes it possible to illuminate one of the main reasons for this ascendancy. In *La Sagesse* he has no qualms about introducing Machiavelli – 'in a certain sense at least' – as 'the first of the democrats', because 'the master of modern politics' was the one who advised the Prince 'not only to take popular passions into account, but to base rulers' authority on them'. Hence the question: which 'common, popular passions' did the Florentine propose to mobilize on behalf of the Italian national state for which he so ardently called? Should hatred and fear be included in the front rank? I am well aware, replies Ferry in substance, that such was Machiavelli's opinion; but despite everything, there has been a change in modern humanity. It is therefore necessary to 'reinterpret' the Machiavellian principle, retaining only such popular passions as have been 'civilized by two more or less republican centuries of history: the democratic passions'. Comte-Sponville agrees, albeit with reservations and nuances: 'What you call the "democratic passions" partially overlap with what I call the "interests".'[182]

Poor Machiavelli, who alone precisely enables us to see clearly in the mystificatory metanarrative on the genesis of the state recounted by modern political philosophers, nourished as they are on juridical culture. Admirable and scandalous author of *The Prince*, he brought to light the interplay of the violent, 'uncivilized' passions – hatred, avarice and fear, as well as love – presiding over the genesis and stabilization of modern states.[183] Niccolò Machiavelli did not deserve

181 So many binary oppositions that have been construed as those of Evil and Good, at the cost of seeing nothing of the impending internal decomposition of the allegedly totalitarian regimes of the Eastern bloc.

182 *La Sagesse des modernes*, pp. 484–7.

183 See *The Prince* (1513), ed. Quentin Skinner and Russell Price, trans. Russell Price, Cambridge University Press, Cambridge 1988.

to be thus summoned in his carpet slippers to sing the praises of a politics of love! But at least the summons allows us to understand what this political conception does not want to admit the existence and persistence of: the relations of force at the heart of our 'democratic' societies; and the violence daily exercised therein under the most 'civilized' appearances, and despite the calm rationality of most official political discourse.

In his time, Althusser ironized about the thinkers who adopted the 'fairy-tale history of the state' narrated by partisans of natural law:

> A completely mythical history, but one that makes pleasant listening, because in the end it explains to those who live in the state that there is nothing horrific in its origins, only nature and law; that the state is nothing but law, is as pure as the law, and as this law is in human nature, what could be more natural and more humane than the state?[184]

Today there is no more emphatic discourse than that extolling the virtues of the 'state of law': it forms part of the mandatory minimum repertoire of politicians in all countries that like to think themselves 'civilized'. And how could one not subscribe to its main themes, when it involves condemning dictatorships or denouncing corrupt regimes? But the phrase probably owes its success to the ambiguity it harbours rather than to its problematizing or emancipatory value. When we hear encomia to a form of state that respects duly established judicial rules and procedures, another little tune insinuates that the state is 'law' in the sense that the wine is 'Bordeaux' or, if you

---

184 'Machiavelli's Solitude', trans. Ben Brewster, in Louis Althusser, *Machiavelli and Us*, Verso, London and New York 1999, pp. 115–30 (p. 124).

prefer, as the material is 'cotton'. This thesis is highly serviceable. It authorizes neo-liberals to maintain that if, in the last analysis, law constitutes the essence of the state, today it is sufficient to let it operate on a planetary scale, borne along by the globalization of trade, without any longer resorting to the form of the nation-state, which has supposedly been rendered obsolete by history.[185]

Our philosophers have in fact rallied to the Weberian notion that modern Western societies are secularized or disenchanted.[186] On this basis they build a whole history that parallels the progress of this disenchantment, the secularization of the state, the expansion of individualism, and the birth of modern love. But is this not to be deceived by appearances? Has the structure via which the normativity of juridical and political institutions operates in the West really changed? Has the absolute reference point constituted by God remained vacant?

In order to establish and maintain itself, any political regime must draw on the instinctual pool of each individual. Through an

185 As always in such matters, the ambiguity thus proves dangerous. It should be noted that the Soviet state, so roundly condemned as totalitarian, was equipped with a legal code that it in no way flouted, but on the contrary respected unswervingly. The same goes for the Nazi state, since – contrary to a too widely held opinion – there existed a very rich and constraining body of Nazi law. Both of these reviled regimes could therefore have presented themselves as states of law! It is useless repeating this formula if we want to avoid the repetition of such horrors! Any political thought worthy of the name should today, on the contrary, profit from the collapse of the Eastern bloc countries to take up the analysis of the genealogy of the state, but also of the categories of the subject of law, liberty, equality and property.

186 Weber's term is *Entzauberung*. See F.-A. Isambert's clarification, 'Le désenchantement du monde: le non-sens ou renouveau du sens', *Archives de sciences sociales des religions*, vol. 61, 1986, pp. 83–103; cited by Pierre Legendre in *Le Désir politique de Dieu: études sur les montages de l'État et du droit*, Fayard, Paris 1988, p. 21.

adequate discourse, embodied in institutions that address everyone, it must deal with the violence of the affects that bind each of us to the other members of the social body.

In the West the techniques of adherence – if not adhesion, as Legendre says – to the state are juridical techniques that have been meticulously refined over centuries, employing the arsenal of Roman-canonical notions. These techniques have undergone various adjustments, depending on the individual cases of the nations concerned. They aim to elicit from subjects or citizens a political passion directed to the supreme guarantor of the social body thus instituted and constituted. This love neutralizes the hatred that can nevertheless always reawaken to rend the social body. The circumstances in which the state replaced the Church as guarantor of citizens' 'marital status' are familiar. It took its place in order to register filiations, and hence also sexual identities.[187] In this sense it plays the role of a phantasy Father for each of us, and arouses the ambivalent feelings attaching to this station.[188]

This is the mechanism that is totally eclipsed in the case of modern democracies. Tocqueville expressed the point very well in *Democracy in America*: 'Thus, not only does democracy make men forget their ancestors, but also clouds their view of their descendants and isolates them from their contemporaries. Each man is forever

187 The bitterness of the debates over the PACS proposed by parliamentary deputies in 1998 finds part of its explanation here. Another part consists in the historical episode, evoked above, which saw marriage become an issue in the confrontation between the Catholic Church and the French state. [The PACS, or *pacte civile de solidarité*, recognizing the legal status of homosexual couples, was eventually passed into law by the left-wing majority in the National Assembly in 1999 – Trans.]

188 See Pierre Legendre, *L'inestimable objet de la transmission: études sur le principe généalogique en Occident*, Fayard, Paris 1985.

thrown back on himself alone, and there is danger that he may be shut up in the solitude of his own heart.'[189]

Contemporary theoreticians of democracy commit the great error of indifference to this genealogical loss. Concentrating their efforts on the modes of rationalization and optimization of procedures for popular representation, delegation of power, and regulation of decisions, they have contributed significantly to ratifying this genealogical oblivion. The behavioural sciences (electoral or otherwise) do not want to know anything about these mysteries of the state,[190] whose functioning they believe to be utterly transparent and fully rationalizable in the perspective of the utmost efficiency. Promoted to the rank of 'sovereign-subjects' (Legendre), individuals are encouraged to maintain relations that are in reality governed by two scarcely Christian maxims, vigorously mocked by Gilles Châtelet: 'Mistrust one another!' and – more discreetly – 'Envy one another!'[191] Thus politics is converted into the aggressive management of interests, which in turn provokes fearful murderous or suicidal explosions by those who endure the flagrant inequalities obtaining in this world, which has simultaneously made equality one of its canonical values.[192]

Is such violence to be warded off by preaching compassion? By extolling the virtues of love as experienced in the modern home? It is doubtful, given the state of a world that constantly exacerbates the poverty of some in order to enhance still further the wealth of

189 Charles Alexis Clérel de Tocqueville (1805–59), *Democracy in America*, ed. J. P. Mayer, trans. George Lawrence, Fontana, London 1994, p. 508.

190 See Ernst Kantorowicz, *Mourir pour la patrie et autres textes*, Presses Universitaires de France, Paris 1984.

191 *Vivre et penser comme des porcs. De l'incitation à l'envie et à l'ennui dans les démocraties-marchés*, Exils, Paris 1998.

192 See Dominique Lecourt, *Contre la peur: de la science à l'éthique, une aventure infinie*, Presses Universitaires de France, Paris 1999.

others. And when one realizes the condition of the modern Western family, one wonders about the value of the *philia* that is supposed to prevail there and the springs of the *agapē* it is thought to harbour. The available statistics on the duration of marriages and the number of divorces are stark.

In these conditions, how can the ambition displayed by Luc Ferry at the end of *L'homme-Dieu* not be considered somewhat arrogant? Always ready to laud our 'pacified' societies, he writes: 'In the current state of things, the urge to extend the humanist and secular system that has proved itself so well in postwar Europe to the entire universe would, for a variety of reasons, seem an ambitious design, not to say a beautiful utopia.' And he concludes: 'Commitment to human rights, political liberty, peace, relative prosperity, respect for other cultures and a critical attitude towards oneself – is not this the ideal our modest continent could offer the rest of the world, if the rest of the world took it into its head to be inspired by it?'[193]

You read it right: 'modest'!

---

193 *L'homme-Dieu*, p. 214.

Epilogue

I do not know if I have answered your questions properly, but I have at least tried to satisfy your demands. Why this trajectory of French philosophers? How to account for the disquiet inspired in you by a thought incapable of grasping the world as it is – and as it sweeps us along?

We have had to make various detours, and frequently revert to the past. I have had to employ several levels of analysis – conceptual filiations, intellectual affinities, political solidarities – and invoke some of the major social, ideological, technological and political upheavals experienced by France over the last thirty years. Naturally, my judgement is dependent upon my viewpoint – that is to say, upon my own personal history within this larger history. Hence an inevitable and irreducible bias. I have sought to get the measure of it in order to control, as far as is possible, its effects on my analysis. I have laid my cards on the table; and it is for you to judge.

At all events, I have tried not to succumb in my turn to the illusion of bringing the pure gaze of some absolute spectator to bear on the world. I am not in the least content with society as it is, or with the way in which it makes me adjust my own being in order to subject me to its dynamic. I know that history itself, to which you have encouraged me to attend, contains the interwoven elements within whose interplay I have not ceased determining myself, and which make me what I am.

I believe I am in a position to suggest that, philosophically speaking, the era of the mediocracy opened with the return of the fiction of the 'subject', in the different forms in which it is supposed to encapsulate the sovereignty of the human individual over itself and its world. These philosophers found it intolerable that in the 1960s and 1970s the subject of (modern) classical philosophy, whether psychological or transcendental, suffered the onslaughts of a whole generation of Nietzscheans, Freudians, Marxists, Freudo–Marxists, Nietzscheo–Marxists, and others. They now apply themselves with the utmost energy to accomplishing a veritable labour of restoration. They have reinstated this fine subject – so punctilious, so well centred on itself, so sleek, so upright, so pure, with its battery of faculties and gamut of feelings – to the foreground.

In tune with a period that consumes it in great quantity, they thus promote the word 'spirituality', borrowed by contemporary philosophy from the vocabulary of the religious life. They have read Chateaubriand only too well – Chateaubriand who, writing about love in *Le Génie du christianisme* (II.3.ii), suggested that we owe the notion of perfection to Christianity, which, with its incessant propensity to purify the heart, managed to inject spirituality into the very predilection that seemed least susceptible to it.

What they raise to honorific status is a new spiritualism – a hymn to the 'liberty of the spirit' and its mystery that is easily the equal of those which earned renown in their time for René Le Senne

(1882–1954) and Louis Lavelle (1883–1951), for example, when they jointly signed their *Manifeste de la philosophie de l'esprit*, published by Aubier in 1934. How, when reading *La Sagesse des modernes*, can we not think precisely of Lavelle, who endeavoured in *Le Mal et la souffrance* to depict philosophy as a 'life discipline'? Lavelle, for whom the metaphysical experience I have of my being is that of an entity which transcends me and in which I participate; and who conceived the discovery of value as that of the immanence of transcendence.[194] As a good neo-Kantian, Lavelle, like Luc Ferry, could have played the card of upstream and downstream: transcendence is no longer situated upstream of ethics, but downstream. If one follows them both, the movement of modernity thus boils down to the transition from the theologico-ethical to the ethico-religious!

In truth, this is an extraordinary irony of history. Thus is reborn, brand-new, on the eve of the twenty-first century and on television sets, the philosophy that ended up triumphing on the dais of our universities at the beginning of the twentieth century. A philosophy wonderfully ignorant of the great upheavals that had marked the mathematical and physical sciences;[195] a philosophy that had hardened into a principled hostility towards the claims of the human and social sciences. We should not be surprised if it looks down on the revolution currently affecting the life sciences. Developments in genetics, like the progress of neurophysiology, merely afford our philosophers pretexts for holding forth on free will and determinism; and the

194 See *De l'acte*, Aubier, Paris 1937, ch. 9, devoted to 'La transcendance'.
195 The epistemological *œuvre* of Gaston Bachelard was elaborated on the basis of a rejection of this 'philosophy of values', which ignored the philosophical lessons to be drawn from the theory of relativity and quantum mechanics.

questions of bioethics, raised by biomedical research, an occasion to be appalled by any attempt 'to improve the human species'.

André Comte-Sponville and Luc Ferry jointly declare their horror at the prospect of human cloning. They use the term 'eugenics', and the terror it arouses because it has become associated with the criminal practices of Nazi doctors. As if the first duty of a philosopher did not consist in taking some distance from the affects that engulf us! Why this fear? What does it signify? At what point does the artificialization of the reproductive process become intolerable? Can today's eugenics be identified with the Nazis? Or even that of the English and American 'progressivists' at the end of the nineteenth century?[196]

Does philosophizing consist in translating the spontaneous expression of these affects into noble discourse? In dramatizing death, massacres, tortures, to justify the discourse of reason and wisdom in response?

Should we resume the path of our elders, who consigned the output of those philosophers whom Paul Nizan (1905–40) denounced as 'watchdogs' to oblivion?[197] Let us wager that the task will be a lot harder, for the entertainment industry is well aware of the frantic desire for identification affecting our contemporaries. When, in between two chain-saw massacres and scenes of family rape, a French philosopher appears on a TV set to perform on the subject, meditating aloud on himself, the tragic character of existence, and the enigma of life and death, media success is guaranteed. We are sorely in need of reference points!

---

196 See Daniel Kevles, *Au nom de l'eugénisme. Génétique et politique dans le monde anglo-saxon*, Presses Universitaires de France, Paris 1995.

197 See Paul Nizan, *The Watchdogs: Philosophers and the Established Order* (1932), trans. Paul Fittingoff, Monthly Review Press, New York 1971.

But this is to turn our backs on the immense unfinished work begun by our predecessors: analysis of the development into a subject of the unique being that is every human being, as a function of the dialogue they necessarily maintain with the world in which it is given them to live. Without referring to the works of Foucault or Deleuze again, is it not high time to resume the lines of investigation opened up by Georges Canguilhem in his reflections on the normative polarity of the living being;[198] and by Gilbert Simondon when he drew attention to the part played by technological objects in the way human beings become individualized?[199]

Predictably, the return of the fiction of the sovereign-subject has been accompanied by that of the 'myth of interiority', so relentlessly condemned by Ludwig Wittgenstein in his time.[200] At the end of the twentieth century we thus see flourishing some belated offspring of that delicate, pseudo-concrete psychology to which our stiff-collared philosophers were partial in its first decade.[201] And this revival is occurring at the very moment when, through a crucial debate with the psychoanalytical schools, the cognitivist movement, attempting to combine the lessons of artificial intelligence and neurophysiology as renovated by molecular biology, is proclaiming a new 'science of the mind', which is rich in promise as well as menace for our capacity to think and act.

198 *The Normal and the Pathological* (1943), trans. Carolyn R. Fawcett with Robert S. Cohen, Zone Books, New York 1989.

199 Gilbert Simondon (1924–89), *Du monde d'existence des objets techniques*, Aubier-Montaigne, Paris 1958; *L'individu et sa genèse physico-biologique*, Presses Universitaires de France, Paris 1964; and *L'individuation psychique et collective*, Aubier, Paris 1989.

200 See Jacques Bouveresse, *Le Mythe de l'intériorité: expérience, signification et langage privé chez Wittgenstein*, Éditions de Minuit, Paris 1976.

201 See Georges Canguilhem's 'historic' article, 'What is Psychology?' (1958), trans. H. Davies, *Ideology and Consciousness*, no. 7, 1980, pp. 37–50.

For our philosophers this merely affords an opportunity to cite their classics once more and debate the subject of the freedom of the spirit. Ethics, you will tell me, is their sole concern. But in this domain we have seen that they merely manipulate what have been the central terms of the tradition for centuries – the sacred, love, happiness, and so forth – and juggle with the established doctrines – materialism, idealism, hedonism, asceticism, and so on.

By contrast, would not an examination of the determinants that bring the subject into existence – including in the guise of moral subject – open up a path to inventive ethical thinking? To wrest some rational, hence controllable, knowledge of these determinants would be to obtain the power to inflect them in a direction we adjudge preferable to the way they currently operate – at our own risk, obviously.

Accomplishing this could contribute to the advent of a new manner of being, original ways of forming relations of love, kinship, friendship, or labour. This has already happened more than once in the history of humanity. Even in France.

Appendix:

Dissidence or

Revolution?

1

The Dissidence of the Dissidents and the Imperialist Crusade for Freedom

What is 'dissidence'?

In the first instance, it is a novel feature of the class struggle in the USSR and Soviet-style social formations. It involves the constitution and regular reproduction of a nonconformist fraction of the intelligentsia – teachers, researchers, writers, artists, and so on – who bypass official channels of communication and distribution to express their rejection of the ideological and political 'rules of the game', which the overwhelming majority of intellectuals in their countries still obey. It comprises figures whose philosophical affiliations and political positions range from 'oppositional' Marxism to utterly reactionary Slavophile messianism, but who all, on the basis of a common rejection, publicly challenge the principles of the social system they live under. Unlike the 'oppositionists' or 'revisionists' of yesteryear, however, they no longer entertain hopes for a democratic evolution of the party and state apparatus. 'Dissidence' involves the heroic struggle of an opposition hounded and reduced to political despair by a system that permits no escape other than silence, madness, or exile.

Far from being a response to the simple prolongation of the Stalinist terror, dissidence is a *recent* phenomenon, which emerged as a result of the partial relaxation of its principal ideological mechanisms after the Twentieth Congress of the Soviet Communist Party in 1956.[1] It developed as a 'by-product' of the new regime of ideological controls that was gradually established and institutionalized, and has now been reinforced, to 'rein in' a social stratum that is ever more numerous and diversified.

A *restricted* phenomenon, dissidence has hitherto remained an elite movement which, among the intellectuals themselves, has affected only the narrow stratum directly linked to scientific and cultural production. It has not disturbed the tacit compromise reached between the state apparatus and the mass of 'specialists' – engineers, cadres, and production technicians. Above all, its themes would seem to have found virtually no echo among the popular masses, whose struggles are largely channelled and contained by the subtle system of bargaining and counter-powers that has replaced the 'classical' Stalinist regime of massive ideological mobilizations and waves of repression.

Once its concrete historical characteristics are taken into account, it is apparent that the long-term political significance of dissidence is neither straightforward nor transparent. In particular – contrary to what people in the West are too readily led to believe – it does not obviously portend an imminent generalized revolt against the Eastern regimes. Indeed, in the immediate present it could even serve as an alibi for a reinforcement of the state. Eastern bloc leaders do not squander the opportunity to exploit the dissidents' isolation, in an attempt to incite the mass of 'ordinary citizens' against a social stratum – the intellectuals – who in fact possess certain privileges; and thus to reinvigorate the workerist component in Soviet ideology – a traditional instrument for mobilizing the party around its apparatus and the masses around the state.

Rakovski has put it very well: the political trajectory of dissidence remains ambiguous.[2] Everything will depend upon its ability to join in a revolutionary movement with the massive, silent and obstinate resistance to oppression of Eastern bloc workers and peasants. Persistent symptoms of this resistance are visible in literary and artistic works. They can be clearly read as so many poorly masked admissions in official documents – absenteeism, stagnation or decline in industrial and agrarian productivity, black markets, youth demoralization, generalized alcoholism, and so on – when they do not take the dramatic form of a strike like that of the Romanian miners in 1977, or an insurrection like that of the Baltic Sea workers in Poland in 1971.

But in less than two years, dissidence has also become *a reality of a quite different kind*: the central theme of an ideological mobilization in the grand style in the West, punctuated by spectacular conferences and congresses (the Venice Biennale, Honolulu, etc.) and fostered by a profusion of diverse publications. This campaign has no qualms about appropriating for its own propagandistic ends the personal tragedy of the dissidents, the dangers and misery that befall their families and friends, the physical and moral torture inflicted on them in the name (or in violation) of 'socialist legality', and the scandalous 'choice' ultimately confronting them: prison (when it is not insanity) or exile.

Dissidence has been turned into a pretext for large-scale manoeuvres in international politics; the conclusion of the Helsinki Accords in 1975 marked their official inception, and the exchange of the Soviet dissident Bukovsky for the Chilean Communist leader Corvalan their most garish episode to date. It has furnished the opportunity for a campaign of massive mystification, launched by the ideologues of the imperialist countries to pursue the moral rearmament of their own camp.[3]

Is it necessary to recall some facts?

From the 1960s onwards, the ideological foundations of imperialist domination had suffered an impressive series of blows. The rout of the most powerful imperialist army in the world in Vietnam had impaired the myth of American military and technological omnipotence. Simultaneously, it provoked a revolt by young intellectuals in the USA against the ideals, rendered patently hypocritical in their eyes, under whose banner they were to be enlisted for the struggle. As if echoing these events, the great upheaval of 1968, rousing students throughout the metropolitan countries, had challenged the existence and operation of those pillars of capitalist domination, the school and the family. Such was the profundity of the upheaval that it rapidly affected what Althusser referred to at the time as 'ideological state apparatuses'.[4] The renewed combativity of the working classes of Western Europe (especially in France and Italy), which had rather too hastily been declared 'bourgeoisified', simultaneously destroyed the technocratic reveries of the ideologues of advanced capitalism. The methodical subversion conducted by the CIA and the Pentagon against Salvador Allende's Popular Unity government in Chile;[5] the bloody terror with which American imperialism was complicit, as in Greece a few years earlier or in Argentina thereafter; the Watergate scandal coming on top of the enigma of the Kennedy assassination – these had all struck directly at the pacific and democratic ideals whose model embodiment and intransigent defender the USA has prided itself on being since the war. Finally, the economic slump of recent years, which has strewn the metropolis with millions of unemployed, had just delivered a decisive blow to the ideals of 'growth' promoted by licensed economists and sociologists for close on three decades.

In short, if the imperialist system retained formidable material and military power, scarcely any of the themes in its propaganda arsenal had resisted the ideological collapse: neither Freedom, nor Democracy, nor Family, nor Work. . . . The functioning of the ideological state apparatuses was everywhere chronically jammed by what has been called 'contestation' in France since 1968, and which today tends, symptomatically, to be dubbed 'dissidence'.

The experts of the Trilateral Commission, assembled in 1975, registered the results. Read their astonishing report. Things are clearly expressed there, with a candour that apparently frightened them afterwards. There is a 'crisis of democracy': the Western democracies have become 'ungovernable', because the essential values that underpinned the social 'consensus' in them have collapsed. This crisis is attributable not only to the persistent hold of revolutionary ideology over the working classes in Europe, but also to the existence of a growing mass of intellectuals who, even in the USA, have entered into rebellion against the ideals they ought to be defending, and are in a state of permanent opposition to established institutions:

> In an age of widespread secondary school and university education, the pervasiveness of the mass media, and the displacement of manual labor by clerical and professional employees, this development constitutes a challenge to democratic government which is, potentially at least, as serious as those posed in the past by the aristocratic cliques, fascist movements, and communist parties.[6]

So much for the diagnosis. The remedy is simple, and possibly brutal: it is advisable to 'limit' the extension of democracy, prior to identifying the new values and inventing the new objectives that might restore the 'consensus'.

Given this crisis, and the analysis of it by Western experts, the godsend afforded to a crumbling system by the emergence of dissidence in the East is understandable. At one go, it permitted the imperialists once again to present themselves, in all seriousness, as the defenders of human rights and freedom. The political astuteness of President Carter, supported by banking circles and the experts of American and world capitalism (Brzezinski, Rockefeller & Co.), was fully to appreciate the advantages it offered from the outset. To work the theme effectively, it would suffice to dismiss some 'black sheep' from the staff of the US administration, reorganize the discredited and cumbersome apparatus of the CIA, absorbing it into the Pentagon's more discreet operations, distance himself verbally from the bloodiest Latin American dictatorships, and construct the image of an 'honest man' taken up with his religious musings. From the start he performed marvellously and, as is well known, made his political fortune.

Yes, as David Cooper exclaims in a courageous little book, 'dissidence – what a wonderful alibi!'[7] Cooper denounces the 'imposture' of the 'World Congress of Psychiatry' organized last summer in Honolulu. It is well known, he explains, that certain Soviet dissidents have been subjected to psychiatric violence. For example, Leonid Plyushch, whose only delirious act was to search for communism in a country ruled by a party that is officially communist, was incarcerated and tortured by psychiatric means – insulin-induced comas, and so on. And then here are the psychiatrists from the capitalist countries, the Anglo-Americans at their head, who daily employ such procedures – and many others – on an experimental scale that now extends to millions of human beings. They have had no qualms about putting their clinical and surgical skills at the service of preventing any rebellion in the ghettos of North America, or repressing guerrillas in Latin America. These psychiatrists, whose 'science' has been contested for over a decade by all that is progressive in their own ranks, have now discovered a way of deflecting criticism and restoring the unity of the profession ('leftists' included), likewise presenting themselves as defenders of freedom and human rights against those in the Soviet Union who are, in the fullest sense of the word, their *colleagues*.

Cooper comments: 'Psychiatrists in the capitalist orbit salve their consciences by supporting the Soviet dissidents who are victims of psychiatric treatment. This is sheer imposture.' What an alibi, and what a remarkable weapon! For the 'inspired' speeches of the American President have indeed given the signal for a veritable international crusade, orchestrated to celebrate the *rehabilitation* of the traditional values of imperialist bourgeois ideology: human rights, freedom and democracy.

Should anyone doubt the truly mystificatory nature of this crusade and its actual objectives, which consist in ideological deterrence; should anyone be misled by its promoters' humanitarian professions of faith; should anyone not realize that while pretending to defend 'human rights' in the Eastern bloc, it aims in reality to counter any revolutionary movement within the imperialist system, then it suffices to note that fundamentally, in its themes and its parameters, it is merely the repetition of the great campaign in 'defence of the free world' launched on the morrow of World War II by the same imperialist powers.

In fact, from one crusade to another, the propaganda is predominantly organized around the same central theme: the critique of *totalitarianism*. Need we recall the immediate political ends for which this critique was originally developed, around a notion – 'totalitarianism' – deliberately concocted to identify the Soviet regime with the Nazi regime, and the Communist parties with the fascist movements?[8]

By artificially inventing a special category of political regimes with their own particular character (the 'totalitarian' regimes), on the one hand Western ideologues diverted attention from the *capitalist* base of the Hitlerite regime and the *imperialist* nature of the contradiction that had opposed it to the Anglo-American allies. On the other hand, they armed themselves with an ideological weapon to counter the audience won by the Western Communist parties during the Resistance, and more generally to withstand the pressure of the masses, which here and there was threatening imperialist hegemony in its heartlands. Finally, it provided them with an ideological justification for the military operations that were being conducted at the time to consolidate and extend the American 'sphere of influence', especially in South-East Asia, by presenting them as designed to 'protect' and 'defend' freedom.

In short, this theme was an instrument for the aggressive ideological rehabilitation of a system which, having plunged millions of human beings into death and desolation in order to surmount its contradictions and experience a new boom, was able to exploit the tragic impasses of the Communist movement and present itself, even before the end of hostilities, as the champion of peoples' freedom.

The repetition, thirty years later, of the same theme in a full-scale campaign may be construed as a symptom. By exploiting the fact of dissidence to brandish the bugbear of 'totalitarianism' once more in front of the masses, and to set themselves up as defenders of freedom, our ideologues seek to obtain the same result of ideological rehabilitation.

*

In my view, paradoxically it is at this level, at a certain remove, by attending to strategic manoeuvres for which dissidence is simply the pretext, as well as their historical antecedents, that it is possible to understand the motivation and illuminate the significance of an operation that is seemingly very French – very 'Parisian,' even. This is the operation for which the band of young intellectuals dubbed 'New Philosophers' has offered, as it were, to be the agents.[9]

People have rightly been astonished by the extent of the immediate and deliberate media impact of works that are obscure, if not baroque, and whose arguments are often abstract and sophisticated. They have asked whether it should be attributed to the undeniable rhetorical talent of the best representatives of the New Philosophy; to the genius for publicity of their commercial backers; to the anticipated political effects of their stance in the electoral context in which their books have been launched on the market; or to the 'divine surprise' for the capitalist world of discovering French intellectuals who are hostile to Marxism, when their 'fascination' with Communism has been a source of complaint for some three decades.[10]

All these explanations have been proposed. But none of them, however legitimate, identifies what is unquestionably the underlying reason for their astonishing success.

I am referring to the *junction* that has been effected between the slogans advanced by the New Philosophers in conclusion to their speculations, and the classical themes of 'anti-totalitarianism', recently 'rediscovered' in the Anglo-Saxon world in the context of its campaign on behalf of 'human rights'. For despite the great fuss over the novelty of their philosophy, we shall see that it too is, in part, merely the repetition of 'Cold War' commonplaces.

But the decisive thing, which has summoned them to an international role, is that their philosophy is not reducible to such repetition, but integrates Cold War themes into a set of arguments that can legitimately pride itself on its novelty, even if it ultimately tips them over into a very old political tradition whose complexion they deny.

The arguments offered by the New Philosophers are subject to certain theoretical and political constraints on account of the parameters and rules of ideological engagement in France – the 'public' they must address, and the theoretical questions and political uncertainties it has inherited from its own history. What is crucial is that these constraints have enabled them to introduce a *variant* into the campaign for the ideological rehabilitation of the imperialist system, which makes it possible to extend and amplify it.

To summarize the point, before I seek to prove it: they have benefited from identifying the way in which this campaign can reach social strata whom the crises of the imperialist system have rendered deaf, even refractory, to the classical ideals of the bourgeoisie, in the form in which the US President and his brains trust have resumed their celebration. These social strata are sometimes characterized as the 'new petty bourgeoisie', and their key role in the crisis of the Western 'democracies' was underscored in the report of the Trilateral Commission.

This represents a veritable *tour de force*, which has consisted in shaping what Robert Linhart quite rightly calls 'Western "dissidence" ideology' – a novel ideological formation that ends up making 'dissidence' the slogan for a major political disengagement by the intellectuals, in favour of a 'revolt' ('resistance' or 'rebellion') that is nothing more than the name for a *refusal*: a refusal to participate in the mass struggles that could yield a revolutionary outcome to the crisis we are living through.

The following chapters are devoted to an analysis of this ideological formation and what is at stake in it politically, which can be summed up in the alternative: 'dissidence or revolution?'.

2

Western Dissidence Ideology: 'Radical Anti-Marxism'

Here they are: self-professed heroes of contestation suddenly converted into heralds of dissidence; troubled young intellectuals who have seen it all, and are inspired by what Rousseau – denouncing the Parisian literary world – once called 'the mania for standing out'. For some months now they have been haunting households with their sombre prophecies, as amplified, multiplied and trotted out by the media, starting with television.

The spectacle that unfolds before us comprises 'characters' out of Dostoevsky, who reveal the torment inflicted on them by their own thinking; characters terrified of reasoning, even as they go through the motions of doing it, on the brink of the Apocalypse; characters so preoccupied by their conscience that one would think them consumed by the dramas supposedly lacerating it. Their skill consists in presenting themselves as the sorrowful heirs to human history in its entirety – its tragedies, its deaths by the million, its hopes, but also – and above all – its disillusions.

We are all familiar with the ritual of their performance.

First of all, there is the great passage about modesty: we are merely a few individuals, they announce, lending our voices to all the oppressed and outcast of the earth. We are simply echoing, in so far as we can, the cries of the tortured, of all those whom one has sought to silence.

The speech then takes a lyrical turn: if we recognize this mission as a duty, they confess, it is because we ourselves have aided the torturers, however marginally. Blinded as we were, within our capabilities we became the accomplices of the executioners. Each of us, mistaken, made his contribution to the general climate of universal illusion. In short, we too were Marxists. And ours was not some insipid or perverted Marxism, but 'pure' and radical; as post-1968 intellectuals, we were 'Maoists'! What more compelling proof of our present sincerity could there be?

All modesty now forgotten, the voice swells for the peroration. They were addressing their own generation, but now they do not hesitate to apostrophize 'our century', arraign 'the West', and brandish the threat of a universal cataclysm. Great Priests of Humanity, they excel at conferring on themselves an eternal actuality.

All this can be misleading and pass for a cry from the heart, for rebellion and despair. But fundamentally it is merely designed to impress; it is a carefully refined artifice whereby each of them meticulously adjusts posture, targets and arguments in line with an evaluation of the balance of forces and what their audience is likely to accept.

Take André Glucksmann, who has built a reputation since 1975 for having 'proved', as *Le Point* subsequently put it, that 'Marxism produced the Gulag'. Having indeed written in black and white in *La Cuisinière et le mangeur d'hommes* in 1975 that 'Marxism generates not only scientific paradoxes, but also concentration camps'; having constructed a 'proof' of this thesis over two hundred pages; having allowed the press to fête him for this theme, here is the same Glucksmann giving an interview to *L'Express* in July 1977 and declaring:

> I reproach Marx, and the other German master thinkers, with having plotted a certain number of intellectual paths: the cult of the total, definitive revolution; of the state that terrorizes for the collective good; of the (social) Science that allows the masses to be guided despite themselves. . . . The master thinkers disarm us before the first outbreaks of the terrorism that precisely invokes the authority of revolution, science and state.[11]

Now this is a subtle and qualified version of the earlier thesis, which gives us to understand that Marx did not, strictly speaking, 'produce the Gulag', but aided its appearance and facilitated its extension. It is a version that 'restrains' the thesis from the overtly reactionary slope down which some imprudent emulators rushed to push it.

This can go a very long way, as we observe when we read the account of a round table organized in Italy this summer by *Espresso*. This time Glucksmann, confronting Lucio Colletti, has no qualms about taking the diametrically opposite view to his master thesis: 'I shall not say that Marxism automatically leads to the Gulag. I do say that it renders people deaf and blind to the development of the Gulag!'[12]

However much care the New Philosophers take composing their characters, what matters is neither their moods nor their tactical subtleties, but the organization of the themes and arrangement of the slogans they offer, inasmuch as they have conferred theoretical form and political efficacy on the novel ideological formation represented by the Western ideology of dissidence.

I shall state the thesis I wish to defend forthwith: dissidence is invested with a dual function in this ideology. It is the pretext for a 'radical' critique of Marxist theory, which exploits the impact of the latest developments in the crisis of the Communist movement on the ideology of Western intellectuals. And it is the name for an apparently anarchist conception of freedom which tends to neutralize and divert some of the novel, potentially revolutionary forms of ideological and political class struggle released in recent years by the crisis of the imperialist system.

Some have detected a return to irrationalism in the philosophy of the New Philosophers, imposed by the current crisis of the capitalist system. But this is to forget that despite their repeated attacks on Reason, the Enlightenment, Science, and so on, their avowed target is not rationalism, but Marxism. Their 'irrationalism' is merely the instrument for their anti-Marxism.

Time magazine was not mistaken when it put 'Marx is Dead' on its front cover on 5 September 1977 to introduce the New Philosophers to the American public. The burial of Marx is indeed the main thing, and it is on his tomb that everyone of them comes to throw a philosophical handful of earth. And this 'radical anti-Marxism' – to adopt the expression employed by one of their number – is the bond that unites them over and above any differences of philosophical detail that might divide them. It is what determines the principal characteristics of the polemical foundation of the Western ideology of dissidence, as we might call it.

First characteristic: the offensive apparently has as its point of departure the dissidents' testimony about the Soviet regime. This testimony is suitably 'filtered', deployed and interpreted, so that it coincides as neatly as possible with a certain image of the dissidents – and their 'philosophy' – taken for the most part from Solzhenitsyn's characters. And when it turns out to be unsuitable – when Plyushch

or Medvedev, for example, persists in defending the idea of socialism – then, in line with the method employed by Glucksmann in *La
Cuisinière*, these characters are themselves called into the witness
box, stripped for the occasion of their novelistic trappings. Ivan and
Matriona appear. 'Hell testifies,' proclaims Glucksmann. And what
does it say? What are these characters, real or fictional, supposed to
tell us?

The truth, the whole truth, and nothing but the truth: about
themselves and their history; about our history; finally, and above
all, about Marxism. We are living – so we are assured – in the age
of the Great Revelation. We are finally discovering what, blinded
by Marxism, we were oblivious of for more than half a century.
Today, 'Marxism is naked', explains Glucksmann in his *Espresso*
interview; and its nakedness is appalling. In its conceptual constructions we can see outlined the terrifying profile of the
concentration camps.

In fact, notwithstanding his recent tactical evasions, this is the
theme Glucksmann has put into circulation. This is the slogan
charged with inducing polemical effects and changes in the French
ideological conjuncture. Through it our philosophers take a position, in their blunt, deterrent fashion, in the debates provoked by the
history of the Soviet Union over recent years.

To some participants in these debates, the New Philosophers
riposte that the camps are not *Russian*: the system of domination
established and reinforced in the USSR is not the bitter fruit of the
specific national conditions (economic backwardness, bureaucratic
traditions, absence of democratic 'fabric', capitalist encirclement,
and so on) in which socialism was historically constrained to take its
first steps. The camps are *Marxist*, engendered by the theoretical
premisses of Marxist doctrine itself.

To others they object that the history of the USSR is in no way that of a 'deviation' which gradually, after a long and contradictory historical process, converted Marxist theory into its opposite: from a theory of the emancipation of the masses, grouped around the proletariat, into the ideological guarantee of their oppression. Consequently, there is no point in seeking to analyse the actual history of this 'deviation', or racking one's brains to uncover its theoretical conditions of possibility and identify its historical causes. As one of them puts it, that would be sheer 'theoretical cretinism'. According to them, the history of the USSR – with which the history of Marxism and socialism in general is allegedly coterminous – is simply the straightforward *repetition*, all contradictions suppressed, of one and the same aberration that was to go on producing and magnifying its effects of terror. It coincides with the empty time of an immense reclusion: the suspended time of Hell. In short, what we have here is history as nothingness.

Second characteristic: all the New Philosophers tackle the 'classical' question of the scientificity of Marxism. But whereas Popper and his followers (like, in the opposite sense, Althusser and his collaborators in 1965) emphasized 'epistemological' arguments,[13] our ideologues employ a type of refutation that could pass for being original. They contrive to prove that in its claims to be a science, 'historical materialism' is, *in its philosophical premises*, nothing more than the rationalization of a practical knowledge [*savoir*], which is allegedly the knowledge of rulers. They hammer out their words and repeat that Marxism is reducible to the Knowledge pertaining to a form of Power, missing no opportunity to make this conceptual pair resonate so that they are better placed to appropriate certain of Michel Foucault's conclusions.

And in order to make the slogan acceptable, they offer some 'proof' – which is always the same, and invariably taken from the history of the USSR. Is not Marxism the official state ideology there? Is it not in its name that the people are oppressed? Not, once again,

because the doctrine has been perverted, emptied of its revolutionary substance, but because it had preprogrammed the methods that
made it possible to conquer, preserve and consolidate power in the
twentieth century. According to their common refrain, Lenin,
spelling out the implications of Kautsky, had understood Marx only
too well, when he asserted in *What is to be Done?* that theory must be
imported into the workers' movement 'from without'.[14] Marx,
who, Glucksmann finally discovers, despite a hundred texts to the
contrary and his consistent practice in the First International, had
promised 'all power to public functionaries! – when he is not claiming, in all seriousness, that *Capital* is the best political economy
manual capitalists have ever had at their disposal.

Third characteristic: if Marxism is an especially dangerous 'science', it is because it fosters a Great Illusion – the illusion of being
not only a science, but a science of *The* Revolution. This, our
philosophers proclaim, is how Marxism becomes the 'opium of the
people'. It incites the masses to believe that in entrusting themselves to 'Marxist leaders' they are going to strive for their
emancipation, when in fact they are merely contributing, unawares,
to their own ruination. By appropriating the ideas of the insurgent
people the better to digest them, and by deluding the masses with
the eternally disappointed hope for a 'last fight', Marxists have supposedly hit upon the ideal means of enslaving them. They succeed in
securing the masses' consent to their own oppression by a state that
dubs itself 'of a new type' solely in order to disguise its antique
essence: a machine of violence and oppression.

For ultimately, they conclude, belying Marxists' noisy declarations of the glory of the revolution, the state they are silently
planning is outlined even before the seizure of power in the organizations they construct to that end. The proof? Once again, look at
the Soviet Union. Who will deny that the people, mobilized by the

Bolsheviks in 1917 to 'make the revolution', let itself be fooled by these same Bolsheviks' proclamations about the 'withering away of the state' that was, in good Marxist doctrine, to ensue?

As everyone knows, this is the real story for our philosophers: *the state*. This is the only word on their lips, and they adopt it to a man: we are against the state, every state; against the very idea of the state. The 'radical' critique of the state is their business; it is simultaneously presented as the ultimate lesson in dissidence and the cornerstone of their philosophy.

It is Glucksmann who asserts in *Le Nouvel Observateur* that '[t]oday, if your heart escapes the state's clutches, you will understand Solzhenitsyn'; and in *Les maîtres penseurs* – a section of which is parodically entitled 'I think, therefore the State is' – he writes: 'On the pretext of educating the subjects and turning each one into a statesman, the eye of the State is installed within each head.' Hence his conclusion: 'Science of the State, science of the Revolution, science of setting to work – three variants of a single body of knowledge.'[15]

Setting aside for now the silences and ambiguities around which these formulas are constructed; setting aside their unavowed theoretical presuppositions and real political meaning, and restricting ourselves to the 'logic' that governs their organization in the unity of a determinate ideological formation, it must be noted that their repetition is not groundless. For they perform a *pivotal* role. It is in fact around them that we find articulated with the critique of Marxism a 'positive' elaboration of the ideology of freedom, which confers philosophical shape on the notion of dissidence, while wrenching it from its immediate political reality and suppressing the main problems posed by the historical fact of dissidence.

Reduced to the bare bones, the operation is simple, and can be summed up in an elementary linguistic-philosophical sleight of hand.

If you assume, as they do, that Marxism is by its very nature the terroristic negation of all freedom because it is at root a 'science of the state',[16] a definition of freedom as the radical *repudiation* not just of Marxism, but of 'the state', follows. To be free, explains Glucksmann with the aid of a great many quotations (Rabelais, Plato, Hegel, Foucault, Legendre, and so on), is to say *no*, to refuse to recognize the state's norms as one's own.

What does it mean 'to be dissident' if not, literally, to 'sit apart'; hence to refuse one's consent to the state; in short, to 'say no'?

The trick has worked: on the basis of this simple (linguistic) fact, something that is experienced and thought of by the most informed intellectuals in the Eastern bloc as the confession of a dramatic political *powerlessness* to transform the world of their oppression supplies the professedly *positive* foundation for a metaphysical conception of Freedom. We thus witness a kind of philosophical transmutation that ends up making dissidence not a delimited historical phenomenon, but the 'concrete' image of the timeless affirmation of a Freedom which, as good metaphysics, is defined via absolute counterposition to its Other – that is to say, the state.

It then only remains to unfold the theoretical implications and practical consequences of this conception of freedom: it represents a rejection of the state, but above all, in the final analysis, of politics itself; and the only form of action that is guaranteed not to see its results rebound on it is 'rebellion', because of the strictly individual limits within which it is contained.

But let us leave the reasoning of our philosophers, in the language peculiar to each of them, there. It is enough for us to have defined the overall contours of the Western ideology of dissidence.

Its novelty consists in *combining* in a single theoretical apparatus a critique of 'totalitarianism' that enlists them in the imperialist crusade on behalf of human rights, and is extended into a 'radical' critique of the philosophical bases of Marxism; and a seemingly anarchist conception of freedom as rebellion, which can deceive as to the real political significance of the operation.

The actual political meaning emerges clearly when we proceed, as we are now going to, to analyse the constitutive elements of this ideology, while relating them to the conjuncture of a dual, overt crisis – of the Communist movement and of the imperialist system – in which their combination is called upon to produce its effects.

The favourite theme of the New Philosophers, when they have to address the masses, is well known. It might be called the 'Gulag argument', which boils down to identifying 'socialism' with the Soviet system and reducing the reality of the Soviet system to that of the camps, just as the reality of the Nazi system is reduced to the existence of Auschwitz or Buchenwald. The effect of horror is thereby guaranteed – all the more so given that the argument, in its various facets, has been well rehearsed. It already constituted the nerve centre of the theory of 'totalitarianism', as developed thirty years ago for the immediate political purposes recalled above.

In her famous book on *The Origins of Totalitarianism* Hannah Arendt, for example, had already explained that the camps are the central, distinguishing institution of all totalitarian regimes; and that the common essence of the Nazi and Bolshevik regimes could be discerned in them. The camps, she wrote in some arresting pages, 'are not only "*la société la plus totalitaire encore réalisée*" (David Rousset) but the guiding social ideal of total domination in general'.[17] Contrary to what some people believe, she continued, the camps are not 'irrational', a result of the mechanism of Terror racing out of control. Quite the reverse: they are laboratories. Proof of this

is the way in which prisoners are selected and classified, the seemingly 'gratuitous' use of torture, and so on, which demonstrate that
they possess an experimental function. What is involved is the
reduction of individuals, through the progressive, systematic
destruction of their juridical and moral persons, to the immediacy
of basic reactions that are meticulously observed and codified, hence
methodically predictable and reproducible at will. The camp thus
makes it possible to develop a 'pure model' of the behaviour of all
members of society.

Arendt concluded that if this was the case, it was because the
essence of social relations in such regimes consisted in the 'total
domination' of their members, ensured by the exercise of a specific
form of terror whose ultimate objective was the radical dissolution
of social structures and bonds. The purpose was the creation of an
atomized and 'amorphous' mass of citizens, each of whom lived
their solitude in a total withdrawal into the self.

Raymond Aron undertook the French version and immediate
political translation of these themes – a version expressly intended
to counter the mass audience of the Communist Party at the
Liberation, while providing the Right, discredited by collaboration,
with an alternative ideology. Reread his lectures of 1957–58, subsequently published under the title *Démocratie et totalitarisme*
(1965).[18] Against the 'anti-anti-Communism' of Sartre and the existentialists, and then in opposition to Merleau-Ponty's
'a-Communism',[19] Aron seized on the theme of totalitarianism, in
order to equip intellectually a vast movement opposed to the
'Communist project'. Forget their role in the Resistance – this is the
essence of his message to 'simple citizens' – and remember that the
Communists are, just as the Nazis were, implacable enemies of freedom. Not simply because they are 'foreign agents', but precisely by
virtue of their 'totalitarian' conception of the state: the state which,

when it is fused with the single party, itself becomes partisan, and crushes individuals.

This suffices – or so it seems to me – to demonstrate that the themes of anti-totalitarianism, which today are such a popular topic for our New Philosophers, dramatized by dissidents' testimony and Solzhenitsyn's novels, are in reality Cold War commonplaces adapted for contemporary tastes.

It is time to proceed to what constitutes, strictly speaking, the first novel feature of the ideological formation into which they are integrated. Earlier quotations have indicated it. In the mouth of Carter and the theoreticians of human rights – as yesterday in the speeches of crusaders for the 'free world' – these themes were self-sufficient, scarcely requiring the reinforcement of a verbal humanism to be valid as a direct political argument for 'democracy' and in praise of the 'liberal' state. In our philosophers' discourse, by contrast, they are *subordinated* to an 'abstract' argument directed at Marxism. For them anti-totalitarianism is merely the starting-point, the pseudo-historical guarantee of philosophical 'demonstrations' whose avowed target is represented by what they reckon to be the philosophical foundations of Marxism.

Anyone who has read their works will be familiar with the conceptual acrobatics they indulge in to identify and describe these philosophical 'foundations'. Leapfrogging *Capital*, they work back directly from 'real socialism' (the Eastern bloc countries!) to 'Marxist philosophy', conceived as a unified body of doctrine whose immediate paternity they attribute to Marx; and then back from this philosophy to that of Hegel, from Hegel to the Enlightenment, and thence to Plato. This is an old refrain,[20] whose theme is open to all sorts of variations, depending on the culture of the author concerned, but invariably with the same result: exposure of Marxism as a sheer ideological construct hatched by intellectuals to enslave the masses; as a theoretical 'apologia' for the state, which cloaks its aim of domination in the mystificatory language of Revolution.[21]

In the final analysis, however, the founding principle of all these stylistic compositions is just a single argument, which derives its force from the 'obviousness' of a 'fact': that 'Marxist philosophy' is the state philosophy of the Soviet Union. Its maxims figure on the pediments of the Siberian camps. Open your eyes, they are their Marxist signature, explained Glucksmann in *La Cuisinière*. It was the infernal 'logic' of 'dialectical materialism' that extracted the staggering confessions from Bukharin and the other accused in the great show trials, announces Lévy. Experimental proof, they both conclude, of the congenital vice of Marx's philosophy. It only remains to explain how this philosophy produced these horrors to establish its dominion over the people.

Yet before even considering the conclusions Glucksmann & Co. draw from it, and the conception of history implied by them, the supposedly overwhelming self-evidence of this 'fact' is, to say the very least, suspect. How can one ignore the reality that it purely and simply recycles the imposture maintained by the Soviet leadership itself about the nature of its regime?

Yes, for them, the Soviet Union is a 'Marxist state', underwritten by its philosophy. For Brezhnev and his academicians, as once for Stalin and his (they are often identical), the 'construction of socialism' was simply the 'application' of the laws of dialectical materialism. The New Philosophers take them at their word, and vindicate them! In their own terms, they render themselves complicit with an illusion that contributes to maintaining the Soviet system – and this at the very moment when they claim to be defending the dissidents.

For ultimately, what is this state philosophy of the Soviet Union, which proclaimed itself 'Marxist' only to supply a symbolic guarantee of continuity in the institutions of state and party, and to profit abroad from the colossal historical impact of the October Revolution? Is it, as Lévy claims, Marx's philosophy 'in power'? The premises of the Marxist conception of history 'embodied in reality'?

Were our philosophers not carried away by their interpretative idealism; were they prepared to concede that the Soviet Union, like every other social formation, does indeed possess a *history*; were they to take the trouble and acquire the means to study it, they would realize that the constitution of this body of doctrine under the name of 'Marxist philosophy' precisely coincided with the *abandonment* of the theoretical core of Marx's *œuvre* – that is to say, the theory of the global process of the class struggle, whose paving stones were laid down in *Capital* via an analysis of the mechanisms of capitalist exploitation.

To be crystal clear: they would realize that this 'Marxist philosophy' was systematized, and made official, precisely in order to conceal this abandonment and provide ideological 'cover' for the repressive practices accompanying it. For even if we restrict ourselves to theoretical formulations and the letter of the official texts, the link between the codification of the principles of 'dialectical materialism' and the abandonment of Marx's theory emerges.

Let us reread the texts. From the 1930s onwards a formula appears in them that was consecrated by Stalin in the *History of the Communist Party of the Soviet Union*: the celebrated formula, still in force, according to which 'historical materialism' is a 'component part' of dialectical materialism.[22] Its meaning is clear: the theory of the conditions and forms of class struggle is henceforth integrated, as one of its 'particular cases', into a more general 'science'. It is regarded simply as one application among others of the supposedly universal laws of a philosophy of nature and history (dialectical materialism), dignified with the title of 'the first scientific philoso-phy'. The scenario here is of a philosophy that presents itself, like all idealist philosophies, as being 'without any exterior' (Althusser) – as a theoretical system which, even if it acknowledges the external world, recognizes it only for the purposes of completely absorbing and dominating it by claiming the truth of everything past, present and future in advance.

In reality, this 'integration' was a veritable disintegration of Marx's theory, which in practice made it possible to declare the class struggle extinct in the USSR (1936 Constitution) and to justify, through the theory of 'conspiracies', the great show trials. At the same time it led to the transformation of 'historical materialism' into a vulgar economic theory of planning and administering the pro-ductive apparatus: the putative 'Marxist political economy' whose 'experts' today still enjoy so much credit (and power) even in the ranks of the Western Communist parties. This is a theoretical mon-strosity inherited from their Stalinist patrimony, which will never be anything more than the 'scientific' good conscience of an economic policy whose practices all rest on a monumental 'oversight'. This consists in forgetting the antagonism of the Marxist theory of the class struggle towards any political economy – the fact that this theory was precisely based upon a 'critique of political economy' (subtitle of *Capital*). Not in the sense that such and such a variety of political economy (the bourgeois sort) is 'erroneous', so that it is a question of substituting for it another variety (the variety expounded for the first time in *Capital*), but in the far more radical sense that there is no 'object' in the global process of the class struggle that corresponds to 'purely' economic phenomena: the very phenomena whose existence must be posited by any 'political economy' if it is to construct the science of them. For Marx, the very idea of a 'politi-cal economy' is merely the rationalization of an illusion induced by the appearances of the capitalist mode of production: one of the illusions that enable it to secure and conceal its own conditions of reproduction by separating 'the economy' from 'politics'.

This straightforward observation could, it seems to me, open up some perspectives for the New Philosophers. For the abandonment of the core of Marxist theory was itself only the end product and outcome of a long historical process. And if they wanted to explain it, they would have to take into account some of the extraordinarily difficult conditions governing the genesis of the first dictatorship of the proletariat: capitalist encirclement, the civil war, the epidemics and, above all, the famine that compelled the Bolsheviks to multiply emergency measures on an *ad hoc* basis for several years. The pressure of objective conditions was crushing, and it contributed to pushing their policies down paths whose impasses Lenin himself did not always perceive – impasses where they risked diverting and obstructing the revolutionary movement.

But that is not all. These external limitations were compounded by the internal limits of the Bolsheviks' ideology. For it is manifestly a crude caricature to portray them as pure executors of a 'Marxist project' whose main contours they had derived from a mere reading of Marx's texts.

Certainly the Bolsheviks strove to be Marxists. Yet this was not some 'ideal' Marxism but, rather, the Marxism bequeathed them by history, Marxism such as it had begun to fuse, in the highly contradictory forms with which we are familiar, with the European workers' movement. And in particular, there is no doubt that – despite the repeated *coups de force* Lenin was able to effect against it – on some sensitive points the Bolsheviks remained heirs to Second International orthodoxy – in other words, to a form of 'Marxist' theory and practice profoundly contaminated by the effects of bourgeois ideology in the ranks of the workers' movement.

They were Marxists but, in a word, as *Bolsheviks*. That is to say, they integrated and combined the already contradictory elements of the Marxist tradition they drew on with another set of ideas, practices and political reflexes derived from another tradition: that of the Russian revolutionary movement. This yielded a unique ideological formation.

Contrary to what people tend to believe, the Bolsheviks' strategy was not the methodical realization of a 'plan' laid down half a century earlier. It was the dramatic testing out in practice of a global conception, mined with contradictions, of the mass movement, the working class, the peasantry, socialism, labour, technology, and so on, whose elements 'interacted' with – and against – one another. Some ideas were abandoned, others were rectified; but some remained intact. Historical hindsight permits us to state that various of these ideas had represented an obstacle to the mass movement from the first, prior to presiding over its destruction.

Some examples? That the Bolsheviks' agrarian policy was heavily informed by the anti-peasant animus of a revolutionary intelligentsia enduringly marked by the failure of populism is well known. This instinctive political reflex[23] ended up combining with the workerist elements in Second International ideology to impede a correct analysis of the crisis of grain deliveries from 1918 onwards.[24] After Lenin's death it dictated the disastrous policy of coercion employed against the peasantry, under the cover of the 'Marxist theory' which had been developed for the occasion: 'socialist accumulation', first offspring of 'Marxist political economy'.

We also know the price the Bolsheviks had to pay for their 'technicist' conception of technology, or the idea that a whole dimension of the productive forces is neutral and can serve capitalism and socialism equally well without any qualitative modification. This idea – which Lenin derived via Plekhanov from certain of Marx and

Engels's texts – led him to bank on the adoption and extension of 'modern' ('rational', 'scientific') forms of labour organization in large-scale capitalist industry, in order to reconstitute a Russian proletariat decimated by war. But he did not realize that it was impossible to dissociate these seemingly 'technical' methods from the mass expropriation of working-class practical knowledge, leading to a gigantic bureaucratization of production.

Finally, one knows about Lenin's distress at the threat represented by the hypertrophy of the state apparatus inherited from Tsarism. One remembers his last writings, and the panic that seized him when he was faced with the results of the 'solution' he thought he had hit upon, when he discovered that the mass entry of proletarians into the administration was no solution to the political problem posed: that of the bond between Soviet power and the masses.

Whether we like it or not, history is never reducible to the transcription of a text; the history of revolutions least of all. The history of the Bolshevik Revolution is no exception to this rule. The concrete 'fusion' initiated at the beginning of the century between the theory of the class struggle and the mass movement in Russia led to the tremendous victory of October, which has continued to shake the imperialist world. But the very forms in which this fusion began, the external and internal limits it encountered – these simultaneously triggered a process of derailment that yielded a dual outcome: the movement was frozen, then destroyed; and the theory was buried.

It could not be easier to understand why the funeral shroud selected should be 'Marxist' in colour. The beneficiaries of this derailment – the functionaries of the party and state apparatus – derived the requisite moral credit from it to keep the masses at bay and justify their dictatorship. This imposture, which took shape from the 1930s onwards, consisted in foregrounding a putative 'Marxist philosophy', introduced as a general 'methodology' of the sciences, seconded by its obligatory 'ontological' complement.[25] Nowhere to be found in this form in the Marxist classics, it had been cobbled together by some professional philosophers over the previous ten years, to impose the party's ideological leadership on specialists in the sciences of nature.[26] Its field of application was then extended when 'historical materialism' was brought under its jurisdiction in such a way as to found the leadership's power over the party, and the party's over the masses, on an inviolable system of universal truths.

As we can see, to make the Soviet state a 'product' of 'Marxist philosophy', or simply to claim that 'Marxist theory' 'facilitated' the development of the Soviet state's repressive forms of politics, is to view history the wrong way round. The Soviet state assumed the form it did only at the end of a process of abandonment of Marxist theory, and foregrounded 'Marxist' philosophy only when it had to conceal the class motives and results of this abandonment, by passing off as 'Marxist' a philosophical 'system' that had been constructed for the occasion.

Please do not misunderstand me: as the reader will appreciate, I do not mean that there ever existed something like a 'pure' Marxist theory, which the historical experience of 'real socialism' one day left by the wayside. I do not imagine that today it is enough to condemn the 'Marxist' imposture of the Eastern bloc, and sideline fifty years of history, in order to 'return' to a science only waiting to be awoken from its slumber to experience its 'recommencement'.

On the contrary, it is vital to uncover the *contradictions* that do indeed run through Marx's *œuvre*; the possibility of the masses reappropriating Marxism, and getting the process of its transformation under way, depends on this. And these contradictions do not simply pertain to formal logic, as some of our sophists claim. Rather, they represent the mark of the conditions and forms of the class struggle – the terrain on which Marx took up his position – in the theory of that struggle. They became the stake of a bitter class struggle within the workers' movement; thus 'worked', they contributed (as I have just recalled) to disarming Lenin when he was confronted by new aspects of the class struggle after the October Revolution. In short, these contradictions constituted the theoretical basis of the Soviet derailment. That is why it is important to identify in Marx's theory the effects of the concrete conditions in which its 'encounter' with the workers' movement occurred, if we want a chance to understand the divorce that ensued and to avoid any repetition of it in new forms.

Althusser's abiding historical achievement was to open the way to such an investigation. For whatever may have been claimed, when he enjoined us to 'read *Capital*', it was not in order to restore some hypothetical purity of Marxism, but precisely in order to try to uncover the traces of the ideological class struggle of which Marx's text was itself a site, at the very moment and in the very forms in which Marx established the concepts that made it possible to theorize this struggle for the first time.

In his first texts Althusser, in turn, committed the error of endeavouring to constitute a 'Marxist philosophy' in the shape of a system 'overhanging' historical materialism, in order to guarantee and control its results.[27] Nevertheless, to his credit, he immediately drew attention to the fact that the theoretical class struggle had crystallized in the interplay of the philosophical positions that run through the 'classical' texts of Marxism (revolutionary materialism, but also economism, humanism, evolutionism, and so on). Finally, starting from this interplay of positions, he also – to his credit – illuminated the limits and silences of 'historical materialism' on a certain number of decisive issues: the nature of the capitalist state, of the practical and theoretical ideologies, of philosophy itself.

Work on these questions, and various others, is still in hand. But once again, in order to pose them we must stop regarding the state philosophy of the Soviet Union as the revealed truth of Marx's philosophy, and the history of the Eastern bloc countries as its inexorable 'realization'. We must rid ourselves of the absolute idealist phantasmagoria whereby 'theory' *produces* reality, so that we can analyse the discrepancy that opened up, and then widened, between theory and reality. It widened to the point where this theory has ceased to be the theory of that reality; where it has ceased, by the same token, to be a *theory* (producing effects of a knowledge of reality), and degenerated into an *ideology* (inducing effects of a misrecognition of reality), to the advantage of the holders of state power.

In truth, our philosophers are scarcely concerned with these questions, on the answers to which hangs the fate of millions of human beings who are struggling in the dark. For them it is enough that Soviet leaders proclaim their state 'Marxist', that Stalin was fêted as 'the greatest Marxist of his time', that Lenin and the Bolshevik old guard were Marxists. It is of little moment to them if the cart is taken for the horse.

This is not out of laziness or ignorance, but because they need this 'Marxism' to be presented as the truth of Marxism if they are to settle their accounts with a quite different history. And it is here that the real political meaning of their speculations begins to emerge.

This history is in fact that of the 'Marxism' of their generation of French intellectuals. Now what exactly was this 'Marxism'? Not, obviously, the imposing theoretical edifice built by the Soviets: it only ever had followers in the ranks of the Communist Party apparatus, which derived its own political advantages from it for internal purposes. Not even, despite Althusser's efforts to shape it, a well-contained theory built on a 'left' critique of the 'Stalinian deviation' and its effects. No. The Marxism in question is the one that Lévy claims has been 'elevated to the status of hegemonic culture in Western societies' – in other words, the diffuse Marxism that has (as he explains elsewhere without beating about the bush) shaped the 'image of the revolutionary intellectual'. Let us translate: this Marxism is the ideological element in which intellectuals – especially French intellectuals – reflected the positions they adopted in the great political struggles of the age; the Marxism that supplied theoretical justification, more or less clearly elaborated, for their engagement alongside the masses in the struggle against the various forms of capitalist exploitation and imperialism.

From the Resistance to the Algerian War, from the Algerian War to May '68, this Marxism had in effect cemented their political imaginary, despite the Soviet Union and the Eastern bloc, despite the Stalinist practices of the PCF. It drew its strength from the fact that – attached to such reference points as October, Cuba, Vietnam, or China – it embodied the idea of a revolutionary exit from the crisis of the imperialist system. It allowed them to connect their own struggles as intellectuals with the global process of capitalist exploitation, to locate and orientate themselves in the political conjuncture with reference to the struggles of the working class and oppressed peoples.

In and through their 'theoretical' attacks on Marxism, the New Philosophers are in reality aiming at nothing other than this political engagement by the intellectuals. In the closing pages of his book, in the form of a profession of faith, Lévy puts it in black and white:

> We will never again place ourselves at the 'service' of the rebels. . . . In fact, the 'revolutionary' intellectual is a pitiful figure. . . . The lesson is clear: We must, forever, give up

'serving the people.' . . . This and simply this is left for us: that we are the species which the West names Intellectuals, that we have to spell out that name, and take on that status, that it is urgent to accept it and to resign ourselves to its misery.[28]

We can understand why this ideology immediately enjoyed solid support in the mass media. Does it not arrive just in time to gratify the desires of the 'experts' in democracy of the imperialist world, who considered in the Trilateral Commission report that 'the effective operation of a democratic political system usually requires some measure of apathy and non-involvement on the part of some individuals and groups', and that such apathy was preferable to the existence of a group of citizens who rejected the rules of the game?[29]

But if such words as 'renunciation' and 'resignation' – inaudible yesterday – can now find an echo from those to whom they are addressed, it is because they express in their fashion a profound alteration of the ideological conjuncture which can, in the final analysis, be related to developments in the crisis of the Communist movement. It is because they register the direct consequences of an event of great historical significance.

The pathetic discourses in which they figure are in fact the twisted symptoms of the way in which *the 'Marxist' political imaginary of Western intellectuals has collapsed*; in the space of a few years, this imaginary has found itself brutally deprived of any external historical 'guarantee'. October? Rumours of the Gulag have now drowned out the salvos of the Bolshevik Revolution in which, notwithstanding all the Zhdanovite obstacles, Sartre and the existentialists still found the courage of their 'Marxist' convictions in the 1950s. Cuba? The revolution is grappling with inextricable difficulties that threaten at any moment to get it stuck in the Soviet rut. China itself, the China of the

Red Guards and the Cultural Revolution, last bastion of their dreams, has just fallen. Need we mention Vietnam? And Chile? Portugal? In a word, we are witnessing the tremendous shock, which might ultimately be productive, of the long-delayed encounter between Western intellectuals and the reality of a pitiless history. This reality consists of the terrible political and theoretical difficulties, inherited from the history of the workers' movement, which continue to impede revolutionary movements in the imperialist heartlands, while inducing their failure elsewhere despite their initial triumph.

Renunciation, resignation: under the cover of its 'radical anti-Marxism', the Western ideology of 'dissidence' is an ideology of the political abdication of the intellectuals. It 'reflects' this new conjuncture, in which their 'Marxism' has lost its imaginary dynamic. It reflects it, in order to inflect it.

It inflects it in the direction of *flight* when it is confronted with the 'discovery' of the crisis of Marxism. Rather than analysing the real history of this crisis in order to identify what is at issue in it, the New Philosophers prefer to proclaim that 'the class struggle has disappeared', explaining that ultimately it existed solely in the theoretical imagination of Marx and his successors. [30] They are like the physicists of the past who, 'discovering' the crisis of physics, declared that 'matter' had 'disappeared', and claimed that it had only ever existed in the implicit philosophy of their predecessors.

It inflects the conjuncture in the direction of flight from the demands of the immediate political struggle. I shall take only two examples, touching directly on the human rights whose ardent defenders the New Philosophers profess to be. The first is spectacular: their incredible discretion when it came to raising their voices against the scandalous procedure involved in the extradition to West Germany of Red Army Faction defence lawyer Klaus Croissant. The second is yet more significant: their indifference to the shocking conditions in which several million immigrant workers live in France. This indifference is explicable. For this is what Glucksmann has no qualms about writing in *Les maîtres penseurs*, to 'refute' the Marxist thesis of the deskilling of labour in large-scale industry:

> To say . . . that this corresponds to *reality* would mean deluding oneself. At the bottom of the ladder, in the most completely de-intellectualized kind of work, modern industry places . . . the worker who of all the workers is the most intellectual, an individual who usually speaks several languages, has known several countries, has lived through several historical epochs, who does not let himself be shut up within a narrowly local horizon, and who often possesses a sense of community and solidarity unknown to those around him: namely, the immigrant.[31]

The immigrant as 'pure' worker, relieved of the stigmata of capitalist barbarism. . . . The cost in cynicism of this intellectual fantasy is evident.

Flight all along the line, then, but camouflaged, as we shall see, under the *illusion of action-packed slogans* in which their dissidence, at the same time as acquiring a 'positive' content, commits the New Philosophers to a political path where their 'resignation' assumes its full significance.

3

Dissidence against Revolution

The flight is disguised as 'rebellion', the abdication as (spiritual) 'resistance': in the New Philosophers' prose, the theme of 'dissidence' acquires libertarian overtones.

I shall not be the first to observe that the content of their idea of 'rebellion', regardless of the actual term employed, is, in several key respects, borrowed from Camus. The filiation is direct and striking.

In one sense, the positions they adopt are indeed related to those of the author of 'Neither Victims nor Executioners' (1946) and especially *The Rebel* (1951)[32] – the Camus who, likewise meditating on the Nazi and Soviet concentration camps after the Liberation, rejected the 'Marxism' of Sartre and the existentialists, without adhering to Raymond Aron's anti-Communism and its technocratic extensions.

Reread the third part of *The Rebel*. The issue is 'Historical Rebellion'. To begin with, Camus states how all attempts over two centuries to impart substance to revolutionary hopes have failed. Worse – they have invariably engendered terror, war and despotism. The explanation of this arresting 'inversion' follows: obstinately 'absolutist' in their thinking, revolutionaries have been led astray by the myth of an 'absolute justice', and have constructed around this idea – which is Christian in origin – the imaginary edifices of their perfect polities, wherein the interest of all will supposedly coincide with the interest of each. In this, adds Camus, they have forgotten that individuals are not amenable to being reduced to their 'social, rational ego, object of calculation'. In short, individuals are free, and this freedom involves differences and divergences. And Camus encapsulates the thinking of revolutionaries in the following formula: 'all freedom must be crushed in order to conquer the empire and one day the empire will be the equivalent of freedom'.[33] The 'New' Philosophy is already fully upon us. . . .

But the parallel is more precise still. Camus further explains that at the root of such convictions is a whole philosophy of history: the Hegelian idea of history as 'development of the Absolute', and of the Absolute as totality. This notion supposedly dooms any revolutionary politics to being totalitarian in essence. We are familiar with the famous pages where it is shown that should the revolutionary persist in the face of refutations by historical reality, and the resistance of individual differences, then he is bound to become a tyrant, and resort to terror to seek to 'embody' his historical ideal of unanimity. As we know very well, Camus denounced this unanimity as 'boundless slavery'.

Against the 'logic' of revolutionary thought (which in his view is merely 'revolutionary aberration'), Camus then proposes recourse to the spirit of *rebellion*, which revolutionary thought had literally 'confiscated', the better to counter and dominate it. 'The revolution', he writes, 'first of all proposes to satisfy the spirit of rebellion which has given rise to it; then it is compelled to deny it, the better to affirm itself.'[34] The spirit of rebellion, he concludes, is the 'will not to surrender': '[w]e all carry within us our places of exile, our crimes, and our ravages. But our task is not to unleash them on the world; it is to fight them in ourselves and in others. Rebellion, the secular will not to surrender of which Barrès speaks, is still, today, at the basis of the struggle.'[35]

All the 'positive' themes of *Les maîtres penseurs* and *La Barbarie à visage humain* are already here, in connection with the Soviet camps, and they culminate in an encomium to freedom as individual resistance and an invitation to disengage from politics in order 'to fight [our ravages] in ourselves'.

The most important thing, however, is not this repetition, which in a further respect refutes the New Philosophers' pretensions to originality. It consists in the fact that in their work such themes are built on to a *metaphysics of the state*.

Consequently, over and above Camus, it is to another political tradition that they are affiliated in their fashion – a tradition that likewise counterposes rebellion to revolution within a metaphysics of the state: that of Max Stirner.[36]

Max Stirner, pseudonym of the obscure Johann Caspar Schmidt, was the author of a sensational book, *The Ego and Its Own*, published in 1844. A veritable anti-Feuerbachian manifesto, among the 'radical' German intellectuals of the 1840s it was reputed to be the theoretical foundation for an 'absolute' opposition to Prussian absolutism as well as the liberal-bourgeois state. It would not take long for people to discover that the opposition involved was illusory, because it was purely metaphysical. In 1848 the proletariat made its entrance on to the historical stage as an organized force, and the exigencies of its struggle dictated a concrete analysis of the contradictory forms in which capitalism was developing. Marx and Engels's brutal judgement on Stirner is well known: he represented the paradigmatic example of those petty-bourgeois intellectuals who are convinced that history is made 'in thought', who are incapable of comprehending the profound social transformations occurring before their very eyes, and who take refuge in speculation to rationalize their theoretical and political impotence.

The New Philosophers revive Stirner. The guiding thread of *The Ego and Its Own* is denunciation of the secret bond – a mortal threat to the individual – which ties any revolutionary project to the institution of a new state.[37]

'The revolution', Stirner wrote, 'commands one to make *arrangements*, the insurrection [*Empörung*] demands that he *rise or exalt himself*.'[38] And if the 'arrangements' the revolutionaries want to make – if their 'organizations' (in particular, parties) – are fated to yield a 'new despotism', it is because the party is always 'a state within a state'. Stirner attempted to prove that the state was 'an enemy and murderer of *ownness*', constructing a whole spectral history of humanity to that end:

> The state is the lord of my spirit, who demands faith and prescribes to me articles of faith, the creed of legality; it exerts moral influence, dominates my spirit, drives away my ego to put itself in its place as 'my true ego' – in short, the state is *sacred*, and, as against me, the individual man, it is the true man, the spirit, the ghost. . . .[39]

Perhaps you will forgive me for quoting a final passage:

> But what concept is the highest to the state? Doubtless that of being a really human society, a society in which every one who is really a man, that is, *not an un-man*, can obtain admission as a member. Let a state's tolerance go ever so far, toward an un-man and toward what is inhuman it ceases. And yet this 'un-man' is a man, yet the 'inhuman' itself is something human, yes, possibly

only to a man, not to any beast; it is, in fact, something 'possible to man'. But, although every un-man is a man, yet the state excludes him; it locks him up, or transforms him from an inhabitant of the state into an inhabitant of the prison (inhabitant of the lunatic asylum or hospital, according to communism).[40]

Surprising lines for 1844 – style apart, they could have come from an ideologue of dissidence.

Max Stirner is claimed as a spiritual ancestor by the anarchist movement. No doubt it could be shown that this is at the cost of a number of misinterpretations of an *œuvre* which is basically devoted to a metaphysical construction of the notion of the individual, and hardly seems to lend itself to the role of doctrinal basis for a movement that has been, and still remains (whether we like it or not), 'revolutionary' in the sense criticized in *The Ego and Its Own*. However that may be, if I have quoted these passages, it is not to tax our ideologues with anarchism (that would be to do an injustice to genuine anarchists), but to reveal the metaphysical slope down which the mechanics of their slogans sends them.

Meanwhile, those – like Glucksmann – who have ventured to push the philosophical elaboration of their positions somewhat further have 'spontaneously' rediscovered Stirner's language and themes. Here is an example of how far this has gone. The formula at the centre of *Les maîtres penseurs*, the key formula that is alleged to encapsulate the 'circle' in which the 'four aces' (Fichte, Hegel, Marx, Nietzsche) have constrained us to turn for a century and a half, is stated as follows: 'to conceive is to dominate'. Presented as the heart of Hegelian logic, the better to damn Marx with it, this formula manifestly does not figure in *The Science of Logic*, but is indeed employed by Stirner in *The Ego and Its Own*, in the section devoted to 'The hierarchy', in a passage where he refutes . . . Hegel![41]

But this time it would be to do Stirner an injustice were we to present the New Philosophers as 'Stirnerians' in disguise. As we shall see, in one respect our ideologues actually *invert* Stirner's arguments.

In Stirner's system, the opposition between rebellion and revolution is simply a consequence of the imposing metaphysical theory of the state he constructs. While he seeks to prop up his theory of individuality (itself metaphysical) on it, in their case the critique of revolution has priority, and their 'theory' of the state is merely an instrument for this critique.

But before proceeding to this key issue, we must indicate a first point of interest in this Stirnerian filiation. For over and above the intellectual biography of any particular New Philosopher, it makes it possible to disclose the historical and political conditions, as well as the theoretical bases, of their flight into metaphysics.

To put it plainly: if their repudiation of Marxism leads them straight to Stirner, it is because – in the name of 'Marxism' under the guise of 'Maoism' – after 1968 they were in fact professing a perfunctory variety of Bakuninite anarchism – at least, those of them who have not purely and simply invented this politico-theoretical past for the self-critical purposes with which we are familiar. If we reread the 'doctrinal' texts of French Maoism post-May '68, we find among them – from the pen of André Glucksmann, a 'master thinker' already – the so-called theory of the 'new fascism' and the 'new resistance'. This guided the practice of the Gauche prolétarienne, prior to inspiring the political analyses of Andreas Baader and Ulrike Meinhof, founders of the Red Army Faction.

Let us reread the special issue of *Les Temps Modernes* published under this title ('Nouveau fascisme, nouvelle résistance') in May 1972. The 'new fascism' the popular masses in France had to confront was described as a 'fascism from above' (in contrast to the older variety, supposed to have derived 'from below'): a fascism that allegedly issued directly from the state apparatus and its functionaries. Hence the strategy of the 'new resistance': 'The struggle against the police and a deepening of the crisis affecting them; confrontation with the state machine's other systems – these are not matters of detail, but the decisive battle of the period.' For it was a matter of mounting a violent 'block' to fascism – the task the Italian and German Communists had failed to carry out in the past, because they did not understand the principles of a people's war. The advantage of such a strategy was 'to force fascism publicly to reveal its contradictions *before* the seizure of power, by weakening it accordingly'.[42]

These political hallucinations, which extended to identifying President Pompidou as 'a Napoleon of the new fascism', started out from an analysis of May '68 that attributed the failure of the 'movement' to the Communist Party's desire not to take power. They made violence the exclusive touchstone of revolutionary politics – the sole criterion of demarcation between living Marxism–Leninism and 'revisionism'. From their perspective, the PCF's policy since the Liberation had had as its aim to expel the idea of violent action from the consciousness of the masses. They thus brandished the banner of the *Resistance*: a mythologized Resistance, supposedly embodying the political virtues of violence in unadulterated form. Accordingly, they proposed to revive its memory through a series of 'exemplary actions'.[43]

Whether the policy of the French Communist leadership has contributed to obstructing or diverting the revolutionary violence of the masses on several occasions is a legitimate question. But the most flagrant instance is perhaps precisely that of the Resistance. Fernando Claudin has shown very clearly how the narrowly 'patriotic' objectives assigned to the PCF by the international Communist movement, as a function of Soviet policy, had the effect of repressing such revolutionary potential as the masses' initiatives may have possessed from the very outset.[44] The political perceptiveness of our post-'68 Maoists can be gauged forthwith. Through their propaganda they were perpetuating an ambiguity that has weighed heavily on our political history for more than thirty years.

The ignorance of the facts and the absence of any class analysis, for which they substitute a mythical conception of history, boiled down in their texts to the realization of ideas (violence, reformism, revisionism, and so on) which are supposed to contest and succeed one another – these sufficiently indicate the limitations of this 'Marxism', even this 'Maoism'. (Think, for example, of Mao's *Report on an Investigation of the Peasant Movement in Hunan*, which remains a model of concrete analysis.[45])

In truth – to repeat the point – by virtue of the 'anti-authoritarian' themes of their propaganda, their appeals to violence, their exclusive political faith in *déclassé* elements, they belonged to the tradition of Bakunin rather than that of Marx or Mao.

In effecting their current metaphysical withdrawal – as indicated in their public stance by total condemnation of violence as a political means, accompanied by an apologia for what Glucksmann calls 'interruption' as well as 'resistance' (but now in the sense of a 'spiritual', moral or intellectual, resistance),[46] and the avowedly 'intransigent' defence of human rights – the New Philosophers are engaged in a peculiar regression. For in elaborating the 'positive' content of the Western ideological theme of 'dissidence', the move they are involved in, which they are careful to present as a renunciation of Marxist theory out of a concern for political efficacy, is in fact simply a *regression on the very terrain of the anarchist tradition where they were already located*: a regression from Bakunin to Stirner, from anarchism as a revolutionary movement to the metaphysical speculations of absolute individualism.

But that is not all. They regress not to Stirner's theses themselves but to an 'inverted' version of these theses, through an inversion of the argument underpinning them. Now, this reversal or inversion, which subordinates the critique of the state to denunciation of the idea of revolution, has the immediate and unavoidable effect of inscribing the logic of their discourse in a political current to which Stirner had already unwittingly found himself tributary (as Marx and Engels remarked in passing in *The German Ideology*): the ultra-reactionary tradition of Joseph de Maistre and Louis de Bonald.[47]

To those who are offended by such a comparison, or who regard it as a purely polemical gesture, I offer the observation that one of the leitmotivs of our ideologues, jointly adopted by Glucksmann and Lévy in the *Espresso* round table, is to say: if we must 'have done with the schema of the revolutionary intellectual', it is because the revolutionary intellectual has always wanted 'to begin history all over again', in the name of the putative 'science of the revolution' whose duly recorded text he brandishes in his writings, ready and waiting to 'lay down the law'.

'*To break history in two*' (a Nietzschean formula): this, they announce, invoking Mao, is the underlying thought that defines the revolutionary project in its invariant essence. What revolutionaries want – so Glucksmann asserts – is to 'reduce society, with all its variety of traditions, its diversity, its homosexuals, drug addicts, poets, to a blank sheet, on which they can then write the poem of the science of the collective happiness of humanity, the mastery of the world, etc.' This, he adds, is why the roots of the Terror, to which the world was to give birth in the name of their ideal, is to be found in the thought of these philosophers.

Now, this theme, which Stirner had sketched in passing on the basis of his theory of the individual and the state, is the centrepiece of Joseph de Maistre's attack on the 'principles' of the French

Revolution. His opuscule *Des Constitutions politiques*, written in 1809, opens with these words: 'One of the great errors of a century that professed them all was to believe that a political constitution could be written and created *a priori*.'[48] And de Bonald echoed him, in identical terms, in his *Législation primitive*. Although he had obviously not read *Capital*, Bonald wrote: '[f]rom the Gospels to the *Social Contract* it is books that have made revolutions'. This has been a classical theme of the counter-revolutionaries for a century and more: the people of 1789 committed a crime and a folly in wanting to 'break history in two' – to abolish the various traditions, the diversity, and so on, of society.

It will be objected that the Western ideology of dissidence 'officially' holds the state, order, elites, and so on, in contempt, whereas right-wing thought makes respect for them an inviolable principle. This was Glucksmann's rejoinder to Jacques Attali, when the latter referred to a 'French New Right' with him in mind. Now, in one sense this is true – and we shall see why. But it nevertheless remains the case that the theoretical stock of their arguments is borrowed from the great tradition of counter-revolutionary thought, from Burke to the present.[49] For if this intellectual tradition contains one invariant theme, it is indeed the condemnation of revolutionary 'optimism', and the idea that this optimism is rooted in the disastrous illusion that man can 'recommence' history and impose on it laws fashioned by the unaided powers of his own reason. We should add that there is scarcely a theoretician of counter-revolution since 1789 who has not attributed the genesis of this illusion to the evil genius of various philosophical 'master thinkers'.

Should ultimate proof be required, we could simply note the alliance formed between the New Philosophy and a man who, day by day, derives arguments from it on behalf of a philosophy of an overtly religious, and frankly reactionary, stamp: Maurice Clavel.

A veritable master of the game, Clavel has from the outset ensured the 'promotion' of their books. But he has also seconded, interpreted and commented on their theses in a series of works of his own, discovering in them weapons for his own campaign for a new religious fundamentalism. Reread *Ce que je crois*, and then especially *Dieu est Dieu, nom de Dieu!*. These are so many manifestos addressed to the Catholic hierarchy, in order that it might rediscover the purity of its principles.[50]

The accord between Clavel and the New Philosophers goes far deeper than has hitherto been noticed. It is not dictated solely by the interests of a literary coterie, but rests on the theoretical resources they share with counter-revolutionary thought. Clavel proclaims loud and clear the *truth* of a position which – as in Burke, Maistre or Bonald – has only ever been defensible by reference to an order, founded in God, transcending nature and society.

Whereas Glucksmann is silent on the subject of what accounts for the value of the 'traditions' he intends to preserve from revolutionary demolition,[51] Clavel offers the only coherent response: a Divine guarantee.

I can hear the objections: Clavel's political themes are 'left-wing', even if the official Left – the left-wing parties – does not enjoy his support, even if Marxism seems diabolical to him; the 'opening to the world' he enjoins upon the Catholic hierarchy is an opening to the 'poor' against clericalism; the paradigm of the political action for which he calls is the long strike of the Lip watchmakers, and he sets the 'refreshing' figure of 'his friend Ranguènes', worker-priest of Lip, against those he regards as 'ageing beaux' – that is to say, the bishops.[52]

Apart from the fact that this is not the issue, you will admit that Clavel's Lip is a rather uncommon one. Witness his eulogy of Raguènes for 'yawning in meetings'. What does it matter, in his opinion, if the one of the most remarkable features of the Lip workers' struggle was its extraordinary *organization*, which enabled it to resist all provocations (whether from Left or Right)? What does it matter if it was precisely the organizational forms invented and tested by them that made an original contribution to the history of class struggle in France – forms that have been adopted and imitated in other enterprises? Maurice Clavel's sympathy is attracted by Raguènes's yawns – his yawns *in meetings*. And it would not occur to him to put them down to the fatigue induced by a struggle without any respite. He 'detects' a symbolic value in them: rejection of *any* organization of the working class, the kind of organization displayed in meetings.

In politics, one cannot escape the logic of one's premisses. What Clavel pushes to the point of caricature is the precise contradiction that haunts the thinking of the ideologues of dissidence.

It is impossible simultaneously to profess, as they do, to be renouncing the role of 'guides' or 'educators' of the masses, and then to draw one's arguments from a theoretical tradition whose main inspiration is a reaction against any organized mass movement intent on changing the existing social order, and whose objective is to sanction the power of an elite over 'the Plebs'.

The New Philosophers are themselves trapped in this circle – all the more so in that they can thus persist in the comforting illusion that, while deserting the battles of real history, they remain their metaphysical masters. Thus they open an 'exit' for the flight of the intellectuals which, as we have seen, is the real motive for their 'radical anti-Marxism'.

It remains the case that their slogans had the capacity to mislead people as to their ultimate political meaning. In the last analysis, the reasons for this are inherent in the ideological crisis of the imperialist system, but in the first instance in the theoretical guarantee they have thought it possible to find in the work of Michel Foucault.

4

The Foucault Factor

When, on the basis of monumental research, Foucault prudently proceeds to venture various hypotheses on power or knowledge, our master thinkers rush to appropriate them as demonstrated truths. Their aim is to impart the weight of authority to their speculations, and supply them with an imaginary historical foundation that is made to measure.

We shall see that the operation is facilitated both by Foucault's own theoretical oscillations and by the fact that in order to pursue his research to a successful conclusion, he has found it necessary to challenge a certain representation of the state, its power and apparatuses, which has been presented as 'Marxist' for more than thirty years. I have already had occasion to signal that it is further aided by the attitude of ignorance or repudiation adopted by the majority of 'official' Marxists towards this 'embarrassing' *œuvre*; they have declined to appreciate the good use they could make of it (in large part, it is true, self-critical). None the less, the signature and certain texts of Michel Foucault function as an *alibi* in this affair, and are repaid with a veritable hijacking of the best results he has obtained over the last fifteen years.

What does this 'hijacking' consist in? It boils down to appropriating two sets of theses proposed as working hypotheses by Foucault. These are, first, the sketch of a theory of *power* that features in his latest works – what he characterizes as a 'micro-physics of power'; and, second, the series of theses, patiently developed and rectified since *Histoire de la folie*, on the relations between *knowledge* and *power*.

We shall not be astonished to find that our ideologues once again take the liberty of neglecting all the 'details', and simplifying Foucault's positions in the extreme, in order to press them into the service of their own. These (as we shall see) are in direct contradiction with Foucault's in various essential respects.

Today, no one is unaware that Foucault's first two books – *Histoire de la folie* and *Naissance de la clinique* – written in a climate epistemologically still profoundly marked by the Lysenko affair, inaugurated a long reflection, initially solitary, on the relations between power and knowledge, even though he was able to formulate 'his' problem in these terms only considerably later, after 1968.

What, in effect, was the first of these texts concerned with, if not to disentangle what Foucault now calls 'the entanglement of the effects of power and knowledge' in the case – seemingly amenable to such analysis – of 'psychiatric knowledge', such as its object was constituted in the early nineteenth century? What was the aim of the second, in an extension of the works of Georges Canguilhem, if not to expose the possible imbrication between certain political and juridical reforms, which affected the entire social formation, and the constitution of an 'object' of clinical medicine?

Since then we have had *Les Mots et les choses*, which was wrongly interpreted as a 'structuralist' work, and *L'archéologie du savoir*, in which Foucault clarified the theoretical misunderstandings occasioned by it. These were both 'methodological' works. It was then that the emphasis of Foucault's research shifted towards the history of the constitution and operation of the judicial and penal apparatus, largely under the impact of the events of May '68. And so it was that the question of *power* came to the forefront.

On the basis of the provisional conclusions he reached in this domain, Foucault has now reverted to his 'old' question about the relationship between knowledge and power. Witness the interviews he gave on the occasion of the publication of *Surveiller et punir*, and especially the programmatic text of the first volume of his *Histoire de la sexualité*.

So what we have is a labour that follows the spiral of any research, returning to its premisses in order to 'elucidate' them: a grand tour that has taken fifteen years, during which some questions have been opened up, and certain theses refined, which may be considered so many results.

In a recent interview, Foucault has suggested that:

> Mechanisms of power in general have never been much studied by history. History has studied those who held power – anecdotal histories of kings and generals; contrasted with this there has been the history of economic processes and infrastructures. Again, distinct from this, we have had histories of institutions, of what has been viewed as a superstructural level in relation to the economy. But power in its strategies, at once general and detailed, and its mechanisms has never been studied.[53]

From this diagnosis, which is ambiguous in many respects, let us retain the programme it encompasses: an investigation conceived as an 'analytics' or 'economy' of power. This involves the analysis of power as a 'more or less pyramidalized, more or less organized, more or less co-ordinated bundle of relations'; an investigation into the 'exercise of power' such as it was instituted in the eighteenth century, when there occurred what Foucault, extrapolating from the prison system to society in its entirety, calls the transition from punishment to surveillance:

> We all know about the great upheavals, the institutional changes which constitute a change of political regime, the way in which the delegation of power right to the top of the state system is modified. But in thinking of the mechanisms of power, I am thinking rather of its capillary form of existence, the point where power reaches into the grain of individuals, touches their bodies and inserts itself into their actions and attitudes, their discourses, learning processes and everyday lives. The eighteenth century invented, so to speak, a synaptic regime of power, a regime of its exercise *within* the social body, rather than *from above* it. The change in official forms of political power was linked to this process, but only via inter-vening shifts and displacements. This more-or-less coherent modification in the small-scale modes of exercise of power was made possible only by a fundamental structural change.[54]

Remarkably, the 'link' between the 'change in the official forms of political power' and the 'modification in the small-scale modes of exercise of power' is theorized neither in this text nor in *Surveiller et punir*, whose theses are summarized here. But it is nevertheless the case that Foucault introduces a domain of research in part unexplored prior to him: that of the power relations within which all forms of social practice in a given social formation are conducted.

This is so even if the periodization Foucault believes he can establish is open to question; and even if the alteration he evokes is arguably not as radical as he claims. It is not obvious that prior to the eighteenth century there did not exist 'small-scale modes of exercise of power', which were just as refined as the ones instituted then, even if they were regulated by a different regime. We may inquire whether, in order to back up his argument, Foucault has not constructed a fictional representation of the 'absolute monarchy' as a 'wide-meshed' power structure.

But before proceeding to this point of contention, we must stress that these theses involve a whole polemic against a determinate representation of power that Foucault designates – not without good reason – as 'Marxist'. Initially muffled, the polemic becomes open in his last two books, notably in the first chapter of *Surveiller et punir*:

> The study of this micro-physics presupposes that the power exercised on the body is conceived not as a property, but as a strategy, that its effects of domination are attributed not to 'appropriation', but to dispositions, manoeuvres, tactics, techniques, functionings. . . . In short, this power is exercised rather than possessed; it is not the 'privilege', acquired or preserved, of the dominant class, but the overall effect of its strategic positions – an effect that is manifested and sometimes extended by the position of those who are dominated. Furthermore, this power is not exercised simply as an obligation or a prohibition on those who 'do not have it'; it invests them, is transmitted by them and through them; it exerts pressure upon them, just as they themselves, in their struggle against it, resist the grip it has on them.[55]

As you can see, the critique does indeed bear on the 'Marxist' representation of state power (and its apparatuses) as a separate machine, located 'above' the social body and regulating the mechanisms of class domination 'from without'. Strictly speaking, this representation does not figure in the work of Marx himself.[56] However, Foucault can legitimately qualify it as 'Marxist', since it is Marxists who have perfected it, on the basis of Marx's silences, in order to justify a certain type of exercise of state power.

In reality, the thesis that state power is exercised *on the basis* of a multiplicity of ideological class relations, referring in the last instance to the *fact* of domination by a class, is in no way incompatible with the bases of a theory of ideological class relations such as they can be established in the light of the classical Marxist texts.

At the appropriate moment, we shall see what prompts Foucault to decline to recognize this – to the extent of abandoning any reference to *state* power, the *dominant* class, and the *dominant* ideology. These refusals are dictated by theoretical considerations that ultimately weigh on his historical analyses. In any event, they possess political implications that the ideologues of dissidence do not fail to exploit.

Foucault's second great thesis concerns the imbrication of effects of power and effects of knowledge.

It goes without saying that what is peculiar to Foucault is not that he has established that the possession of knowledge is equivalent to the acquisition of power: this is a classical theme among eighteenth-century philosophers. On the other hand, there is a theme running throughout his *œuvre* which he is indeed the first to have theorized and developed as such: that power is *productive* of knowledge. It complements the previous thesis by imparting a directly political significance to it.

Against the 'negative' and 'repressive' conception – which is fundamentally juridical – of power as content to *prohibit*, to say 'no', Foucault establishes 'the productive character of power'. This is a central theme in *La Volonté de savoir*, and is summarized thus: 'What makes power hold good, what makes it accepted, is simply the fact that it doesn't only weigh on us as a force that says no, but that it traverses and produces things, it induces pleasure, forms of knowledge, produces discourse.'[57] It could be formulated by saying that all knowledge is produced *under* (by the effect and under the constraint of) power relations.

Now, this theme, once again, has some obvious polemical implications. It is directed against the rationalist interpretation of the 'science/ideology' couple as it haunted Althusser's first texts, and was manipulated and exploited by epigones. But over and above this opposition, it is also directed against the notion of *ideology* once again.

Foucault has never stopped wrestling with this notion. And some of the main features of his theoretical constructions can be explained by his ambition to circumvent it[58] – even if, as a recent interview attests, his position basically remains nuanced:

The notion of ideology appears to me to be difficult to make use of, for three reasons. The first is that, like it or not, it always stands in virtual opposition to something else which is supposed to count as the truth. Now I believe that the problem does not consist in drawing the line between that in a discourse which falls under the category of scientificity or truth, and that which comes under some other category, but in seeing historically how effects of truth are produced within discourses which in themselves are neither true nor false. The second drawback is that the concept of ideology refers, I think necessarily, to something of the order of a subject. Thirdly, ideology stands in a secondary position relative to something which functions as its infrastructure, as its material, economic determinant, etc. For these three reasons, I think that this is a notion that cannot be used without circumspection.[59]

Once again, it is true that a certain 'Marxism', exploiting the ambiguities of some extremely allusive texts by Marx,[60] succumbs to this critique. But as we know, on the first two points Althusser's latest works indicate a path that is identical to the one taken by Foucault, in the categories and idiom peculiar to him. *Practical ideology* figures fully there as one social practice among others, articulated with the other social practices of the social formation in question, as a function of the requisite 'subjection' of individuals (their constitution-interpellation as subjects) to the ideological social relations characteristic of it. And all this involves no consideration (even 'virtual') of 'the truth'.

As for the category of the *subject*, everyone knows that right from the start, one of the angles of Althusser's attack on the encroachments of idealist philosophy within Marxism was to demonstrate its inadmissibility there, since it brings with it the trace of its (bourgeois) juridical origins in philosophical disguise. The theses subsequently advanced on practical ideology, far from implying (as Foucault supposes) 'something of the order of a subject', instead establish, according to a now famous formula, that this practice (like any other) is 'a process without a subject'. It is the process (without a subject) of the constitution of individuals as 'subjects'.

Finally, as for the relationship between ideology and something like an 'infrastructure', this is indeed the sensitive point. For it is true that for a Marxist, although it is endowed with relative autonomy, practical ideology (which is indissociably a practice of transformation and of ideological class *struggle*) can be analysed only according to the other forms of class struggle, which are all, in the last instance, rooted in the practice of production of material goods.

To get the measure of our disagreement here is to specify the theoretical limits within which historical materialism can profit from Foucault's work.

Let us work back up the chain. Foucault declines to connect the system of practical ideologies with the relations of production which, in the last instance, determine the character and form of class domination in a given social formation. It is for this reason that he refuses to speak of the *dominant* ideology. For the same reason, when he considers the power effects conveyed, produced and reproduced in the *state apparatus*, which ensure the domination of this ideology, he refuses to link the power effects that – to his credit – he has exposed in the family, schools, hospitals, and so on (when the effect of the dominant ideology is to conceal them), to the nature of the state in question. His grounds are that this would be to make them the product of a single (fictive) centre.

Hence the theory of the 'microphysics of power' such as he defends it: a theory of foci of power that are discontinuous, diffused throughout the 'social body', without it being possible to identify any global mechanism underlying this process of production, which consequently assumes the appearance of a veritable spontaneous generation. As a result, 'Power', stripped of any class character, emerges as a universally serviceable, metaphysical substance. When – in the interview I quoted at the outset – Foucault evokes the 'link' established between the change at the level of state power and the functioning of its apparatuses, he provides no specification apart from signalling 'intervening shifts and displacements'. This is because he is unable to analyse the

contradictory historical process of the constitution of these apparatuses, and the perfection of the articulation of their mechanisms
in contemporary class struggle.

But a mere declaration of such theoretical differences, even when it
is accompanied by the political reasons adduced for them, cannot act
as a substitute for the exacting task in which Foucault anticipates us:
to treat with our own theoretical instruments the enormous quantity of historical material he handles in his inquiries. I shall restrict
myself to a very limited example here – albeit one that is crucial to
the interpretation of *Surveiller et punir* – simply to give some idea of
the nature of the requisite critical work.[61]

Foucault's book opens with a chapter on 'torture' – the role of
torture in his argument is well known. Foucault lays out the ground
plan of the 'political technology of the body' (an element of the
'microphysics of power'), the modification of whose form and functions will serve to explain the prison system and discipline. Whereas
the body is the direct, public object of torture, prison, Foucault
explains, involves a 'discreet grip' on the body, which is touched 'as
little as possible'. On this basis he invites us to think of prison as a
new type of torture, *vis-à-vis* which – and this is the second theoretical function of the book's opening – we are supposed to
conduct ourselves in the same way as the spectators of torture, zealously supporting an institution we endow with a power we ourselves
do not possess.

As you can see, Foucault's entire theory of power is involved in
these initial pages. But in his description of the ritual of torture this
theory precisely commits him to emphasizing all the features related
to the marks (of power) that are inscribed on the flesh of the condemned man. He therefore focuses attention on the relationship

between the condemned man (his body) and his executioner. And the executioner himself comes on stage as executor of the will of a 'king' who, because his role as holder of state power in the service of domination by a class is ignored, takes on a quasi-mythical appearance.

Simultaneously, other features and characters highlighted in the sources to which Foucault refers fade into the background. Their presence is blurred and their role in the ritual is virtually abolished. This is the case with the highly significant role of the Church. Obviously, it is not absent from Foucault's depiction of punishment, but he 'slides' over the sources' insistence upon the presence of the clergy as its *central*, omnipresent character.

The site (the church square) where the *amende honorable* is made is not taken into account theoretically; nor is the fact that priests accompany the condemned man to the scaffold in procession; nor is the presence at his side of the confessor who, up until his last sigh, murmurs words of consolation. In short, as a result of Foucault's theoretical objectives, the pair of the condemned man and the priest (vice and virtue), central to the descriptions on which he bases his work, finds itself relegated to the background, ceding to the pair of the condemned man and his executioner.

If we restore to the clerical apparatus the full prominence expressly allotted it by contemporaries, the whole 'economy' of the ritual topples over, and its significance alters. Far from being simply a component of a 'technology of bodies', conceived as an element in a microphysics of power that has no origin, in an exclusively juridical framework of crime and punishment, torture emerges as an exemplary *mise en scène*, intended to capture the 'gaze' of the masses. It stages the regular operation of the different ideological apparatuses of a given state (here the feudal state). It is organized by the major ideological apparatus of the time: the Church, which naturally assigns itself the principal role in the spectacle and brings into play, in the situation of extreme tension thus induced, the full system of its own ideological themes: Hell, Heaven, Good, Evil, Sin, Forgiveness, and so on. And this involves a contrived opening, whether soothing or threatening, of the earthly tribunal on to the calculated decisions of the Heavenly Tribunal.

In short, if we want to endow it with its full historical substance, torture is subject to a class analysis which implies that we should not decline, as Foucault contrives to, all reference to a state, its power and apparatuses. No doubt they functioned differently in the feudal period, but neither 'less well' nor less intensely than in the classical age when the bourgeoisie established the machinery of its domination.[62]

These sketchy comments certainly remain insufficient, but at least they make it possible to bring out the theoretical core of our disagreements. If Foucault, with the results we have just glimpsed, constructs a theory of power as a bundle of infinitesimal relations without any overall mechanism regulating the small-scale modes of its exercise, it is for this reason: he does not take into consideration *the general process of the class struggle*, whose dominant tendency the operation of the state's different ideological and repressive apparatuses has the function of realizing, via regulated effects of power.

In the case of a theoretician of Foucault's calibre, we have reason to doubt whether this position is thought through, and whether this refusal is deliberate. In fact, this is what he stated in a recent interview:

If one accepts that the form – both general and concrete – of struggle is contradiction, then clearly everything which allows the contradiction to be localised or narrowed down will be seen as a brake or a blockage. But the problem is precisely as to whether *the logic of contradiction* can actually serve as a principle of intelligibility and rule of action in political struggle. This touches on a momentous political question: how is it that since the nineteenth century *the specific problems of struggle and the strategy of struggle have tended so constantly to be dissolved into the meagre logic of contradiction?* . . . In any case, one must try to think struggle and its forms, objectives, means and processes in terms of a logic free of the sterilising constraints of the dialectic.[63]

The issue is whether it is not, rather, the Foucauldian conception of 'contradiction' that is meagre; and whether the dialectic – which, we can readily agree, contains 'sterilising constraints' in its idealist form – cannot be released from these constraints on the basis of materialist philosophical positions. But however that may be, these pronouncements bring us to the *political crux* of our disagreements.

This can be summed up as follows. Foucault's theory of the microphysics of power possesses a dual importance. First, it exposes the presence of 'power relations' where they had remained invisible, and thereby challenges the 'liberal' illusions fostered by certain reforms (e.g. Pinel's reforms in the case of psychiatric hospitals). Second, it has the merit of demolishing any mechanistic representation of the 'dominant ideology' whereby it is a mystification exclusively perpetrated 'from above', whose cogs are meticulously perfected in secret in some ideological headquarters. This misrepresents the dominant ideology, which is an outcome – invariably contested in the struggle in which it finds its motivation and inscribes its effects – of a process of *ongoing unification*; and in this process, according to a global dynamic that is invariably impeded, ideological elements are adjusted that are *already present* 'below', where the dominant ideology has a direct purchase on the imaginary relations individuals maintain with their real conditions of existence. Now if Foucault's theory possesses these merits, on the other hand it cannot inspire any overall organization of the masses for emancipatory struggle, only a strategy of 'minor repulsions' which, denying its existence, excludes the major stake in any political struggle aimed at transforming the bases of a given social formation: *state power*.

Sketching the contours of his 'politics' in the Preface he has written to a recent book, Foucault states: 'The thing is to multiply the "points of repulsion" in the political fabric and increase the surface area of potential dissidence. In the battle against the institutions of power, it is a question of employing what tacticians used to call "*l'ordre mince*". As we know, it has secured some victories.'[64]

We have thus reached a point where, on the basis of his own theoretical positions, Foucault openly lends a hand to 'Operation Dissidence', and consequently facilitates our ideologues' exploitation of his work.

Yet for all that, nothing would be more fallacious than to identify their theoretical positions with those of the author of *L'histoire de la folie*. This exploitation is indeed an *exploitation*, conducted on the basis of a misinterpretation that the New Philosophers strive to preserve, while Foucault has not as yet seen fit to defend himself against it. If such a misinterpretation is possible, it is (as we have seen) because of the veritable metaphysics of power Foucault wants to construct, tying himself in knots in the process; and because of the political conclusions he has the consistency immediately to draw from it. But it is at the cost (I repeat) of a hijacking of some of the theses that govern the totality of his inquiries.

Obviously, I am not referring to Foucault's positions with respect to Marxism: as we have just seen, they in no way amount to the pure and simple repudiation that has made our master thinkers' fortune. Foucault does not waver in maintaining that Marx laid the foundations of a theory of exploitation (he omits to specify: capitalist exploitation); and under the very nose of Lévy, who questions him in *Les Nouvelles littéraires*, he asserts that being a historian and being a Marxist are well-nigh synonymous. In short, he evinces no desire to cede to blackmail on this score.

I am, however, referring to his own concepts. Foucault's *œuvre* investigates the 'small-scale modes of the exercise of power' in order the better to refute a 'centralist', 'centralizing' conception of the state as an exclusive organ of command. How, ultimately, other than through imposture, can it be pressed into service to corroborate what we have characterized as a *metaphysics of the state*, which discovers the definitive explanation of the whole history of the West in the universal and inexorable logic of a centralized state?[65]

Yet this is what our philosophers have no qualms about doing when, to cloud the issue, they appropriate an example from *Surveiller et punir* in a way that is contrary to the spirit and letter of Foucault's own declarations: the example of Bentham's panopticon.[66]

If Foucault has exhumed this wholly forgotten text of Bentham's, it is because he reckoned that he had discovered in the idea of the panopticon as formulated by Bentham the paradigm of the novel 'technology' of power, based on surveillance, established in the eighteenth century; a paradigm that is all the more striking in so far as Bentham's 'plans' have been realized in the architecture of prisons, hospitals and boarding schools.

But unlike our philosophers, Foucault has never elevated the panopticon into an archetype of state power. On the contrary, in the preface to the French reprint of Bentham he is very careful in his formulations. Foucault states that Bentham 'invented a technology of power designed to solve the problems of surveillance', and considered 'his optical system . . . the *great* innovation needed for the easy and effective exercise of power'. Nevertheless, it was necessary to bear in mind that 'the procedures of power that are at work in modern societies are much more numerous, diverse and rich'; and hence that '[i]t would be wrong to say that the principle of visibility governs all technologies of power used since the nineteenth century'.[67]

Now, this is precisely what Glucksmann claims and repeats at length in *Les maîtres penseurs*, where he takes the opportunity to load Foucault with responsibility for Hegelian theses on the state under the emblem of a 'generalized panopticism'![68]

It is therefore legitimate – or so it seems to me – to speak of a hijacking of Foucault's results, even if he, for his own reasons – in the 'non-contradictory' logic of his metaphysical conception of power – has more or less been able to go along with it.

Our philosophers find in Foucault a 'left' theoretical guarantee which – in conjunction with their apparently anarchist *démarche* – helps to confuse the issue and instil illusions about the political core of their positions. And so it is that their 'discourse' can, in its way, register the effects of the ideological crisis of the imperialist system, while disconnecting them from any revolutionary political outcome to that crisis.

5

Conclusion:
The America in Our Heads

Now that the final mask has slipped, the Western ideology of dissidence is exposed for what it is: a polemical ideological formation whose theoretical stock is derived directly from the ultra-reactionary political tradition which, for a century and a half, has fed off the original theoreticians of counter-revolution. It is an ideological formation that 'legitimates' and accentuates the flight of Western intellectuals when they are faced with the 'crisis' of their Marxism, by rooting it in a metaphysics of the state. It translates and inflects this reaction in the direction of a 'radical', mass disengagement. It thus intervenes 'on the spot' over an issue that the development and transformation of capitalism have rendered critical for the outcome of contemporary class struggles in the imperialist countries: the question of the alliance between the workers' movement and an ever more numerous and diversified social stratum, dubbed 'value-oriented intellectuals' by the experts of the Trilateral Commission.[69] It intervenes not to try to make them abide by the 'rules of the game' they have been challenging for fifteen years, but – registering their 'refusal' – to equip them with an ideology that at least permits these rules to operate: an ideology of non-intervention, of withdrawal into the self, of 'dissidence'.

It is here that the anarchist *guise* of their discourse assumes its full significance – their anti-statism, their anti-technocratism, their indictment of the human sciences, and so on, which at first sight distinguish them so sharply from such classical critics of totalitarianism as Popper or Aron. For the system encompassing these denunciations rests on a metaphysical base that prompts them to propose, as a substitute for 'politics', a 'morality' which, at root, is ultimately nothing more than a variant of the most traditional bourgeois morality.

To be more precise, it is a morality that solders around the unreserved exaltation of 'private life' (a constant refrain of Glucksmann's) elements of the decomposition affecting this ideology since 1968. This represents a major recuperation, in which such original forms of struggle as the women's movement, the ecological movement, and the gay movement are pressed into the service of an apologia for the underlying kernel of the dominant bourgeois ideology against which these struggles are engaged.

What is this 'private life', if not the key notion in the moral ideology that 'rounds off' bourgeois juridical ideology? As such, it transposes the central distinction of bourgeois law (public/private) as organized around *private* law – that is to say, property law.

And how did these forms of struggle – which, ten years on, remain one of the vital legacies of the May of the intellectual petty bourgeoisie – win a mass audience, if not by exposing the *political* nature of matters hitherto regarded as 'private' (abortion, contraception, sexuality, and so on), while relating them to the general process of the class struggle?

Our ideologues propose, quite simply, to retreat. But once again, the substance of their slogans and their impact lie in the fact that they 'reflect', in order to inflect, an objective situation: the *limits* which these struggles continue to come up against, and which for the most part relate to the inability of the workers' movement to date to reappropriate their positive content. Isolated, their revolutionary potential is constantly menaced with repression.

To account for it, we must once again advert to the crisis of the Communist movement – that is to say, to the shadow cast by the Stalinist period over the French Communist Party. To take but one recent example: what happened at its Twenty-second Congress over these issues. The party leadership submitted a discussion document containing one paragraph devoted to 'morality'. Written in terms that have been traditional for half a century, it condemned the 'degeneracy' of bourgeois ideology. Thousands of amendments were proposed by cells through which, ten years after the event, the currents of May '68 were blowing. Not one was accepted. And the final document retains a solemn condemnation of the 'perversion' induced by the decomposition of this ideology. No mention is made of the 'positive' content of the ideological crisis of the imperialist system, or of the challenge we are witnessing to the mechanisms of ideological subjection. Nothing is said to help distil a revolutionary 'outcome' from these struggles from the standpoint of the working class.

Yet this is a question of great significance. For it involves the *ideological revolution* that must be undertaken before the seizure of state power, in order to avoid the ideological superstructures inherited from capitalism subsequently, retroactively, blocking and diverting the process of socialist transition, as happened in the Soviet Union.

At any rate, what is certain is that in the immediate present the positions of the PCF, like the silence of Marxist theoreticians on these questions, has allowed the ideologues of dissidence to profit

from the stasis of such movements, and open up a different path for
them: a regression to the forms of bourgeois ideology whose
'regime' has already been tested out in the United States.

For ultimately, such is the future promised us by this whole operation: under the cover of 'expelling the Russia in our heads', the
installation of America there.

A few indiscreet intellectuals have just made this crystal clear.

When one has made a speciality of being an 'avant-garde thinker',
and built a reputation on a terrain that is by definition shifting, there
is nothing more catastrophic than to see oneself overtaken; at a
stroke, one's *raison d'être* is lost. This is what the editors of the journal *Tel Quel* have just realized. Having lacked intuition, and having
allowed the train of dissidence to speed past, here they are abruptly
dubbing themselves 'dissident intellectuals' and seeking to get to the
front of the next one. This kind of volte-face would be derisory if
their precipitation did not contain some revealing indiscretions.
Thus, by comparison with the politically cautious and compara-
tively controlled *démarche* of the New Philosophers, the special issue
of *Tel Quel* devoted to the United States may be construed as an
extraordinary *political lapsus*.[70] In their haste to find a new vocation,
Philippe Sollers, Julia Kristeva, and their little *équipe* candidly disclose the long-term objective of the operation that we have to
confront.

To read their 'discussions' is to encounter one surprise after
another. First of all we learn that in the USA, 'the state lacks the
repressive structures' that exist everywhere else in the world. Never
mind the pitiless repression of strikes (like that of the Kentucky
miners) displayed before our very eyes in *Harlem County U.S.A.*;
never mind the physical liquidation, in a veritable bloodbath, of the

Black Panthers; never mind the systematic repression of the student movement after 1968; never mind the sinister ghettos in which all the more or less 'subversive' minorities are forced (or, more subtly, 'invited') to rot; never mind the mass psychiatrization of the population. In a remarkable instance of selective amnesia, our intellectuals of the eternal avant-garde have suddenly lost all memory of them.

Meanwhile, they inform us that what interests them about this country, which in their prose assumes the image of Paradise (in sum: the 'Free World'), is its ability to let an almost limitless diversity of 'cultural products' bloom – unlike 'totalitarian Marxism'. Never mind, once again, the incredible cultural and political *void* of the life of the majority of American intellectuals, who can escape the sterilization imposed on them by their narrow specialization in the service of the dominant technocracy only at the cost of heroic efforts, which are most often pathetic. 'We felt ourselves summoned when standing before this void,' confide the editors, who go into raptures over having discovered a 'culture' that reaches a peak below the 'threshold of verbalization'!

All this builds up to the conclusion that, through the fault of Christianity and Marxism, we merely inhabit an 'archaic subset' of contemporary American society. And since such diagnoses require a minimum of pseudo-historical justification, the editors have no trepidation in explaining that the 'European avant-garde' was definitively grafted on to the United States, as a result of two world wars and the intellectual emigrations they prompted. We had simply forgotten it. . . .

To repeat: the interest of these recantations lies in the fact that they give explicit expression to the objective tendency of the Western ideology of dissidence: to facilitate the unification and harmonization of the ideological bases of the imperialist system. The masses can have the scarecrow of 'totalitarianism', while the intellectuals have a 'choice': on the one hand, positivism and technocratism; on the other, 'dissidence' behind the *cordon sanitaire* of 'private life'. There is no doubt that this system of 'permanent recuperation' – which makes it possible to avoid and reabsorb all 'critical' ideological and political confrontations, and is so loudly trumpeted by the editors of *Tel Quel* – is the secret dream shared in common by 'our' capitalists in Western Europe and their American colleagues; that what they point to as a modality of the coherent pluralism of modernist ideology gives accurate expression to the tendency to 'social prophylaxis', whose instruments we observe being set in place even here.

Unquestionably, the real dissidents are a long way away. For what we are dealing with is the fabrication of a novel 'ideological formation' whose efficacy can be measured by the sudden success of the term 'dissident', which functions as a symptom in it. Far from being, as some have thought, merely a pre-electoral operation, whose scope would be restricted by the approaching French general election of March 1978, it involves the refinement of a long-range battle plan. In it imperialism finds a way of exploiting both the crisis of the Communist movement and its own crisis to its advantage. By playing on *the fact* of dissidence, it can impart renewed vigour to the old themes of the critique of 'totalitarianism', and once again present itself as the defender of democracy. By exploiting this fact philosophically, it can simultaneously counter the influence of Marxism over the new petty-bourgeois intellectual strata produced by the development of capitalism, and confer a 'positive' content on an ideology of 'rebellion' that recuperates the positive aspects of the ideological crisis experienced by these strata since 1968. The ultimate objective of this recuperation is revealed by the illusory slogans with which our ideologues conclude their interventions: over and above the critique of Marxism occupying the front of the stage, the real objective is a *depoliticization* of the intellectuals, to complement a *demobilization* of the masses.

This is a general strategy, as I indicated at the outset. But because of the services expected of it, and the manner in which it has responded to that expectation, the French variant is set to be exported: exported in some form or another, whether it is the New Philosophy or not, to all those countries where an organized mass movement and a Marxist tradition (old or recent) coexist among intellectuals.

Notes

Chapter 1   The Dissidence of the Dissidents and the Imperialist Crusade for Freedom

1. For reasons that we will have plenty of time to study later, people in the West readily imagine that nothing has changed in the USSR and the Eastern bloc countries since Stalin; in particular, the great crisis that shook these social formations during the Khrushchev period, and the subsequent economic and political restructuring, are ignored. On these points, among others, readers are referred to Roy and Zhores Medvedev's *Khrushchev: The Years in Power*, trans. Andrew R. Durkin, Oxford University Press, Oxford 1977.

2. Marc Rakovski's remarkable little book *Towards an East European Marxism* (Allison & Busby, London 1978) is well worth reading. Changes in the social composition of the Soviet intelligentsia are particularly well analysed in it.

3. My argument here adopts and develops that of Robert Linhart's contribution to the Venice conference organized by *Il Manifesto* in autumn 1977. See his 'Western "Dissidence" Ideology and the Protection of Bourgeois Order', in *Il Manifesto*, ed., *Power and Opposition in Post-*

Revolutionary Societies, trans. Patrick Camiller and Jon Rothschild, Ink Links, London 1979, pp. 249–60.

4. See Louis Althusser, 'Ideology and Ideological State Apparatuses', trans. Ben Brewster, in Althusser, *Essays on Ideology*, Verso, London 1984, pp. 1–60.

5. For a 'dissection' of this operation, see the admirable film *The Spiral*, by Armand Mattelart, Chris Marker and others.

6. Michel Crozier, Samuel P. Huntington and Joji Watanuki, *The Crisis of Democracy: Report on the Governability of Democracies to the Trilateral Commission*, New York University Press, New York 1975, p. 7. The Trilateral Commission, whose headquarters are in the USA, comprises economists, bankers, industrialists, politicians and intellectuals. In addition to Jimmy Carter, its members include Raymond Barre, Giovanni Agnelli, and the president of the Japanese consortium Mitsubishi. No translation rights having been granted for *The Crisis of Democracy*, the PCF publishing house, Éditions Sociales, published extracts from it with a commentary, under the title *Démocratie croissance zéro*.

7. David Cooper, *Qui sont les dissidents?*, Galilée, Paris 1977.

8. The notion of totalitarianism was first elaborated in the form with which we are familiar by Sigmund Neumann in 1942, in a book entitled *Permanent Revolution: The Total State in a World at War* (Harper, New York and London 1942), to designate the common characteristics of authoritarian movements and dictatorial regimes in the interwar period. It passed into the standard idiom of political theorists after the war, giving rise to many works. In addition to those I cite later, I should mention those of Kautsky and von Deutsch, as well as the book by Zbigniew Brzezinski, Carter's current national security adviser: *Ideology and Power in Soviet Politics* (Thames & Hudson, London 1962). For fuller information, readers are referred to Jean-Pierre Faye's documentary study *Les Langages totalitaires* (Herman, Paris 1973), and to Nicos Poulantzas's very interesting observations in his last work, *State, Power, Socialism* (trans. Patrick Camiller, New Left Books, London 1978).

9. Since I am dealing with the political significance of the 'New Philosophy', I shall refer exclusively to the works of André Glucksmann and Bernard-Henri Lévy, the two political leaders of the movement. For an exposition of the philosophical texts of the New Philosophers, readers can consult Aubral and Delcourt's *Contre la nouvelle philosophie* (Gallimard, Paris

1977), which nevertheless has the drawback that it does not make the authors' own position clear.

10. See especially Raymond Aron, *The Opium of the Intellectuals* (1955), trans. Terence Kilmartin, Secker & Warburg, London 1957.

Chapter 2   Western Dissidence Ideology: 'Radical Anti-Marxism'

11. André Glucksmann, *L'Express*, 18–24 July 1977; see also Glucksmann, *La Cuisinière et le mangeur d'hommes: essai sur l'État, le marxisme, les camps de concentration*, Seuil, Paris 1975.

12. André Glucksmann, *L'Espresso*, 24 July 1977.

13. Popper condemned Marxism (as well as psychoanalysis) in the name of the conception of science developed in *The Logic of Scientific Discovery* (1934). As is well known, against the dominant tradition of neo-positivism (that of the Vienna Circle, to which he was the 'official opposition'), Popper proposed in this work a new demarcation criterion between science and metaphysics. It no longer consisted in the 'verifiability' of propositions (supposedly revealed on inspection to be 'meaningful' or 'meaningless'), but in their 'falsifiability': a theory could be adjudged scientific, so Popper explained, only if some of its statements (at least potential) can be falsified by a certain number of suitable tests. This criterion, which 'inverts' classical neo-positivism, remains no less firmly attached to the juridical question of the 'credentials' of knowledge: the question of right traditionally posed to scientific practice by idealist philosophy. It allows Popper to disqualify the scientific claims of Marxism: unlike 'classical' neo-positivism, whose way of engaging in politics was to profess not to do so, Popperianism is thus a polemical philosophy. It is extended in a philosophy of history, expounded in *The Open Society and its Enemies* (1945), and in the defence and illustration of the human sciences as theoretical bases for a rational 'social engineering'. This is how Popper has become the 'official' philosopher of Helmut Schmidt's Federal Republic of Germany: by supplying a single theoretical foundation for the dual aspects of its politics: anti-Communism and technocratism.

14. Since *What is to be Done?* continues to be a major reference point in the discussion of Marxist positions on the relationship between revolutionary theory and the workers' movement, it should be remembered that

Lenin himself reckoned it appropriate to explain the unilateral character of this text on two occasions: in 1903 in his 'Speech on the Party Programme'; and in 1907 in his preface to the collection *Twelve Years* (compare Lenin, *Collected Works*, Progress Publishers, Moscow 1964, vol. 5, pp. 347–529, with vol. 6, pp. 489–91 and vol. 13, pp. 94–113).

It is impossible, Lenin recalls, properly to appreciate the theses contained in *What is to be Done?* if one ignores the conjuncture in which it was written. For its main target is therewith forgotten: 'economism'. *What is to be Done?* 'bends the stick in the opposite direction', in order to 'correct' economism. This is the perspective in which the 'loan' from Kautsky should be interpreted. For Lenin it was a matter of drawing attention to the 'separation' that existed between Marxist theory and the nascent Russian workers' movement, by sketching an analysis of the historically determinate social conditions that had rendered this separation inevitable. This was not in order to assert and establish some primacy of intellectuals over the workers' movement but, on the contrary, to highlight an urgent problem requiring *practical* resolution, whereby this separation would be overcome.

If these texts pose a question, it consists, rather, in the contradictory forms in which the *fusion* of Marxism and the Russian workers' movement was initiated and then realized, and the transformative effects on the theory itself produced by this 'fusion'. On these points, readers are referred to Étienne Balibar, *Cinq études du matérialisme historique*, François Maspero, Paris 1974.

15. André Glucksmann, *The Master Thinkers*, trans. Brian Pearce, Harvester, Brighton 1980, pp. 162, 149.

16. Jacques Rancière has underlined the paradox involved in the New Philosophers denouncing Marxism as a theory of the state when Marx's *œuvre* remains cursory, to say the least, on the subject. He writes:

Glucksmann is more radical when he has to demonstrate, in the face of all the evidence, that Marx valorizes the state as the opposite of civil society. The impossibility of furnishing the least proof supplies him with his ultimate proof: '[t]he chapter on the state', writes Glucksmann, 'which Marx planned to write is missing, as though by chance, from *Capital*' [*The Master Thinkers*, p. 104]. Well-known Stalinist logic: the best proof that people are guilty is the absence of any proof. For if there is no proof, it is because they have concealed it; and if they have concealed it, it is because they are guilty. (*Le Nouvel Observateur*, 25–31 July 1977)

17. Hannah Arendt, *The Origins of Totalitarianism*, 2nd edn, George Allen & Unwin, London 1958, p. 438.

18. Raymond Aron, *Democracy and Totalitarianism*, trans. Valence Ionescu, Weidenfeld & Nicolson, London 1968.

19. Aron's *Marxismes imaginaires: d'une sainte famille à l'autre* (Gallimard, Paris 1970) contains some of the key texts he devoted to combating French intellectuals' 'fascination' with Marxism. Aron's tactics consisted in demonstrating, without any difficulty, the contradiction between Sartre's existentialism and Marxist philosophy; and then – when Merleau-Ponty offered a self-criticism in *Adventures of the Dialectic* (1955) of his post-Liberation positions, as defended in the editorials of *Les Temps Modernes* and *Humanism and Terror* (1947) – encouraging him to abandon his 'neutral' position of 'a-Communism' and join the ranks of the militant anti-Communism that Aron himself had always championed.

20. I say 'old refrain' because most of the philosophical developments that are received as novelties these days are, in reality, adopted from texts dating from the 1930s. In particular, this is true of the argument according to which Plato foreshadowed the main features of all future totalitarian regimes, and established the theoretical mechanism justifying them. As is well known, from Glucksmann to Maurice Clavel, every New Philosopher revives it in a philosophical purple passage denouncing the author of *The Republic* as the main culprit of our current ills. It should be recalled that this theme made its first appearance in the history of political philosophy in 1920, from the pen of Bertrand Russell in his book on *The Practice and Theory of Bolshevism*. It was adopted by Warner Fite in 1934 in *The Platonic Legend*, before being elaborated by Karl Popper in his celebrated work *The Open Society and its Enemies*, in 1945. Readers are referred to the amazing chapter in which Victor Goldschmidt retraces the episodes of this Platonist 'quarrel', in order to distil its philosophical presuppositions, in a work – *Platonisme et pensée contemporaine* (Aubier-Montaigne, Paris 1970) – whose topicality has only been enhanced by recent events.

21. Bernard-Henri Lévy clearly explains their joint position when he writes:

Marx, then, the Machiavelli of the century. The U.S.S.R., or philosophy in power. It has been proved, in any case, that socialists are not only dreamers, gentle and tireless utopians, projecting into the heaven of ideas the sighs and torments of the humble and humiliated; but that Stalinism is a mode of socialism, socialism's mode of being, socialism as it is embodied in reality. (*Barbarism with a Human Face*, trans. George Holoch, Harper & Row, New York 1979, p. 157)

22. See Stalin, 'Dialectical and Historical Materialism', in *History of the Communist Party of the Soviet Union (Bolsheviks): Short Course*, Foreign Languages Publishing House, Moscow 1939, ch. 4, sect. 2, pp. 105–31.

23. Robert Linhart devotes a chapter of his remarkable *Lénine, les paysans, Taylor: essai d'analyse matérialiste historique de la naissance du système productif soviétique* (Seuil, Paris 1976, pp. 50–61) to the subject, in connection with Gorki.

24. I have emphasized this point, and its dramatic consequences, in *Proletarian Science? The Case of Lysenko*, trans. Ben Brewster, New Left Books, London 1977.

25. On this, see my *Proletarian Science?*; and Rakovski, *Towards an East European Marxism*, which argues identical positions.

26. The essentials of this labour by Soviet academicians, and the debates between them, are recorded in the journal *Under the Banner of Marxism*, which is of the greatest interest for understanding the conditions in which, and the ends to which, this 'Marxist philosophy' was constituted.

27. On several occasions Althusser has explained this error, which took the form in his initial texts of a 'Theory of theoretical practice': in other words, a variant of the positivist project of a 'Science of the sciences', of which Soviet 'dialectical materialism' is an avatar. See Louis Althusser, *Essays in Self-Criticism*, trans. Grahame Lock, New Left Books, London 1976.

28. Lévy, *Barbarism with a Human Face*, pp. 194–5.

29. Crozier *et al.*, *The Crisis of Democracy*, pp. 114–15.

30. Lévy's shock formulas are familiar: 'The idea of a dominant class is meaningless'; 'neither the dominant, nor the dominated' exist. And then there are Glucksmann's: 'Capital does not exist'; 'Labour does not exist'; and so on and so forth.

31. Glucksmann, *The Master Thinkers*, pp. 220–21. The reader can compare this representation of the immigrant with the figure of Ali in Robert Linhart's admirable book *The Assembly Line* (1978), trans. Margaret Crosland, John Calder, London 1981.

Chapter 3   Dissidence against Revolution

32. Albert Camus, 'Neither Victims nor Executioners', in Camus, *Between Hell and Reason: Essays from the Resistance Newspaper 'Combat', 1944–1947*, trans. Alexandre de Gramont, University Press of New England, Hanover, NH 1991, pp. 115–45; *The Rebel*, trans. Anthony Bower, Penguin, Harmondsworth 1971.

33. Camus, *The Rebel*, p. 199.

34. Ibid., p. 252.

35. Ibid., p. 265.

36. On the Stirner–Camus filiation, see Henri Arvon, *Aux sources de l'existentialisme*, Presses Universitaires de France, Paris 1954.

37. It is surprising to find a philosopher as well informed as Michel Foucault attributing the paternity of this thesis to Glucksmann, and heralding it as a veritable novelty.

38. Max Stirner, *The Ego and Its Own*, ed. David Leopold, trans. Steven Tracy Byington, Cambridge University Press, Cambridge 1995, p. 280.

39. Ibid., p. 273. Marx's polemic against Stirner in *The German Ideology* (trans. Clemens Dutt, W. Lough and C. P. Magill, in Marx and Engels, *Collected Works*, vol. 5, Lawrence & Wishart, London 1976) ironizes at length on the purely speculative character of Stirner's history of humanity.

40. *The Ego and Its Own*, pp. 158–9.

41. Ibid., pp. 62–89. I say that the formula is 'manifestly' not to be found in the *Science of Logic*, since the theory of the concept constructed there *precludes* it from figuring. The reason is quite simple: Hegel's theory of the concept – the decisive passage of the work – is constructed *against* the 'subjectivist', Kantian conception of the concept, opposing a subject to an object, implied by the formula.

This is a beautiful example of Glucksmann's manner of philosophizing, because it bears on the central thesis of his book, and his procedure amounts to imposture plain and simple. He attributes the formula to Hegel and does not hesitate to state that it is the cornerstone of his doctrine: '"To think, to conceive, is to dominate" (*Begreifen ist beherrschen*) was the happy thought on which he built up his science. (If you remove the word "concept" from the *Great Logic*, the text drains away)' (*The Master Thinkers*, p. 112). Yet Glucksmann knows as well as I do in which text Hegel had occasion to employ this formula, in the shape of an aphorism: in a draft of *The Spirit of Christianity* – an early work where Hegel sees in it a summary of Jewish thought! As Dominique Janicaud and Jean Wahl – the very commentators to whom Glucksmann refers in a note – explain very well, Hegel was able to constitute his system only by abandoning this formula and rejecting its philosophical implications. Glucksmann – who, in fact, is not unaware of this – writes: 'At first, Hegel recoiled from the idea in horror, proclaiming it to be "Jewish". Then he got used to it.' And this is how one builds a reputation as a 'profound' philosopher in Paris!

42. Glucksmann, 'Fascismes: l'ancien et le nouveau', *Les Temps Modernes*, no. 310 bis, May 1972, pp. 266–340; see also his 'Strategy and Revolution in France 1968', *New Left Review*, no. 52, November/December 1968, pp. 67–121. It was during this period that Alain Geismar and Serge July wrote *Vers la guerre civile* (Lattès, Paris 1969).

43. As is well known, these uncommon 'Marxists' sought to mobilize around this theme all those capable of escaping the 'control' of the traditional working-class organizations: immigrants, young peasants, young workers of peasant origin, school and university students, and so on, who were to act as the instruments of their grand political designs. In the disarray of post-May some were indeed enlisted – to their cost. It is not for me to say how many, subject to incessant intellectual and moral terrorism, lost their lives or their sanity: others will draw up the accounts one day. How will the escapees have been able to read the closing lines of this book by Glucksmann, one of the organizers of this terror? In *The Master Thinkers* (p. 287) he writes:

The master thinkers raised to the level of the speakable that will to power which inspires, more pettily, more covertly, the bosses and under-bosses of disciplinary societies. Because I have not only been subjected to their *mise en scène* but have also played a minor role in setting it up, I cannot hope to be able to draw the curtain with the ironical magic of a Prospero:

. . . These our actors,
As I foretold you, were all spirits and
Are melted into air, into thin air:
And, like the baseless fabric of this vision,
The cloud-capp'd towers, the gorgeous palaces,
The solemn temples, the great globe itself,

> Yea, all which it inherit, shall dissolve
> And, like this insubstantial pageant faded,
> Leave not a rack behind.

44. See Fernando Claudin's great work *The Communist Movement: From Comintern to Cominform*, 2 vols, trans. Brian Pearce and Francis MacDonagh, Monthly Review Press, New York and London 1975, vol. 2, pp. 316–43.

45. *Selected Readings from the Works of Mao Tse-Tung*, Foreign Languages Press, Peking 1967, pp. 20–32.

46. The transition from the historical Resistance (albeit mythologized) to a symbolic resistance as part of a spiritualist metaphysics is effected via an idealist interpretation of Mao's theses on knowledge. Evidence of this is the numerous developed passages in *La Cuisinière et le mangeur d'hommes* where Glucksmann asserts that 'to resist is to know', that knowledge can be acquired solely on the basis of resistance: 'In the beginning was the Resistance' (p. 21). Hence the idea that there is nothing to add to the testimony of the dissidents: that they speak the truth, the whole truth, and nothing but *the truth* about themselves and everything else.

47. See *The German Ideology*, p. 346.

48. Joseph de Maistre, *Des Constitutions politiques*, ed. R. Thomas, Les Belles Lettres, Paris 1959, p. 1.

49. On this, see Thomas Molnar's militant book *La Contre-révolution* (10/18, Paris 1972), which retraces the history of counter-revolutionary thought and seeks to bring out the invariants, or (in his own words) 'the substance of counter-revolutionary theory, which has scarcely varied since the original counter-revolutionaries, such as Maistre and Burke'. This 'substance' corresponds very precisely to the themes summarized here.

50. Since I wrote these lines, Clavel has published a new book – an 'Open Letter to Glucksmann' – whose title is a direct echo of Joseph de Maistre. Clavel refers to *Deux siècles chez Lucifer* (Seuil, Paris 1977), in the same way as de Maistre spoke of a 'Satanic revolution' in his *Considerations on France* (ed. and trans. Richard A. Lebrun, Cambridge University Press, Cambridge 1994).

51. It is worth observing that in his *Espresso* interview Glucksmann responds to Colletti's objection that the Italian Red Brigade terrorists are not Marxist in origin, but Catholic: 'According to me, Marxism is also present in the Vatican bureaucracy.' A quintessential 'Clavelian' theme. . . .

52. [Lip was a micro-mechanics factory in eastern France which, when it was

threatened with closure in 1973, was taken over by its workforce, who continued to produce watches for the best part of a year. This experiment in *autogestion* attracted considerable sympathy and support – Trans.]

One day it will be necessary to examine the ideological manoeuvres that have been conducted over this symbolic Lip, whose image has been constructed and reconstructed by each of our ideologues in accordance with their political volte-faces. Initially, in their 'militant' phase, they erected it into a universal model of action, without taking any account of the concrete conditions involved in this strike, or of the very strong anarcho-syndicalist tradition in the working class in the Besançon region, which is not far from La Chaux-de-Fonds.

Chapter 4   The Foucault Factor

53. Michel Foucault, 'Prison Talk' (1975), trans. Colin Gordon, in Foucault, *Power/Knowledge: Selected Interviews and Other Writings 1972–1977*, ed. Colin Gordon, trans. Colin Gordon and others, Harvester, Brighton 1980, pp. 36–54 (p. 51).

54. Ibid., pp. 38–9.

55. Michel Foucault, *Discipline and Punish: The Birth of the Prison*, trans. Alan Sheridan, Allen Lane, London 1977, pp. 26–7.

56. Foucault declares on several occasions that Marx, theoretician of exploitation, did not develop a theory of power. The historical credit for having been first to pose the issue is assigned to Nietzsche.

57. Michel Foucault, 'Truth and Power' (1977), trans. Colin Gordon, in *Power/Knowledge*, pp. 109–33 (p. 119).

58. See Dominique Lecourt, *Marxism and Epistemology*, trans. Ben Brewster, New Left Books, London 1975, pp. 187–213.

59. Foucault, 'Truth and Power', p. 118.

60. Notably the 1859 Preface to *A Contribution to the Critique of Political Economy*: see Marx, *Early Writings*, ed. Lucio Colletti, trans. Rodney Livingstone and Gregor Benton, Penguin/*New Left Review*, Harmondsworth 1975, pp. 424–8.

61. I borrow this example from an as yet unpublished work by Yves Vargas, *Se battre pour des idées. Gladiateurs, tournois, football*. The interpretation of it offered here is mine alone.

62. I have already indicated the reservations that might be entered about Foucault's idea that 'Monarchy' (?) is a regime of power 'with weak

links', which the bourgeoisie was content to tighten, extend and differentiate. Foucault nurses a predilection for the 'classical age' around which all his inquiries *begin*, because they presuppose a veritable historical *beginning* in it. It would unquestionably be more interesting to ponder, as Althusser proposed in his article on the ideological state apparatuses, the effects induced in the practice of ideological class struggle – its instruments, themes and forms – by the alteration that occurred in the *hierarchy* of these apparatuses with the transition from the feudal to the capitalist mode of production, when the school system replaced the Church as the dominant apparatus. More specifically, in his inquiry, is not Foucault in fact dealing with the mechanism that *redistributes* the topography of the various regions of ideology (religious, juridical, moral, aesthetic), under the domination of a new region (in the event, juridical ideology, which is inseparable from the operation of bourgeois law), as an *effect* of this modification in the order of precedence among the ideological state apparatuses? That this modification and redistribution, which are effected under the impact of the general process of class struggle, induce 'new practices' in the ideological struggle; and that these 'new practices' find their 'regime' and are articulated with one another only according to a series of *discrepancies* (which can ultimately give rise to real derailments), linked to the historical conjuncture in which they are effected – maybe this is what Foucault seeks to explain, while concealing the complexity of the issue under the myth of a 'beginning' declared 'classical', and guaranteed by a 'pre-history' itself fashioned to that end.

63. Michel Foucault, 'Power and Strategies' (1977), trans. Colin Gordon, in *Power/Knowledge*, pp. 134–45 (pp. 143–4; emphasis added).

64. Michel Foucault, Preface to Mireille Debard and Jean-Luc Hennig, *Les Juges Kaki*, Alain Moreau, Paris 1977.

65. It is Foucault who declares that '[o]ne impoverishes the question of power if one poses it solely in terms of legislation and constitution, in terms solely of the state and the state apparatus. Power is quite different from and more complicated, dense and pervasive than a set of laws or a state apparatus': 'The Eye of Power' (1977), trans. Colin Gordon, in *Power/Knowledge*, pp. 146–65 (p. 158). Directed against a certain 'Marxist' representation of the state, these remarks richochet on to the speculations of Glucksmann and the like.

66. The panopticon, whose principle Jeremy Bentham set out in a book he began writing in 1786, is an architectural construct whose main features Foucault summarizes thus:

> at the periphery, an annular building; at the centre, a tower; this tower is pierced with wide windows that open onto the inner side of the ring; the peripheric building is divided into cells, each of which extends the whole width of the building; they have two windows, one on the inside, corresponding to the windows of the tower; the other, on the outside, allows the light to cross the cell from one end to the other. All that is needed, then, is to place a supervisor in a central tower and to shut up in each cell a madman, a patient, a condemned man, a worker or a schoolboy. (*Discipline and Punish*, p. 200)

67. Foucault, 'The Eye of Power', p. 148.

68. See the section entitled 'The panoptic apparatus', which concludes with these lines (*The Master Thinkers*, pp. 109–10):

> It matters little whether there is a warder in the central observatory of the panoptic prison: if it has been constructed according to the rules ('with firmly established laws and a settled organization of the state') it provides the feeling that we are perpetually under surveillance (always and at any moment), in so far as we cannot turn round towards our warders, nor they towards the central warder. The latter can be away as much as he likes: the structure is sufficient and we all sense his gaze upon the back of our necks, whether his eyes are actually open or shut. Hegel places *anyone at all* at the centre of the monarchy: 'A monarch . . . has only to say "yes" and dot the "i".' Here there can be no failure or mistake due to inattention, insuperable irrationality, compromise with reaction. With a single stroke of genius the philosopher has defined the height of (disciplinary) rationality: with the most utter idiot at its head, the prison goes on functioning. There is no contradiction here: Hegel defines his ruler as he who sees without being seen. If Marx perceives a contradiction, he does not perceive the modern state.

Chapter 5   Conclusion: The America in Our Heads

69. Crozier *et al.*, *The Crisis of Democracy*, p. 7.

70. See *Tel Quel*, nos 71–3, Autumn 1977, 'Pourquoi les États-Unis?'.

Bibliography

Abécassis, Éliette, *Petite métaphysique du meurtre*, Presses Universitaires de France, Paris 1998.

Althusser, Louis, ed. and trans., *Ludwig Feuerbach: Manifestes philosophiques (textes choisis 1839–1845)*, Presses Universitaires de France, Paris 1960.

—— *For Marx*, trans. Ben Brewster, Allen Lane, London 1969.

—— *Essays in Self-Criticism*, trans. Grahame Lock, New Left Books, London 1976.

—— *Essays on Ideology*, trans. Ben Brewster and Grahame Lock, Verso, London 1984.

—— *Philosophy and the Spontaneous Philosophy of the Scientists & Other Essays*, ed. Gregory Elliott, trans. Ben Brewster *et al.*, Verso, London and New York 1990.

—— *The Future Lasts a Long Time and The Facts*, ed. Olivier Corpet and Yann Moulier Boutang, trans. Richard Veasey, Chatto & Windus, London 1993.

—— *The Spectre of Hegel: Early Writings*, ed. François Matheron, trans. G. M. Goshgarian, Verso, London and New York 1997.

—— *Lettres à Franca (1961–1973)*, ed. François Matheron and Yann Moulier Boutang, Stock/IMEC, Paris 1998.

—— *Machiavelli and Us*, ed. François Matheron, trans. Gregory Elliott, Verso, London and New York 1999.

Althusser, Louis and Balibar, Étienne, *Reading Capital*, trans. Ben Brewster, New Left Books, London 1970.

Althusser, Louis, Balibar, Étienne, Establet, Roger, Macherey, Pierre and Rancière, Jacques, *Lire le Capital*, Presses Universitaires de France, Paris 1996.

Arendt, Hannah, *The Origins of Totalitarianism*, 2nd edn, George Allen & Unwin, London 1958 .

Aron, Raymond, *The Opium of the Intellectuals* (1955), trans Terence Kilmartin, Secker & Warburg, London 1957.

— *Democracy and Totalitarianism*, trans. Valence Ionescu, Weidenfeld & Nicolson, London 1968.

— *Marxismes imaginaires: d'une sainte famille à l'autre*, Gallimard, Paris 1970.

Arvon, Henri, *Aux sources de l'existentialisme*, Presses Universitaires de France, Paris 1954.

Aubral, François and Delcourt, Xavier, *Contre la nouvelle philosophie*, Gallimard, Paris 1977.

Badiou, Alain, 'Le (re)commencement du matérialisme dialectique', *Critique*, no. 240, May 1967, pp. 438–67.

— *L'éthique. Essai sur la conscience du Mal*, Hatier, Paris 1993.

Balibar, Étienne, *Cinq études du matérialisme historique*, François Maspero, Paris 1974.

Baudrillard, Jean, *Forget Foucault* (1977), Semiotext(e), New York 1987.

— *The System of Objects*, trans. James Benedict, Verso, London and New York 1996.

— *The Consumer Society: Myths and Structures*, Sage Publications, London and Thousand Oaks, CA 1998.

Bennington, Geoffrey and Derrida, Jacques, *Jacques Derrida*, trans. Bennington, University of Chicago Press, Chicago and London 1993.

Benoist, Jean-Marie, *Marx est mort*, Gallimard, Paris 1970.

Boltanski, Luc, *La Souffrance à distance. Morale humanitaire, médias et politique*, Métaillié, Paris 1993.

Bonald, Louis de, *Législation primitive*, 3 vols, Paris 1802.

Bourdieu, Pierre and Passeron, Jean-Claude, *The Inheritors: French Students and their Relation to Culture*, trans. Richard Nice, University of Chicago Press, Chicago and London 1979.

Bouveresse, Jacques, *Le Mythe de l'intériorité: expérience, signification et langage privé chez Wittgenstein*, Éditions de Minuit, Paris 1976.

Brauman, Rony, *Humanitaire le dilemme*, Éditions Textuel, Paris 1996.

Broyelle, Claudie, *Women's Liberation in China*, Harvester, Hassocks 1977.

Broyelle, Claudie and Broyelle, Jacques, *China: A Second Look*, trans. Sarah Mathews, Harvester, Hassocks 1980.

Brzezinski, Zbigniew, *Ideology and Power in Soviet Politics*, Thames & Hudson, London 1962.

Camus, Albert, *The Rebel*, trans. Anthony Bower, Penguin, Harmondsworth 1971.

—— 'Neither Victims nor Executioners', in Camus, *Between Hell and Reason: Essays from the Resistance Newspaper 'Combat', 1944–47*, trans. Alexandre de Gramont, University Press of New England, Hanover (NH) 1991, pp. 115–45.

Canguilhem, Georges, *Études d'histoire et de philosophie des sciences*, J. Vrin, Paris 1968.

—— 'What is Psychology?' (1958), trans. H. Davies, *Ideology and Consciousness*, no. 7, 1980, pp. 37–50.

—— *The Normal and the Pathological* (1943), trans. Carolyn R. Fawcett with Robert S. Cohen, Zone Books, New York 1989.

—— *Vie et mort de Jean Cavaillès*, Allia, Paris 1996.

Châtelet, Gilles, *Vivre et penser comme des porcs. De l'incitation à l'envie et à l'ennui dans les démocraties-marchés*, Exils, Paris 1998.

Chevènement, Jean-Pierre, *Le Vert et le noir: intégrisme, pétrole, dollar*, Grasset, Paris 1995.

Claudin, Fernando, *The Communist Movement: From Comintern to Cominform*, 2 vols, trans. Brian Pearce and Francis MacDonagh, Monthly Review Press, New York and London 1975.

Clavel, Maurice, *Ce que je crois*, Grasset, Paris 1975.

—— *Dieu est Dieu, nom de Dieu!*, Grasset, Paris 1976.

—— *Deux siècles chez Lucifer*, Seuil, Paris 1977.

Clément, Catherine and Kristeva, Julia, *Le Féminin et le sacré*, Stock, Paris 1998.

Comte-Sponville, André, *Traité de désespoir et de la béatitude*, vol. I: *Le Myth d'Icare*, Presses Universitaires de France, Paris 1984.

—— *Traité de désespoir et de la béatitude*, vol. II: *Vivre*, Presses Universitaires de France, Paris 1988.

—— *Petit traité des grandes vertus*, Presses Universitaires de France, Paris 1995.

—— *Impromptus*, Presses Universitaires de France, Paris 1996.

Comte-Sponville, André and Ferry, Luc, *La Sagesse des modernes: dix questions pour notre temps*, Robert Laffont, Paris 1998.

Cooper, David, *Qui sont les dissidents?*, Galilée, Paris 1977.

Crozier, Michel, Huntington Samuel P., and Watanuki, Joji, *The Crisis of Democracy: Report on the Governability of Democracies to the Trilateral Commission*, New York University Press, New York 1975.

Dagognet, François, *Une nouvelle morale: travail, famille, nation*, Les empêcheurs de penser en rond, Paris 1998.

Debord, Guy, *The Society of the Spectacle*, trans. Donald Nicholson-Smith, Zone Books, New York 1994.

Debray, Régis, *Par amour de l'art: une éducation intellectuelle*, Gallimard, Paris 1998.

Deleuze, Gilles, 'À propos des nouveaux philosophes et d'un problème plus général', supplement to *Minuit*, no. 24, 5 June 1977.

— *Nietzsche and Philosophy*, trans. Hugh Tomlinson, Athlone Press, London 1983.

— *Expressionism in Philosophy: Spinoza*, trans. Martin Jouglin, Zone Books, New York 1992.

Deleuze, Gilles and Guattari, Félix, *Anti-Oedipus: Capitalism and Schizophrenia*, trans. Robert Hurley, Mark Seem and Helen R. Lane, Viking Press, New York 1977.

Derrida, Jacques, *Speech and Phenomena and Other Essays on Husserl's Theory of Signs*, trans. David B. Allison, Northwestern University Press, Evanston, IL 1973.

— *Of Grammatology*, trans. Gayatri Chakravorty Spivak, Johns Hopkins University Press, Baltimore and London 1976.

— *Writing and Difference*, trans. Alan Bass, Routledge & Kegan Paul, London 1978.

— *Margins of Philosophy*, trans. Alan Bass, University of Chicago Press, Chicago 1982.

Destexhe, Alain, *L'humanitaire impossible ou deux siècles d'ambiguité*, Armand Colin, Paris 1993.

Dollé, Jean-Paul, *L'insoumis. Vies et légendes de Pierre Goldmann*, Grasset, Paris 1997.

Dubuisson, Daniel, *L'Occident et la religion. Mythes, science et idéologie*, Éditions Complexe, Brussels 1998.

Duranton-Crabol, Anne-Marie, *Visages de la nouvelle droite: le GRECE et son histoire*, Presses de la Fondation Nationale des Sciences Politiques, Paris 1988.

Durkheim, Émile, *The Elementary Forms of the Religious Life: A Study in Religious Sociology*, trans. Joseph Ward, Allen & Unwin, London 1915.

Faye, Jean-Pierre, *Les Langages totalitaires*, Herman, Paris 1973.

Ferry, Luc, *L'homme-Dieu ou le Sens de la vie*, Grasset, Paris 1996.

Ferry, Luc and Renaut, Alain, *French Philosophy of the Sixties: An Essay on Antihumanism*, trans. Mary H. S. Cattani, University of Massachusetts Press, Amherst 1990.

Feuerbach, Ludwig, *The Essence of Christianity*, trans. George Eliot, Harper & Row, New York 1957.

Finkielkraut, Alain, *La Défaite de la pensée*, Gallimard, Paris 1987.

Foucault, Michel, *Folie et déraison. Histoire de la folie à l'âge classique*, Plon, Paris 1961.

— *Madness and Civilization: A History of Insanity in the Age of Reason*, trans. Richard Howard, Tavistock, London 1967.

— *The Order of Things: An Archaeology of the Human Sciences*, Tavistock, London 1970.

— *The Archaeology of Knowledge*, trans. A. M. Sheridan Smith, Tavistock, London 1972.

— *The Birth of the Clinic: An Archaeology of Medical Perception*, trans. A. M. Sheridan, Tavistock, London 1973.

— *Discipline and Punish: The Birth of the Prison* (1975), trans. Alan Sheridan, Allen Lane, London 1977.

— *Language, Counter-Memory, Practice: Selected Essays and Interviews*, ed. Donald F. Bouchard, trans. Bouchard and Sherry Simon, Cornell University Press, Ithaca, NY 1977.

— 'My Body, this Paper, this Fire' (1971), trans. Geoffrey Bennington, *Oxford Literary Review*, vol. IV, no. 1, Autumn 1979, pp. 5–29.

— *The History of Sexuality*, vol. I: *An Introduction* (1976), trans. Robert Hurley, Allen Lane, London, 1979.

— *Power/Knowledge: Selected Interviews and Other Writings 1972–1977*, ed. Colin Gordon, trans. Gordon *et al.*, Harvester, Brighton 1980.

— *The History of Sexuality*, vol. II: *The Use of Pleasure* (1984), trans. Robert Hurley, Viking, London 1986.

— *The History of Sexuality*, vol. III: *The Care of the Self* (1984), trans. Robert Hurley, Viking, London 1986.

— *Politics, Philosophy, Culture: Interviews and Other Writings 1977–1984*, ed. Lawrence D. Kritzman, trans. Alan Sheridan *et al.*, Routledge, New York and London 1988.

— *Foucault Live: Collected Interviews, 1961–1984*, ed. Sylvère Lotringer, trans. Lysa Hochroth, John Johnston *et al.*, Semiotext(e), New York 1989.

— *Remarks on Marx: Conversations with Duccio Trombadori*, trans. R. James Goldstein and James Cascaito, Semiotext(e), New York 1991.

— *Dits et écrits, 1954–1988*, 4 vols, Gallimard, Paris 1994.

Franche, Dominique, *Rwanda, généalogie d'un génocide*, Mille et une nuits, Paris 1997.

Gallo, Max, 'Les intellectuels, la politique et la modernité', *Le Monde*, 26 July 1983.

Geismar, Alain and July, Serge, *Vers la guerre civile*, Lattès, Paris 1969.

Giscard d'Estaing, Valéry, *Démocratie française*, Fayard, Paris 1976.

Glucksmann, André, 'Strategy and Revolution in France 1968', *New Left Review*, no. 52, November/December 1968, pp. 67–121.

— 'Fascismes: l'ancien et le nouveau', *Les Temps Modernes*, no. 310 bis, May 1972, pp. 266–340.

— *La Cuisinière et le mangeur d'hommes: essai sur l'État, le marxisme, les camps de concentration*, Seuil, Paris 1975.

— *The Master Thinkers*, trans. Brian Pearce, Harvester, Brighton 1980.

— *Discours de la guerre*, expanded edn, Le Livre de Poche, Paris 1985.

— *Le Bien et le mal: lettres immorales d'Allemagne et de France*, Robert Laffont, Paris 1997.

Goldmann, Pierre, *Souvenirs obscurs d'un juif polonais né en France*, Seuil, Paris 1975.

Goldschmidt, Victor, *Platonisme et pensée contemporaine*, Aubier-Montaigne, Paris 1970.

Grotius, Hugo, *Prolegomena to the Law of War and Peace*, trans. Francis W. Kelsey, Liberal Arts Press, New York 1957.

Guibert, Hervé, *La Mort propagande*, Régine Deforges, Paris 1977.

Guillebaud, Jean-Claude, *La Tyrannie du plaisir*, Seuil, Paris 1998.

Habermas, Jürgen, *The Philosophical Discourse of Modernity: Twelve Lectures* (1985), trans. Frederick Lawrence, Polity Press, Cambridge 1987.

d'Holbach, Paul Henry, *La Politique naturelle*, Fayard, Paris 1998.

Houellebecq, Michel, *Atomised*, trans. Frank Wynne, Heinemann, London 2000.

Jankélévitch, Vladimir, *Philosophie morale*, Flammarion, Paris 1998.

Jeanneret, Yves, *L'affaire Sokal ou la querelle des impostures*, Presses Universitaires de France, Paris 1998.

Julliard, Jacques, *La Faute aux élites*, Gallimard, Paris 1997.

Kant, Immanuel, *Religion within the Boundaries of Mere Reason and Other Writings*, ed. and trans. Allen Wood and George di Giovanni, Cambridge University Press, Cambridge 1998.

Kantorowicz, Ernst, *Mourir pour la patrie et autres textes*, Presses Universitaires de France, Paris 1984.

Kaspi, André, Bertrand, Jean-Claude and Heffer, Jean, *La Civilisation américaine*, Presses Universitaires de France, Paris 1993.

Kevles, Daniel, *Au nom de l'eugénisme. Génétique et politique dans le monde anglo-saxon*, Presses Universitaires de France, Paris 1995.

Knabb, Ken, ed. and trans., *Situationist International: An Anthology*, Bureau of Public Secrets, Berkeley, CA 1981.

Lacan, Jacques, *Écrits*, Seuil, Paris 1966.

— *Écrits: A Selection*, trans. Alan Sheridan, Tavistock, London 1977.

Lacorne, Denis, *L'invention de la république: le modèle américain*, Hachette/Pluriel, Paris 1991.

— *La Crise de l'identité américaine: du melting pot au multiculturalisme*, Fayard, Paris 1997.

Lavelle, Louis, *De l'acte*, Aubier, Paris 1937.

— *Le Mal et la souffrance*, Plon, Paris 1940.

Lavelle, Louis and Le Senne, René, *Manifeste de la philosophie de l'esprit*, Aubier, Paris 1934.

Lecourt, Dominique, *Marxism and Epistemology: Bachelard, Canguilhem, Foucault*, trans. Ben Brewster, New Left Books, London 1975.

— *Proletarian Science? The Case of Lysenko*, trans. Ben Brewster, New Left Books, London 1977.

— *Dissidence ou révolution?*, François Maspero, Paris 1978.

— *L'ordre et les jeux: le positivisme logique en question*, Grasset, Paris 1981.

— *Contre la peur: de la science à l'éthique, une aventure infinie*, Presses Universitaires de France, Paris 1999.

Legendre, Pierre, *L'inestimable objet de la transmission: études sur le principe généalogique en Occident*, Fayard, Paris 1985.

— *Le Désir politique de Dieu: études sur les montages de l'État et du droit*, Fayard, Paris 1988.

— *Dieu au miroir: études sur l'institution des images*, Fayard, Paris 1994.

Lenin, V. I., *Collected Works*, vols 5, 6, 13, 24 & 25, Progress Publishers, Moscow 1964.

Lévy, Benny, *Visage continu: la pensée du retour chez Emmanuel Lévinas*, Verdier, Paris 1998.

Lévy, Bernard-Henri, *Barbarism with a Human Face*, trans. George Holoch, Harper & Row, New York 1979.

Linhart, Robert, *Lénine, les paysans, Taylor: essai d'analyse matérialiste historique de la naissance du système productif soviétique*, Seuil, Paris 1976.

— 'Western "Dissidence" Ideology and the Protection of Bourgeois Order', in *Il Manifesto*, ed., *Power and Opposition in Post-Revolutionary Societies*, trans. Patrick Camilller and Jon Rothschild, Ink Links, London 1979, pp. 249–60.

— *The Assembly Line*, trans. Margaret Crosland, John Calder, London 1981.

Lipovetsky, Gilles, *L'ère du vide: essais sur l'individualisme contemporain*, Gallimard, Paris 1983.

Lyotard, Jean-François, *The Postmodern Condition: A Report on Knowledge* (1979), trans. Geoff Bennington and Brian Massumi, Manchester University Press, Manchester 1984.

— *Heidegger and 'The Jews'*, trans. Andreas Michel and Mark Roberts, University of Minnesota Press, Minneapolis 1990.

— 'The Tomb of the Intellectual', in Lyotard, *Political Writings*, trans. Bill Readings and Kevin Paul Geiman, UCL Press, London 1993, pp. 3–7.

Macherey, Pierre, *Histoires de dinosaure. Faire de la philosophie 1965–1997*, Presses Universitaires de France, Paris 1999.

Machiavelli, Niccolò, *The Prince*, ed. Quentin Skinner and Russell Price, trans. Russell Price, Cambridge University Press, Cambridge 1988.

Maistre, Joseph de, *Des Constitutions politiques*, ed. R. Thomas, Les Belles Lettres, Paris 1959.

— *Considerations on France*, ed. and trans. Richard A. Lebrun, Cambridge University Press, Cambridge 1994.

Mao Tse-Tung, 'Report on an Investigation of the Peasant Movement in Hunan', in *Selected Readings from the Works of Mao Tse-Tung*, Foreign Languages Press, Peking 1967, pp. 20–32.

Marcuse, Herbert, *Reason and Revolution: Hegel and the Rise of Social Theory*, Oxford University Press, New York 1941.

— *Eros and Civilization: A Philosophical Inquiry into Freud*, Beacon Press, Boston, MA 1955.

—— *One-Dimensional Man: Studies in the Ideology of Advanced Industrial Society*, Beacon Press, Boston, MA 1964.

Marx, Karl, 'Theses on Feuerbach', in Marx, *Early Writings*, ed. Lucio Colletti, trans. Rodney Livingstone and Gregor Benton, Penguin/*New Left Review*, Harmondsworth 1975, pp. 421–3.

—— Preface to *A Contribution to the Critique of Political Economy*, in *Early Writings*, pp. 424–8.

—— *The German Ideology*, trans. Clemens Dutt, W. Lough and C. P. Magill, in Marx and Engels, *Collected Works*, vol. 5, Lawrence & Wishart, London 1976.

Medvedev, Roy and Medvedev, Zhores, *Khrushchev: The Years in Power*, trans. Andrew R. Durkin, Oxford University Press, Oxford 1977.

Merleau-Ponty, Maurice, *Humanism and Terror*, trans. John O'Neill, Beacon Press, Boston 1969.

—— *Adventures of the Dialectic*, trans. Joseph Bien, Northwestern University Press, Evanston, IL 1973.

Molnar, Thomas, *La Contre-révolution*, 10/18, Paris 1972.

Neumann, Sigmund, *Permanent Revolution: The Total State in a World at War*, Harper, New York and London 1942.

Nicolet, Claude, *L'idée républicaine en France (1789–1924). Essai d'histoire critique*, Gallimard, Paris 1982.

Nizan, Paul, *The Watchdogs: Philosophers and the Established Order* (1932), trans. Paul Fittingoff, Monthly Review Press, New York 1971.

Onfray, Michel, *Le Désir d'être un volcan: journal d'un hédoniste*, Grasset, Paris 1996.

—— *Politique du rebelle. Traité de résistance et d'insoumission*, Grasset, Paris 1997.

—— *Les Vertus de la foudre: journal hédoniste II*, Grasset, Paris 1998.

Otto, Rudolf, *The Idea of the Holy: An Inquiry into the Non-Rational Factors in the Idea of the Divine and its Relation to the Rational*, trans. John W. Harvey, 2nd edn, Oxford University Press, London and New York 1950.

Popper, Karl, *The Open Society and its Enemies*, 2 vols, Routledge and Kegan Paul, London 1945.

—— *The Logic of Scientific Discovery* (1934), Hutchinson, London 1959.

Poulantzas, Nicos, *State, Power, Socialism*, trans. Patrick Camiller, New Left Books, London 1978.

Rakovski, Marc, *Towards an East European Marxism*, Allison and Busby, London 1978.

Rancière, Jacques, *Disagreement: Politics and Philosophy*, trans. Julie Rose, University of Minnesota Press, Minneapolis 1998.

Reich, Wilhelm, *La Lutte sexuelle des jeunes*, Maspero, Paris 1972.

— *The Function of the Orgasm: Sex-Economic Problems of Biological Energy*, trans. Vincent R. Carfagno, Souvenir Press, London 1983.

Russell, Bertrand, *The Practice and Theory of Bolshevism*, George Allen & Unwin, London 1920.

de Sade, Donatien-Alphonese-François, *Oeuvres*, Bibliothèque de la Pléiade/Gallimard, Paris 1990.

Sartre, Jean-Paul, *Critique of Dialectical Reason I: Theory of Practical Ensembles*, trans. Alan Sheridan-Smith, ed. Jonathan Rée, New Left Books, London 1976.

Schiwy, Günther, *Les nouveaux philosophes*, Denoël-Gonthier, Paris 1979.

Simondon, Gilbert, *Du Monde d'existence des objets techniques*, Aubier-Montaigne, Paris 1958.

— *L'individu et sa genèse physico-biologique*, Presses Universitaires de France, Paris 1964.

— *L'individuation psychique et collective*, Aubier, Paris 1989.

Sirinelli, Jean-François, ed., *Histoire des droites en France*, 3 vols, Gallimard, Paris 1992.

Situationist International, *The Veritable Split in the International*, Chronos Publications, London 1990.

— *Internationale Situationniste, 1958–1969 (édition augmentée)*, Fayard, Paris 1997.

Solzhenitsyn, Alexander, *The Gulag Archipelago*, trans. Thomas P. Whitney, Collins/Fontana, Glasgow 1974.

Sorman, Guy, *La Révolution conservatrice américaine*, Fayard, Paris 1983.

Stalin, J. V., 'Dialectical and Historical Materialism', in *History of the Communist Party of the Soviet Union (Bolsheviks): Short Course*, Foreign Languages Publishing House, Moscow 1939, ch. 4, sect. 2, pp. 105–31.

Stirner, Max, *The Ego and Its Own*, ed. David Leopold, trans. Steven Tracy Byington, Cambridge University Press, Cambridge 1995.

Tel Quel, nos 71–3, Autumn 1977, 'Pourquoi les États-Unis?'.

Les Temps Modernes, no. 310 bis, May 1972, 'Nouveau fascisme, nouvelle démocratie'.

Terray, Emmanuel, *Le troisième jour du communisme*, Actes Sud, Arles 1992.

Tocqueville, Charles Alexis Clérel de, *Democracy in America*, ed. J. P. Mayer, trans. George Lawrence, Fontana, London 1994.

United Nations, *Universal Declaration of Human Rights*, 1948.

Vaneigem, Raoul, *The Revolution of Everyday Life*, trans. Donald Nicolson-Smith, Left Bank Books and Rebel Press, n. p. 1983.

—— *Résistance au christianisme: les hérésies, des origines au XVIIIᵉ siècle*, Fayard, Paris 1993.

—— *Les Hérésies*, Presses Universitaires de France, Paris 1994.

Vattimo, Gianni, *The End of Modernity: Nihilism and Hermeneutics in Post-Modern Culture* (1985), trans. Jon R. Snyder, Polity, Cambridge 1988.

Veyne, Paul, *Comment on écrit l'histoire* (1971), expanded edn, Seuil, Paris 1978.

Winock, Michel, *Le Siècle des intellectuels*, Seuil, Paris 1997.

Zapata, René, *Luttes philosophiques en URSS 1922–1931*, Presses Universitaires de France, Paris 1983.

—— *La Philosophie russe et soviétique*, Presses Universitaires de France, Paris 1988.

Index